MICROSO
PowerPoint® 2002

Introductory Course

Mastering and Using

H. Albert Napier
Philip J. Judd
Linda Sourek
Susan Lehner

COURSE
TECHNOLOGY

THOMSON LEARNING

Australia • Canada • Mexico • Singapore • Spain • United Kingdom • United States

COURSE TECHNOLOGY
TM
THOMSON LEARNING

Mastering and Using Microsoft® PowerPoint 2002 Introductory Course
by H. Albert Napier, Ph.D. & Philip J. Judd, Susan Lehner, Linda Sourek

Managing Editor:
Melissa Ramondetta

Development Editor:
Robin M. Romer, Pale Moon
Productions

Product Marketing Manager:
Kim Wood

Product Manager:
Robert Gaggin

Editorial Assistant:
Jodi Dreissig

Production Services:
GEX Publishing Services

Copy Editor:
GEX Publishing Services

Cover Design:
Steve Deschene

Compositor:
GEX Publishing Services

What's New in PowerPoint 2002

Office XP

▶ Streamlined, flatter look

▶ Multiple task panes containing command shortcuts

▶ Ask A Question Box Help tool

▶ Smart Tags

▶ AutoCorrect Options

▶ Revised Office Clipboard

▶ Paste Options

▶ Route documents for review with tracked changes via e-mail

▶ Speech Recognition

▶ Improved "crash" recovery features

▶ Search task pane

▶ Digital signatures for documents routed over the Internet

PowerPoint 2002

▶ Collaborative online reviews

▶ Print presentation with comment pages

▶ Merge and compare reviewed presentations

▶ Animation schemes with animation and transitions

▶ New animation effects

▶ Motion paths

▶ Better organization charts

▶ New diagram types (cycle, pyramid, radial, Venn)

▶ Task panes for applying slide and presentation formatting

▶ Outline/Slides tab – Thumbnail of slides in Normal view

▶ Print preview

▶ Multiple design templates per presentation

▶ Visible grids for aligning placeholders, shapes, and pictures

▶ Adjustable spacing between grids for more control

▶ Automatic layout for inserted objects

▶ Embedded fonts (characters within presentation or all font characters)

▶ Text AutoFit improvements to automatically adjust layout for charts, diagrams, and pictures

▶ Picture rotation

▶ Play sounds and animation when a presentation is saved as a Web page

▶ Password protection when opening a presentation

▶ Language indicator in status bar

Napier & Judd

In their over 50 years of combined experience, Al Napier and Phil Judd have developed a tested, realistic approach to mastering and using application software. As both academics and corporate trainers, Al and Phil have the unique ability to help students by teaching them the skills necessary to compete in today's complex business world.

H. Albert Napier, Ph.D. is the Director of the Center on the Management of Information Technology and Professor in the Jesse H. Jones Graduate School of Management at Rice University. In addition, Al is a principal of Napier & Judd, Inc., a consulting company and corporate trainer in Houston, Texas, that has trained more than 120,000 people in computer applications.

Philip J. Judd is a former instructor in the Management Department and the Director of the Research and Instructional Computing Service at the University of Houston. Phil now dedicates himself to consulting and corporate training as a principal of Napier & Judd, Inc.

Philip J. Judd

H. Albert Napier,
Ph.D.

Preface

At Course Technology, we believe that technology will change the way people teach and learn. Today millions of people are using personal computers in their everyday lives—both as tools at work and for recreational activities. As a result, the personal computer has revolutionized the ways in which people interact with each other. The *Mastering and Using* series combines the following distinguishing features to allow people to do amazing things with their personal computers.

Distinguishing Features

All the textbooks in the *Mastering and Using* series share several key pedagogical features:

Case Project Approach. In their more than 20 years of business and corporate training and teaching experience, Napier & Judd have found that students are more enthusiastic about learning a software application if they can see its real-world relevance. The textbook provides bountiful business-based profiles, exercises, and projects. It also emphasizes the skills most in demand by employers.

Comprehensive and Easy to Use. There is thorough coverage of new features. The narrative is clear and concise. Each unit or chapter thoroughly instructs on the concepts that underlie the skills and procedures. The text explains not just the *how*, but the *why*.

Step-by-Step Instructions and Screen Illustrations. All examples in this text include step-by-step instructions that explain how to complete the specific task. Full-color screen illustrations are used extensively to provide students with a realistic picture of the software application feature.

Extensive Tips and Tricks. The authors have placed informational boxes in the margin of the text. These boxes of information provide students with the following helpful tips:

► *Quick Tip*. Extra information provides shortcuts on how to perform common business-related functions.
► *Caution Tip*. This additional information explains how a mistake occurs and provides tips on how to avoid making similar mistakes in the future.
► *Menu Tip*. Additional explanation on how to use menu commands to perform application tasks.
► *Mouse Tip*. Further instructions on how to use the mouse to perform application tasks.
► *Task Pane Tip*. Additional information on using task pane shortcuts.
► *Internet Tip*. This information incorporates the power of the Internet to help students use the Internet as they progress through the text.
► *Design Tip*. Hints for better presentation designs (found in the PowerPoint chapters).

End-of-Chapter Materials. Each book in the *Mastering and Using* series places a heavy emphasis on providing students with the opportunity to practice and reinforce the skills they are learning through extensive exercises. Each chapter has a summary, commands review, concepts review, skills review, and case projects so that the student can master the material by doing. For more information on each of the end-of-chapter elements, see page ix of the How to Use This Book section in this preface.

Appendices. *Mastering and Using* series contains three appendices to further help students prepare to be successful in the classroom or in the workplace. Appendix A teaches students to work with Windows 2000. Appendix B illustrates how to format letters; how to insert a mailing notation; how to format envelopes (referencing the U.S. Postal Service documents); how to format interoffice memorandums; and how to key a formal outline. It also lists popular style guides and describes proofreader's marks. Appendix C describes the new Office XP speech recognition features.

Microsoft Office User Specialist (MOUS) Certification.
What does this logo mean? It means this courseware has been approved by the Microsoft® Office User Specialist Program to be among the finest available for learning Microsoft

Office XP, Microsoft Word 2002, Microsoft Excel 2002, Microsoft PowerPoint® 2002, and Microsoft Access 2002. It also means that upon completion of this courseware, you may be prepared to become a Microsoft Office User Specialist.

What is a Microsoft Office User Specialist? A Microsoft Office User Specialist is an individual who has certified his or her skills in one or more of the Microsoft Office desktop applications of Microsoft Word, Microsoft Excel, Microsoft PowerPoint®, Microsoft Outlook® or Microsoft Access, or in Microsoft Project. The Microsoft Office User Specialist Program typically offers certification exams at the "Core" and "Expert" skill levels. The Microsoft Office User Specialist Program is the only Microsoft approved program in the world for certifying proficiency in Microsoft Office desktop applications and Microsoft Project. This certification can be a valuable asset in any job search or career advancement.

More Information: To learn more about becoming a Microsoft Office User Specialist, visit *www.mous.net*. To purchase a Microsoft Office User Specialist certification exam, visit *www.DesktopIQ.com*.

SCANS. In 1992, the U.S. Department of Labor and Education formed the Secretary's Commission on Achieving Necessary Skills, or SCANS, to study the kinds of competencies and skills that workers must have to succeed in today's marketplace. The results of the study were published in a document entitled *What Work Requires of Schools: A SCANS Report for America 2000.* The in-chapter and end-of-chapter exercises in this book are designed to meet the criteria outlined in the SCANS report and thus help prepare students to be successful in today's workplace.

Instructional Support

All books in the *Mastering and Using* series are supplemented with an ***Instructor's Resource Kit.*** This is a CD-ROM that contains lesson plans with teaching materials and preparation suggestions, along with tips for implementing instruction and assessment ideas; a suggested syllabus; and SCANS workplace know how. The CD also contains:

▶ Career Worksheets
▶ Evaluation Guidelines
▶ Hands-on Solutions
▶ Individual Learning Strategies
▶ Internet Behavior Contract
▶ Lesson Plans
▶ Portfolio Guidelines

▶ PowerPoint Presentations
▶ Solution Files
▶ Student Data Files
▶ Teacher Training Notes
▶ Test Questions
▶ Transparency Graphics Files

ExamView® This textbook is accompanied by ExamView, a powerful testing software package that allows instructors to create and administer printed, computer (LAN-based), and Internet exams. ExamView includes hundreds of questions that correspond to the topics covered in this text, enabling students to generate detailed study guides that include page references for further review. The computer-based and Internet testing components allow students to take exams at their computers, and also save the instructor time by grading each exam automatically.

MyCourse.com. MyCourse.com is an online syllabus builder and course-enhancement tool. Hosted by Course Technology, MyCourse.com is designed to reinforce what you already are teaching. It also adds value to your course by providing content that corresponds with your text. MyCourse.com is flexible: choose how you want to organize the material, by date or by class session; or don't do anything at all, and the material is automatically organized by chapter. Add your own materials, including hyperlinks, assignments, announcements, and course content. If you're using more than one textbook, you can even build a course that includes all your Course Technology texts—in one easy-to-use site! Start building your own course today…just go to *www.mycourse.com/instructor*.

Student Support

Data Disk. To use this book, students must have the Data Disk. Data Files needed to complete exercises in the text are contained on the Review Pack CD-ROM. These files can be copied to a hard drive or posted to a network drive.

How to Use This Book

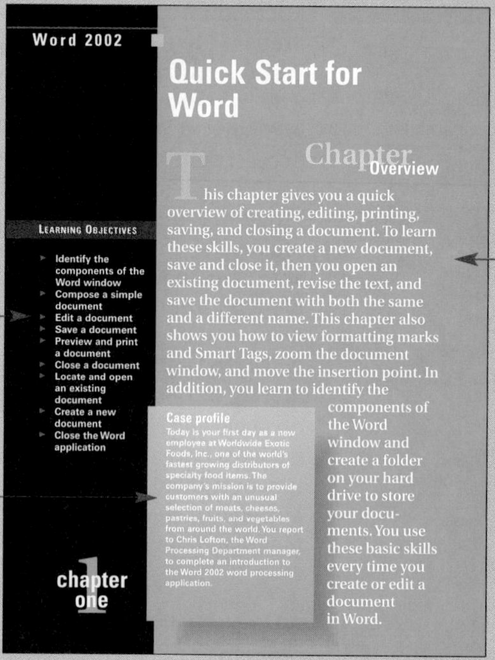

Word 2002

Quick Start for Word

Chapter Overview

This chapter gives you a quick overview of creating, editing, printing, saving, and closing a document. To learn these skills, you create a new document, save and close it, then you open an existing document, revise the text, and save the document with both the same and a different name. This chapter also shows you how to view formatting marks and Smart Tags, zoom the document window, and move the insertion point. In addition, you learn to identify the

LEARNING OBJECTIVES

- Identify the components of the Word window
- Compose a simple document
- Edit a document
- Save a document
- Preview and print a document
- Close a document
- Locate and open an existing document
- Create a new document
- Close the Word application

Case profile
Today is your first day as a new employee at Worldwide Exotic Foods, Inc., one of the world's fastest growing distributors of specialty food items. The company's mission is to provide customers with an unusual selection of meats, cheeses, pastries, fruits, and vegetables from around the world. You report to Chris Lofton, the Word Processing Department manager, to complete an introduction to the Word 2002 word processing application.

components of the Word window and create a folder on your hard drive to store your documents. You use these basic skills every time you create or edit a document in Word.

chapter one 1

Learning Objectives — A quick reference of the major topics learned in the chapter

Case profile — Realistic scenarios that show the real-world application of the material being covered

Chapter Overview — A concise summary of what will be learned in the chapter

Clear step-by-step directions explain how to complete the specific task

Caution Tip — This additional information explains how a mistake occurs and provides tips on how to avoid making similar mistakes in the future

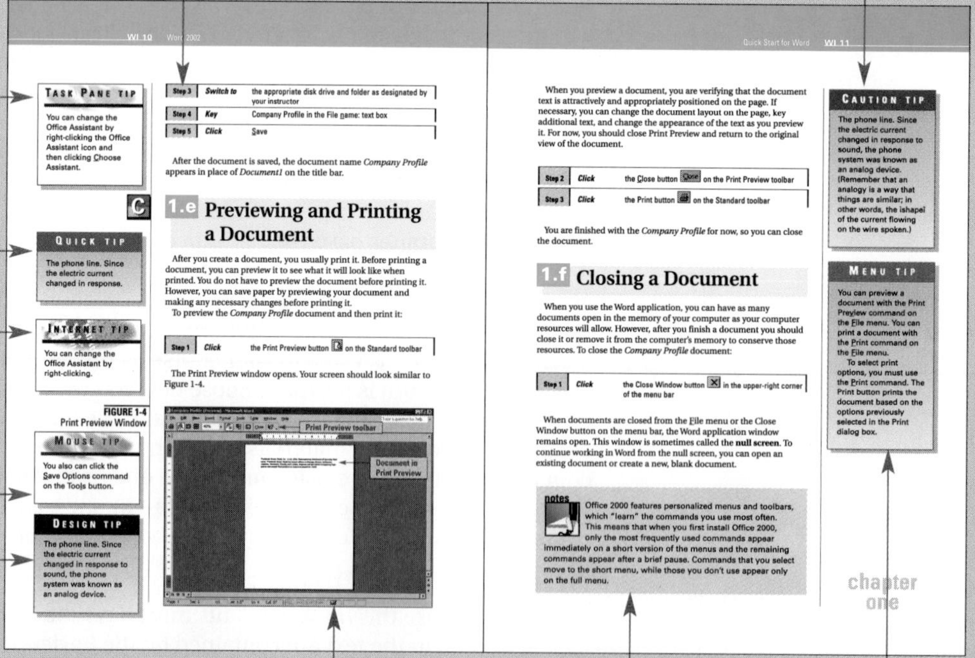

Task Pane Tip — Additional information about using task pane shortcuts

Quick Tip — Extra information provides shortcuts on how to perform common business-related functions

Internet Tip — Information to help students incorporate the power of the Internet as they progress through the text

Mouse Tip — Further instructions on how to use the mouse to perform application tasks

Design Tip — Hints for better presentation designs (found in only the PowerPoint chapters)

Full-color screen illustrations provide a realistic picture to the student

Notes — These boxes provide necessary information to assist you in completing the activities

Menu Tip — Additional explanation on how to use menu commands to perform application tasks

---

WI.10 Word 2002

TASK PANE TIP

You can change the Office Assistant by right-clicking the Office Assistant icon and then clicking Choose Assistant.

Step 3	Switch to	the appropriate disk drive and folder as designated by your instructor
Step 4	Key	Company Profile in the File name: text box
Step 5	Click	Save

After the document is saved, the document name *Company Profile* appears in place of *Document1* on the title bar.

1.e Previewing and Printing a Document

After you create a document, you usually print it. Before printing a document, you can preview it to see what it will look like when printed. You do not have to preview the document before printing it. However, you can save paper by previewing your document and making any necessary changes before printing it.

To preview the *Company Profile* document and then print it:

| Step 1 | Click | the Print Preview button on the Standard toolbar |

The Print Preview window opens. Your screen should look similar to Figure 1-4.

QUICK TIP

The phone line. Since the electric current changed in response.

INTERNET TIP

You can change the Office Assistant by right-clicking.

FIGURE 1-4
Print Preview Window

Print Preview toolbar

Document in Print Preview

MOUSE TIP

You also can click the Save Options command on the Tools button.

DESIGN TIP

The phone line. Since the electric current changed in response to sound, the phone system was known as an analog device.

Quick Start for Word WI.11

When you preview a document, you are verifying that the document text is attractively and appropriately positioned on the page. If necessary, you can change the document layout on the page, key additional text, and change the appearance of the text as you preview it. For now, you should close Print Preview and return to the original view of the document.

| Step 2 | Click | the Close button on the Print Preview toolbar |
| Step 3 | Click | the Print button on the Standard toolbar |

You are finished with the *Company Profile* for now, so you can close the document.

1.f Closing a Document

When you use the Word application, you can have many documents open in the memory of your computer as your computer resources will allow. However, after you finish a document you should close it or remove it from the computer's memory to conserve those resources. To close the *Company Profile* document:

| Step 1 | Click | the Close Window button in the upper-right corner of the menu bar |

When documents are closed from the File menu or the Close Window button on the menu bar, the Word application window remains open. This window is sometimes called the **null screen**. To continue working in Word from the null screen, you can open an existing document or create a new, blank document.

notes
Office 2000 features personalized menus and toolbars, which "learn" the commands you use most often. This means that when you first install Office 2000, only the most frequently used commands appear immediately on a short version of the menus and the remaining commands appear after a brief pause. Commands that you select move to the short menu, while those you don't use appear only on the full menu.

CAUTION TIP

The phone line. Since the electric current changed in response to sound, the phone system was known as an analog device. (Remember that an analogy is a way that things are similar; in other words, the ishapel of the current flowing on the wire spoken.)

MENU TIP

You can preview a document with the Print Preview command on the File menu. You can print a document with the Print command on the File menu.
To select print options, you must use the Print command. The Print button prints the document based on the options previously selected in the Print dialog box.

chapter one

End-of-Chapter Material

Concepts Review — Multiple choice and true or false questions help assess how well the student has learned the chapter material

Summary — Reviews key topics discussed in the chapter

Commands Review — Provides a quick reference and reinforcement tool on multiple methods for performing actions discussed in the chapter

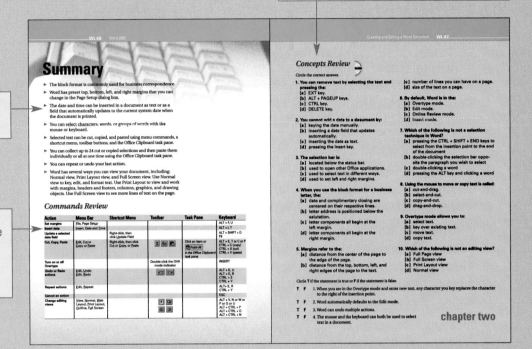

Skills Review — Hands-on exercises provide the ability to practice the skills just learned in the chapter

Case Projects — Asks the student to synthesize the material learned in the chapter and complete an office assignment

SCANS icon — Indicates that the exercise or project meets SCANS competencies and prepares the student to be successful in today's workplace

MOUS Certification icon — Indicates that the exercise or project meets Microsoft's certification objectives that prepare the student for the MOUS exam

Internet Case Projects — Allow the student to practice using the World Wide Web

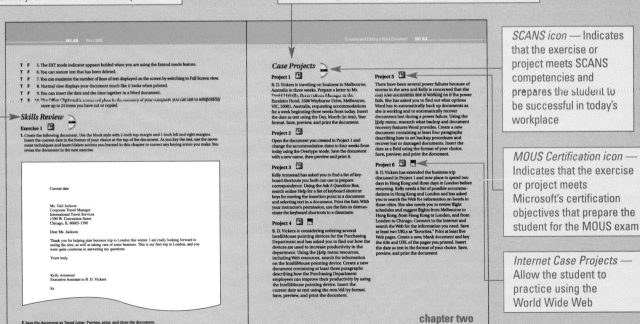

Acknowledgments

We would like to thank and express our appreciation to the many fine individuals who have contributed to the completion of this book.

No book is possible without the motivation and support of an editorial staff. Therefore, we wish to acknowledge with great appreciation the project team at Course Technology: Melissa Ramondetta, managing editor; Robert Gaggin, product manager; and Jodi Dreissig, editorial assistant. Our appreciation also goes to Robin Romer for managing the developmental editing of this series. In addition, we want to acknowledge the team at GEX for their production work, especially Karla Russell, Kendra Neville, Michelle Olson, and Angel Lesiczka.

We are very appreciative of the personnel at Napier & Judd, Inc., who helped to prepare this book. We acknowledge, with great appreciation, the assistance provided by Ollie Rivers and Nancy Onarheim in preparing and checking the many drafts of the Office unit and the Appendixes of this book.

We gratefully acknowledge the work of Linda Sourek and Susan Lehner in writing the PowerPoint unit for this series.

H. Albert Napier
Philip J. Judd

We would like to thank our families—Mick, Roxie, and Peter Sourek; Ed, Michael, Tracy, David, and Tommy Lehner—for their understanding and patience during this endeavor.

In addition, we would like to thank our parents, Gordon and Ruth Pedersen, and Tony and Lorraine Jayne for their encouragement and support.

Linda Sourek
Susan Lehner

Contents

PowerPoint Unit ————————————————————— PI 1

APPENDIX —————————————————————————— AP 1

Microsoft
Office XP

M

icrosoft Office XP provides the ability to enter, record, analyze, display, and present any type of business information. In this chapter, you learn about the capabilities of Microsoft Office XP, including its computer hardware and operating system requirements and elements common to all its applications. You also learn how to open and close those applications and get Help.

LEARNING OBJECTIVES

- ► Describe Microsoft Office XP
- ► Determine hardware and operating system requirements
- ► Identify common elements of Office applications
- ► Start Office applications
- ► Get Help in Office applications
- ► Close Office applications

chapter one

1.a What Is Microsoft Office XP?

Microsoft Office XP is a software suite (or package) that contains a combination of software applications you use to create text documents, analyze numbers, create presentations, manage large files of data, and create Web pages.

The **Word 2002** software application provides you with word processing capabilities. **Word processing** is the preparation and production of text documents such as letters, memorandums, and reports. **Excel 2002** is software you use to analyze numbers with worksheets (sometimes called spreadsheets) and charts and to perform other tasks such as sorting data. A **worksheet** is a grid of columns and rows in which you enter labels and data. A **chart** is a visual or graphical representation of worksheet data. With Excel, you can create financial budgets, reports, and a variety of other forms.

PowerPoint 2002 software is used to create a **presentation**, or collection of slides. A **slide** is the presentation output (actual 35mm slides, transparencies, computer screens, or printed pages) that can contain text, charts, graphics, audio, and video. You can use PowerPoint slides to create a slide show on a computer attached to a projector, to broadcast a presentation over the Internet or company intranet, and to create handout materials for a presentation.

Access 2002 provides database management capabilities, enabling you to store and retrieve a large amount of data. A **database** is a collection of related information. A phone book and an address book are common examples of databases you use every day. Other examples of databases include a price list, school registration information, or an inventory. You can query (or search) an Access database to answer specific questions about the stored data. For example, you can determine which customers in a particular state had sales in excess of a particular value during the month of June.

Outlook 2002 is a **personal information manager** that provides tools for sending and receiving e-mail as well as maintaining a calendar, contacts list, journal, electronic notes, and electronic "to do" list. The **FrontPage 2002** application is used to create and manage Web sites.

QUICK TIP

Office contains a variety of new features designed to minimize the impact of system crashes and freezes, such as one-click save in case of a system crash, timed recoveries, a new document recovery task pane, the Hang Manager, and a new corrupt document recovery feature.

chapter
one

notes   For the remainder of this book, Microsoft Office XP may be called Office. Rather than include the words *Microsoft* and *2002* each time the name of an application is used, the text refers to the respective software package as Word, Excel, PowerPoint, Access, or Outlook.

A major advantage of using the Office suite is the ability to share data between the applications. For example, you can include a portion of an Excel worksheet or chart in a Word document, use an outline created in a Word document as the starting point for a PowerPoint presentation, import an Excel worksheet into Access, and merge names and addresses from an Outlook Address Book with a Word letter.

1.b Hardware and Operating System Requirements

You can install Office applications on computers using the Windows 2000, Windows 98, or Windows NT Workstation 4.0 (with Service Pack 6a installed) operating systems. Office XP applications do not run in the Windows 95, Windows 3.x or the Windows NT Workstation 3.5 environments.

You can install Office on a "x86" computer with a Pentium processor, at least 32 MB of RAM for Windows 98 or 64 MB of RAM for Windows 2000, a CD-ROM drive, Super VGA, 256-color video, Microsoft Mouse, Microsoft IntelliMouse, or another pointing device, a 28,800 (or higher) baud modem, and 350 MB of hard disk space. To access certain features you should have a multimedia computer, e-mail software, and a Web browser. For detailed information on installing Office, see the documentation that comes with the software.

1.c Common Elements of Office Applications

Office applications share many technical features that make it easier for Information Technology (IT) Departments in organizations to manage their Office software installations. Additionally, the Office applications share many features that enable users to move seamlessly between applications and learn one way to perform common tasks, such as creating, saving, and printing documents or moving and copying data.

QUICK TIP

Speech recognition features enable users to speak the names of toolbar buttons, menus, menu items, alerts, dialog box control buttons, and task pane items. Users can switch between two modes— Dictation and Voice command—using the Language bar. For more information on using the Speech Recognition features, see Appendix C.

Office applications share many common elements, making it easier for you to work efficiently in any application. A **window** is a rectangular area on your screen in which you view a software application, such as Excel. All the Office application windows have a similar look and arrangement of shortcuts, menus, and toolbars. In addition, they share many features—such as a common dictionary to check spelling in your work, identical menu commands, toolbar buttons, shortcut menus, and keyboard shortcuts to perform tasks such as copying data from one location to another.

notes

You learn more about the common elements of the Office applications in later chapters of this unit or in specific application units.

Figure 1-1 shows many of the common elements in the Office application windows.

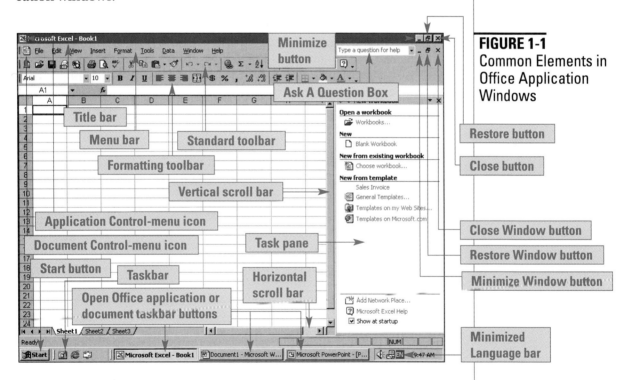

FIGURE 1-1
Common Elements in Office Application Windows

Title Bar

The application **title bar** at the top of the window includes the application Control-menu icon, the application name, the filename of the active document, and the Minimize, Restore (or Maximize), and Close buttons.

The **application Control-menu** icon, located in the upper-left corner of the title bar, displays the Control menu. The Control menu commands manage the application window, and typically include commands such

chapter
one

as Restore, Move, Size, Minimize, Maximize, and Close. Commands that are currently available appear in a dark color. You can view the Control menu by clicking the Control-menu icon or by holding down the ALT key and then pressing the SPACEBAR key.

The **Minimize** button, near the right corner of the title bar reduces the application window to a taskbar button. The **Maximize** button, to the right of the Minimize button, enlarges the application window to fill the entire screen viewing area above the taskbar. If the window is already maximized, the Restore button appears in its place. The **Restore** button reduces the application window to a smaller size on your screen. The **Close** button, located in the right corner of the title bar, closes the application and removes it from the computer's memory.

Menu Bar

The **menu bar** is a special toolbar located at the top of the window below the title bar and contains the menus for the application. A **menu** is list of commands. The menus common to Office applications are File, Edit, View, Insert, Format, Tools, Window, and Help. Other menus vary between applications.

The **document Control-menu** icon, located below the application Control-menu icon, contains the Restore, Move, Size, Minimize, Maximize, and Close menu commands for the document window. You can view the document Control menu by clicking the Control-menu icon or by holding down the ALT key and pressing the HYPHEN (-) key.

The **Minimize Window** button reduces the document window to a title-bar icon inside the document area. It appears on the menu bar below the Minimize button in Excel and PowerPoint. (Word documents open in their own application window and use the Minimize button on the title bar.)

The **Maximize Window** button enlarges the size of the document window to cover the entire application display area and share the application title bar. It appears on the title-bar icon of a minimized Excel workbook or PowerPoint presentation. (Word documents automatically open in their own application window and use the Maximize button on the title bar.) If the window is already maximized, the Restore Window button appears in its place.

The **Restore Window** button changes the size of the document window to a smaller sized window inside the application window. It appears in the menu bar to the right of the Minimize Window button in Excel and PowerPoint. (Word documents automatically open in their own application Window and use the Restore button on the title bar.)

The **Close Window** button closes the document and removes it from the memory of the computer. It appears in the menu bar to the right of the Restore Window or Maximize Window button.

Default Toolbars

The **Standard** and **Formatting toolbars**, located one row below the menu bar, contain a set of icons called buttons. The toolbar buttons represent commonly used commands and are mouse shortcuts that enable you to perform tasks quickly. In addition to the Standard and Formatting toolbars, each application has several other toolbars available. You can customize toolbars by adding or removing buttons and commands.

When the mouse pointer rests on a toolbar button, a **ScreenTip** appears, identifying the name of the button. ScreenTips are also provided as part of online Help to describe a toolbar button, a dialog box option, or a menu command.

Scroll Bars

The vertical scroll bar appears on the right side of the document area. The **vertical scroll bar** is used to view various parts of the document by moving or scrolling the document up or down. It includes scroll arrows and a scroll box. The horizontal scroll bar appears near the bottom of the document area. The **horizontal scroll bar** is used to view various parts of the document by moving or scrolling the document left or right. It includes scroll arrows and a scroll box.

Ask A Question Box

The **Ask A Question Box** is a help tool alternative to the Office Assistant that appears on the menu bar of every Office application. The Ask A Question Box is used to quickly key a help question in plain English and then view a list of relevant Help topics.

Task Pane

Office XP includes a **task pane** feature, a pane of shortcuts, which opens on the right side of the application window. The contents of the task pane vary with the application and the activities being performed. For example, task pane shortcuts can be used to create new Office documents, format Word documents or PowerPoint presentations, or perform a Word mail merge. The task pane can be displayed or hidden as desired.

Taskbar

The **taskbar,** located across the bottom of the Windows desktop, includes the Start button and buttons for each open Office document. The **Start button,** located at the left end of the taskbar, displays the Start menu or list of tasks you can perform and applications you can use.

You can switch between documents, close documents and applications, and view other items, such as the system time and printer status, with buttons or icons on the taskbar. If you are using Windows 2000 or Windows 98, other toolbars, such as the Quick Launch toolbar, may also appear on the taskbar.

QUICK TIP

The **Office Assistant** is an interactive, animated graphic that appears in the Office application windows. When you activate the Office Assistant, a balloon-style dialog box opens to display options for searching online Help by topic. The Office Assistant may also automatically offer suggestions when you begin certain tasks. You can customize the Office Assistant by changing the animated graphic image or turning on or off various options. Any customization is shared by all Office applications.

chapter
one

1.d Starting Office Applications

You access the Office applications through the Windows desktop. The Windows operating system software is automatically loaded into the memory of your computer when you turn on your computer. After turning on your computer, the Windows desktop appears.

You begin by using the Start button on the taskbar to view the Start menu and open the Excel application. To use the Start button to open the Excel application:

Step 1	*Click*	the Start button [Start] on the taskbar
Step 2	*Point to*	Programs
Step 3	*Click*	Microsoft Excel on the Programs menu

The Excel software is placed into the memory of your computer and the Excel window opens. Your screen should look similar to Figure 1-1.

notes
You may sometimes use the keyboard to use Office application features. This book lists all keys, such as the TAB key, in uppercase letters. When the keyboard is used to issue a command, this book lists keystrokes as: Press the ENTER key. When you are to press one key and, while holding down that key, to press another key, this book lists the keystrokes as: Press the SHIFT + F7 keys.

You can open and work in more than one Office application at a time. When Office is installed, two additional commands appear on the Start menu: the Open Office Document command and the New Office Document command. You can use these commands to select the type of document on which you want to work rather than first selecting an Office application. To create a new Word document without first opening the application:

Step 1	*Click*	the Start button [Start] on the taskbar
Step 2	*Click*	New Office Document
Step 3	*Click*	the General tab, if necessary

The New Office Document dialog box on your screen should look similar to Figure 1-2. A **dialog box** is a window that contains options for performing specific tasks.

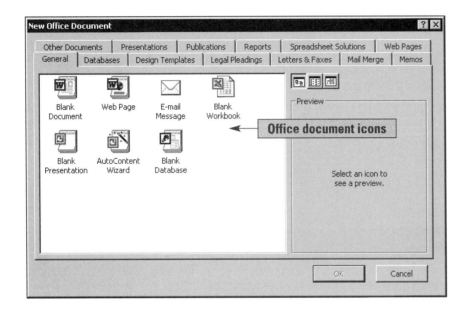

FIGURE 1-2
General Tab in the New Office Document Dialog Box

This dialog box provides options for creating different Office documents. **Icons** (or pictures) represent the Office document options; the number of icons available depends on the Office suite applications you have installed. The icons shown here create a blank Word document, a blank Web page (in Word), an e-mail message (using Outlook or Outlook Express), a blank Excel workbook, a blank PowerPoint presentation, a PowerPoint presentation using the AutoContent Wizard, and a blank Access database. You want to create a blank Word document.

| Step 4 | *Click* | the Blank Document icon to select it, if necessary |
| Step 5 | *Click* | OK |

The Word software is placed in the memory of your computer, the Word application window opens with a blank document. Your screen should look similar to Figure 1-3.

MOUSE TIP

Double-clicking an icon is the same as clicking the icon once to select it and then clicking the OK button.

chapter
one

FIGURE 1-3
Word Application Window

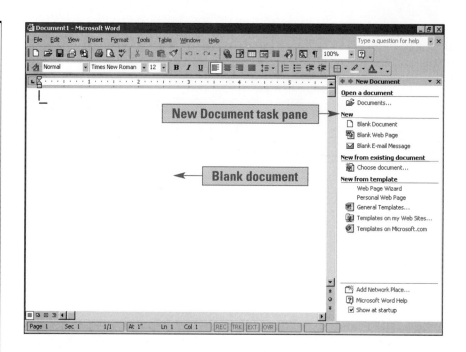

MENU TIP

The task pane containing shortcuts to create new documents or open existing documents opens by default when you launch a Word, Excel, or PowerPoint application. However, if you create or open another document in the same application, the task pane automatically hides. To display it again, click the Tas<u>k</u> Pane command on the <u>V</u>iew menu.

Next you open a blank presentation. To open the PowerPoint application:

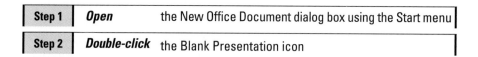

| Step 1 | *Open* | the New Office Document dialog box using the Start menu |
| Step 2 | *Double-click* | the Blank Presentation icon |

Your screen should look similar to Figure 1-4.

FIGURE 1-4
Blank PowerPoint
Presentation

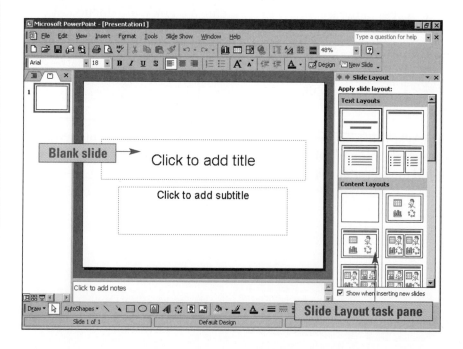

You can also open an Office application by opening an existing Office document from the Start menu. To open an existing Access database:

Step 1	*Click*	the Start button [Start] on the taskbar
Step 2	*Click*	Open Office Document
Step 3	*Click*	the Look in: list arrow in the Open Office Document dialog box
Step 4	*Switch to*	the disk drive and folder where the Data Files are stored
Step 5	*Double-click*	International Sales

The Access application window and Database window that open on your screen should look similar to Figure 1-5.

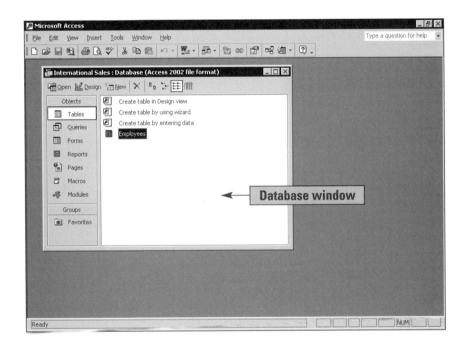

FIGURE 1-5
International Sales Database in Access Window

QUICK TIP

You can have multiple Excel workbooks, PowerPoint presentations, and Word documents open at one time. The number of documents, workbooks, and presentations you can have open at one time is determined by your computer's resources. You can open only one Access database at a time.

You can switch between open Office documents by clicking the appropriate taskbar button. If multiple windows are open, the **active window** has a dark blue title bar. All inactive windows have a gray title bar. To switch to the Excel workbook and then the Word document:

Step 1	*Click*	the Excel button on the taskbar
Step 2	*Observe*	that the Excel application window and workbook are now visible
Step 3	*Click*	the Word Document1 button on the taskbar
Step 4	*Observe*	that the Word application window and document are now visible

chapter
one

1.e Getting Help in Office Applications

You can get help when working in any Office application in several ways. You can use the <u>H</u>elp menu, the Help toolbar button, or the F1 key to display the Office Assistant; get context-sensitive help with the What's <u>T</u>his command or the SHIFT + F1 keys; or launch your Web browser and get Web-based help from Microsoft. You can also key a help question in the Ask A Question Box on the menu bar.

Using the Ask A Question Box

Suppose you want to find out how to use keyboard shortcuts in Word. To get help for keyboard shortcuts using the Ask A Question Box:

Step 1	*Verify*	that the Word document is the active window
Step 2	*Click*	in the Ask A Question Box
Step 3	*Key*	keyboard shortcuts
Step 4	*Press*	the ENTER key

A list of help topics related to keyboard shortcut keys appears. Your list should look similar to the one shown in Figure 1-6.

FIGURE 1-6
List of Help Topics

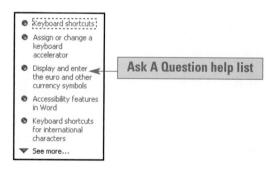

If you want to view the detailed help for any topic, simply click that topic in the list.

Step 5	*Press*	the ESC key
Step 6	*Click*	in the document area to deselect the Ask A Question Box

Using the Help Menu

The Help menu provides commands you can use to view the Office Assistant or Help window, show or hide the Office Assistant, connect to the Microsoft Web site, get context-sensitive help for a menu command or toolbar button, detect and repair font and template files, and view licensing information for the Office application. To review the Help menu commands:

Step 1	*Click*	Help on the menu bar

The Help menu on your screen should look similar to Figure 1-7.

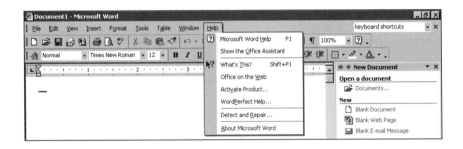

FIGURE 1-7
Help Menu

Step 2	*Observe*	the menu commands
Step 3	*Click*	in the document area outside the menu to close the Help menu

Using What's This?

You can get context-sensitive help for a menu command or toolbar button using the What's This? command on the Help menu. This command changes the mouse pointer to a help pointer, a white mouse pointer with a large black question mark. When you click a toolbar button or menu command with the help pointer, a brief ScreenTip help message appears, describing the command or toolbar button. You can quickly change the mouse pointer to a help pointer by pressing the SHIFT + F1 keys.

To view the help pointer and view a ScreenTip help message for a toolbar button:

Step 1	*Press*	the SHIFT + F1 keys
Step 2	*Observe*	the help mouse pointer with the attached question mark
Step 3	*Click*	the Save button 🖫 on the Standard toolbar
Step 4	*Observe*	the ScreenTip help message describing the Save button

> **QUICK TIP**
>
> You can click the Help button on the title bar in any dialog box to convert the mouse pointer to a What's This help pointer.

chapter
one

Step 5	*Press*	the ESC key to close the ScreenTip help message

1.f Closing Office Applications

There are many ways to close the Access, Excel, and PowerPoint applications (or the Word application with a single document open) and return to the Windows desktop. You can:

- double-click the application Control-menu icon on the title bar.
- click the application Close button on the title bar.
- right-click the application button on the taskbar to display a short-cut menu and then click the Close command.
- press the ALT + F4 keys.
- click the Exit command on the File menu to close Office applications (no matter how many Word documents are open).

To close the Excel application from the taskbar:

Step 1	*Right-click*	the Excel button on the taskbar
Step 2	*Click*	Close

You can close multiple applications at one time from the taskbar by selecting the application buttons using the CTRL key and then using the shortcut menu. To close the PowerPoint and Access applications at one time:

Step 1	*Press & hold*	the CTRL key
Step 2	*Click*	the PowerPoint button and then the Access button on the taskbar
Step 3	*Release*	the CTRL key and observe that both buttons are selected (pressed in)
Step 4	*Right-click*	the PowerPoint or Access button
Step 5	*Click*	Close

Both applications close, leaving only the Word document open. To close the Word document using the menu:

Step 1	*Verify*	that the Word application window is maximized
Step 2	*Click*	File
Step 3	*Click*	Exit

Summary

► The Word application provides word processing capabilities for the preparation of text documents, such as letters, memorandums, and reports.

► The Excel application provides the ability to analyze numbers in worksheets and for creating financial budgets, reports, charts, and forms.

► The PowerPoint application is used to create presentation slides and audience handouts.

► You use the Access databases to store and retrieve collections of data.

► The Outlook application helps you send and receive e-mail and maintain a calendar, "to do" lists, and the names and addresses of contacts—and perform other information management tasks.

► One major advantage of using the Office suite applications is the ability to integrate the applications by sharing information between them.

► Another advantage of the Office suite applications is that they share a number of common elements such as window features, shortcuts, toolbars, and menu commands.

► You can start the Office suite applications from the Programs submenu on the Start menu and from the Open Office Document or New Office Document commands on the Start menu.

► To close the Office applications, you can double-click the application Control-menu icon, single-click the application Close button on the title bar, right-click the application button on the taskbar, press the ALT + F4 keys, or click the Exit command on the File menu.

► To get help in an Office application, you can click commands on the Help menu, press the F1 key or the SHIFT + F1 keys, or click the Microsoft Help button on the Standard toolbar.

chapter one

Concepts Review

SCANS

Circle the correct answer.

1. ScreenTips do not provide:
- [a] the name of a button on a toolbar.
- [b] help for options in a dialog box.
- [c] context-sensitive help for menu commands or toolbar buttons.
- [d] access to the Office Assistant.

2. To manage a Web site, you can use:
- [a] Outlook.
- [b] FrontPage.
- [c] Excel.
- [d] Publisher.

3. The title bar contains the:
- [a] document Control-menu icon.
- [b] Close Window button.
- [c] Standard toolbar.
- [d] application and document name.

4. The Excel application is best used to:
- [a] prepare financial reports.
- [b] maintain a list of tasks to accomplish.
- [c] prepare text documents.
- [d] manage Web sites.

5. A major advantage of using Office applications is the ability to:
- [a] store mailing lists.
- [b] analyze numbers.
- [c] share information between applications.
- [d] sort data.

6. Word processing is used primarily to:
- [a] create presentation slides.
- [b] analyze numbers.
- [c] prepare text documents.
- [d] maintain a calendar and "to do" lists.

7. Right-click means to:
- [a] press the left mouse button twice rapidly.
- [b] place the mouse pointer on a command or item.
- [c] press and hold down the right mouse button and then move the mouse.
- [d] press the right mouse button and then release it.

8. You cannot close Office XP applications by:
- [a] clicking the Exit command on the File menu.
- [b] clicking the Close button on the title bar.
- [c] right-clicking the application button on the taskbar and clicking Close.
- [d] pressing the SHIFT + F4 keys.

Circle **T** if the statement is true or **F** if the statement is false.

T F 1. You use Excel to create newsletters and brochures.

T F 2. Word is used to create presentation slides.

T F 3. The Office Assistant is an interactive graphic used to get online help in Office applications.

T F 4. Access is used to create and format text.

T F 5. You can open and work in only one Office application at a time.

T F 6. When you open multiple documents in an Office application, each document has its own button on the taskbar.

Skills Review

Exercise 1

1. Identify each of the numbered elements of Office application windows in the following figure.

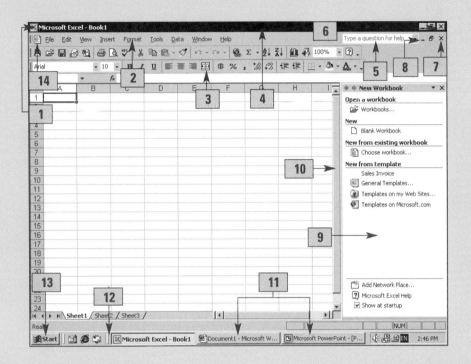

Exercise 2

1. Open the Word application using the Programs command on the Start menu.

2. Close the Word application using the taskbar.

Exercise 3

1. Open the Excel application using the Programs command on the Start menu.

2. Open the PowerPoint application using the Programs command on the Start menu.

3. Open the Access application and the *International Sales* database using the Open Office Document command on the Start menu.

4. Switch to the PowerPoint application using the taskbar button and close it using the Close button on the title bar.

5. Close the Excel and Access applications at the same time using the taskbar.

Exercise 4

1. Create a new, blank Word document using the New Office Document command on the Start menu.

2. Create a new, blank Excel workbook using the New Office Document command on the Start menu.

3. Switch to the Word document using the taskbar and close it using the Close button on the title bar.

4. Close the Excel workbook using the taskbar button.

chapter one

Exercise 5

1. Open the Word application using the Start menu.

2. Show the Office Assistant, if necessary, with a command on the Help menu.

3. Hide the Office Assistant with a shortcut menu.

4. Show the Office Assistant with the Microsoft Word Help button on the Standard toolbar.

5. Search online Help using the search phrase "key text."

6. Click the "Change typing and editing options" link.

7. Review the Help text and then close the Help window.

8. Show the Office Assistant, and then click the Options command on the Office Assistant shortcut menu.

9. Click the Use the Office Assistant check box to remove the check mark and turn off the Office Assistant.

Exercise 6

1. Write a paragraph that describes the different ways to close the Word application.

Exercise 7

1. Open any Office application and use the Ask A Question Box and the keyword "Office Assistant" to search for online Help for information on using the Office Assistant.

2. Write down the instructions for selecting a different Office Assistant graphic image.

Case Projects

SCANS

Project 1

You are the secretary to the marketing manager of High Risk Insurance, an insurance brokerage firm. The marketing manager wants to know how to open and close the Excel application. Write at least two paragraphs describing different ways to open and close the Excel application. With your instructor's permission, use your written description to show a classmate several ways to open and close the Excel application.

Project 2

You work in the administrative offices of Alma Public Relations and the information management department just installed Office XP on your computer. Your supervisor asks you to write down and describe some of the Office Assistant options. Display the Office Assistant. Right-click the Office Assistant graphic, click the Options command, and view the Options tab in the Office Assistant dialog box. Click the What's This? or Help button on the dialog box title bar and review each option. Write at least three paragraphs describing five Office Assistant options.

Project 3

As the new office manager at Hot Wheels Messenger Service, you are learning to use the Word 2002 application and want to learn more about some of the buttons on the Word toolbars. Open Word and use the What's This? command on the Help menu to review the ScreenTip help for five toolbar buttons. Write a brief paragraph for each button describing how it is used.

Project 4

You are the administrative assistant to the vice president of operations for Extreme Sports, Inc., a sports equipment retailer with stores in several cities in your state. The vice president wants to save time and money by performing business tasks more efficiently. She asks you to think of different ways to perform common business tasks by sharing information between the Office XP applications. Write at least three paragraphs describing how the company can use Word, Excel, PowerPoint, Access, and Outlook to improve efficiency by combining information.

Working with Menus, Toolbars, and Task Panes

Chapter Overview

Office tries to make your work life easier by learning how you work. The personalized menus and toolbars in each application remember which commands and buttons you use and add and remove them as needed. Office has two new tools—task panes and Smart Tags—that provide shortcuts for performing different activities. In this chapter, you learn how to work with the personalized menus and toolbars and how to use task panes and Smart Tags.

LEARNING OBJECTIVES

- ▶ Work with personalized menus and toolbars
- ▶ View, hide, dock, and float toolbars
- ▶ Work with task panes
- ▶ Review Smart Tags

chapter two

2.a Working with Personalized Menus and Toolbars

A **menu** is a list of commands you use to perform tasks in the Office applications. Some of the commands also have an associated image, or icon, which appears to the left of each command in the menu. Most menus are found on the menu bar located below the title bar in the Office applications. A **toolbar** contains a set of icons (the same icons you see on the menus) called "buttons" that you click with the mouse pointer to quickly execute a menu command.

notes
The activities in this chapter assume the personalized menus and toolbars are reset to their default settings. As you learn about menus and toolbars, task panes, and Smart Tags you are asked to select menu commands and toolbar buttons by clicking them with the mouse pointer. You do not learn how to use the menu command or toolbar button, task pane, or Smart Tags to perform detailed tasks in this chapter. Using these features to perform detailed tasks is covered in the individual application chapters.

When you first install Office and then open an Office application, the menus on the menu bar initially show only a basic set of commands and the Standard and Formatting toolbars contain only a basic set of buttons. These short versions of the menus and toolbars are called **personalized menus and toolbars**. As you work in the application, the commands and buttons you use most frequently are stored in the personalized settings. The first time you select a menu command or toolbar button that is not part of the basic set, that command or button is automatically added to your personalized settings and appears on the menu or toolbar. If you do not use a command for a while, it is removed from your personalized settings and no longer appears on the menu or toolbar. To view the personalized menus and toolbars in PowerPoint:

Step 1	*Click*	the New Office Document command on the Start menu
Step 2	*Click*	the General tab in the New Office Document dialog box, if necessary
Step 3	*Double-click*	the Blank Presentation icon
Step 4	*Click*	Tools on the menu bar
Step 5	*Observe*	the short personalized menu containing only the basic commands

The Tools menu on your screen should look similar to Figure 2-1.

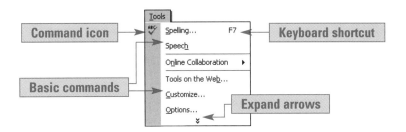

FIGURE 2-1
Personalized Tools Menu

If the command you want to use does not appear on the short personalized menu, you can expand the menu. The fastest way to expand a personalized menu is to double-click the menu command on the menu bar. For example, to quickly expand the Insert menu, you can double-click the Insert command on the menu bar. Another way to expand a menu is to click the Expand arrows that appear at the bottom of the personalized menu when it opens. Finally, after opening a menu, you can pause for a few seconds until the menu automatically expands. To expand the Tools menu:

| Step 1 | *Pause* | until the menu automatically expands *or* click the Expand arrows at the bottom of the menu to expand the menu |

The expanded Tools menu on your screen should look similar to Figure 2-2.

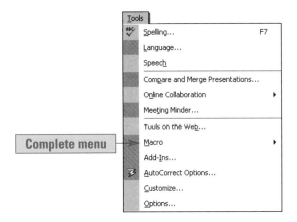

FIGURE 2-2
Expanded Tools Menu

You move a menu command from the expanded menu to the personalized menu simply by selecting it. To add the AutoCorrect Options command to the short personalized Tools menu:

| Step 1 | *Click* | AutoCorrect Options |

chapter
two

Step 2	*Click*	Cancel in the AutoCorrect dialog box to close the dialog box without making any changes
Step 3	*Click*	Tools on the menu bar
Step 4	*Observe*	the updated personalized Tools menu contains the AutoCorrect Options command

The Tools menu on your screen should look similar to Figure 2-3.

FIGURE 2-3
Updated Personalized
Tools Menu

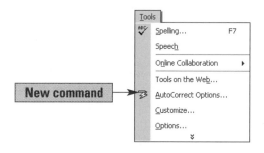

New command

Step 5	*Press*	the ESC key twice to close the menu

The first time you launch most Office applications, the Standard and Formatting toolbars appear on one row below the title bar. In this position, you cannot see all their default buttons. If a toolbar button is not visible, you can resize or reposition one of the toolbars. When the mouse pointer is positioned on a toolbar **move handle** (the gray vertical bar at the left edge of the toolbar), the mouse pointer changes from a white arrow pointer to a **move pointer**, a four-headed black arrow. You can drag the move handle with the move pointer to resize or reposition toolbar. To resize the Formatting toolbar:

Step 1	*Move*	the mouse pointer to the move handle on the Formatting toolbar
Step 2	*Observe*	that the mouse pointer becomes a move pointer

The move pointer on your screen should look similar to Figure 2-4.

FIGURE 2-4
Move Pointer on the
Formatting Toolbar Handle

Step 3	*Click & hold*	the left mouse button
Step 4	*Drag*	the Formatting toolbar to the right as far as you can to view the default buttons on the Standard toolbar

Step 5	*Drag*	the Formatting toolbar to the left as far as you can to view the default buttons on the Formatting toolbar
Step 6	*Release*	the mouse button
Step 7	*Observe*	that you now see three buttons on the Standard toolbar

The buttons that don't fit on the displayed area of a toolbar are collected in a Toolbar Options list. The last button on any toolbar, the Toolbar Options button, is used to display the Toolbar Options list. To view the Toolbar Options list:

| Step 1 | *Click* | the Toolbar Options button list arrow ⬛ on the Standard toolbar |
| Step 2 | *Observe* | the default buttons that are not visible on the toolbar |

The Toolbar Options list on your screen should look similar to Figure 2-5.

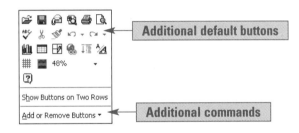

FIGURE 2-5
Toolbar Options List

If you want to display one of the default buttons on a personalized toolbar, you can select it from the Toolbar Options list. To add the Search button to the personalized Standard toolbar:

| Step 1 | *Click* | the Search button 🔍 |
| Step 2 | *Observe* | that the Search button is added to the personalized Standard toolbar |

When you add another button to the personalized Standard toolbar, one of the other buttons might move out of view. This is because of the limited viewing area of the Standard toolbar in its current position. If you want to view all the menu commands instead of a short personalized menu and all the default toolbar buttons on the Standard and Formatting toolbars, you can change options in the Customize dialog box. To view the Customize dialog box:

| Step 1 | *Click* | Tools on the menu bar |

chapter
two

Step 2	*Click*	<u>C</u>ustomize
Step 3	*Click*	the <u>O</u>ptions tab, if necessary

The Customize dialog box on your screen should look similar to Figure 2-6.

FIGURE 2-6
<u>O</u>ptions Tab in the
Customize Dialog Box

Personalized menus and toolbars options

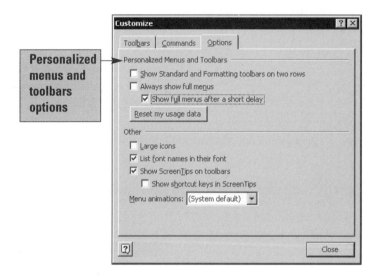

If you reposition the Formatting toolbar below the Standard toolbar, you can view all the default buttons on both toolbars. You can do this by inserting a check mark in the <u>S</u>how Standard and Formatting toolbars on two rows check box. You can insert a check mark in the Always show full me<u>n</u>us check box to view the entire set of menu commands for each menu instead of the short personalized menus. If you do not want the short personalized menus to expand automatically when you pause, you can remove the check mark from the Show f<u>u</u>ll menus after a short delay check box. Then, to show the full menu, you have to double-click the menu or click the expand arrows at the bottom of the menu.

You want to show all the Standard and Formatting toolbar buttons and menu commands.

Step 4	*Click*	the <u>S</u>how Standard and Formatting toolbars on two rows check box to insert a check mark
Step 5	*Click*	the Always show full me<u>n</u>us check box to insert a check mark
Step 6	*Click*	Close to close the dialog box
Step 7	*Observe*	the repositioned and expanded Standard and Formatting toolbars

| Step 8 | Click | Tools to view the entire set of Tools menu commands |
| Step 9 | Press | the ESC key to close the Tools menu |

You can return the menus and toolbars to their initial (or **default**) settings in the Customize dialog box. To open the Customize dialog box and reset the default menus and toolbars:

Step 1	Click	Tools
Step 2	Click	Customize
Step 3	Click	the Options tab, if necessary
Step 4	Remove	the two check marks you just inserted
Step 5	Click	Reset my usage data
Step 6	Click	Yes to confirm you want to reset the menus and toolbars to their default settings
Step 7	Close	the Customize dialog box
Step 8	Observe	that the Tools menu and Standard toolbar are reset to their default settings

2.b Viewing, Hiding, Docking, and Floating Toolbars

Office applications have additional toolbars that you can view when you need them. You can also hide toolbars when you are not using them. You can view or hide toolbars by pointing to the Toolbars command on the View menu and clicking a toolbar name or by using a shortcut menu. A **shortcut menu** is a short list of frequently used menu commands. You view a shortcut menu by pointing to an item on the screen and clicking the right mouse button. This is called right-clicking the item. The commands on shortcut menus vary depending on where you right-click, so that you view only the most frequently used commands for a particular task. An easy way to view or hide toolbars is with a shortcut menu.

notes Although the PowerPoint application is used to illustrate how to customize toolbars, the same techniques are used to customize toolbars and menus in the Word, Excel, and Access applications.

MOUSE TIP

You can use a command on the Toolbar Options list to place the Standard and Formatting toolbars that currently appear on one row on two rows. You can also place the Standard and Formatting toolbars that appear in two rows back to one row with a command on the Toolbar Options list.

chapter two

To view the shortcut menu for toolbars:

| Step 1 | *Right-click* | the menu bar, the Standard toolbar, or the Formatting toolbar |
| Step 2 | *Observe* | the shortcut menu and the check marks next to the names of displayed toolbars |

Your shortcut menu should look similar to Figure 2-7.

FIGURE 2-7
Toolbars Shortcut Menu

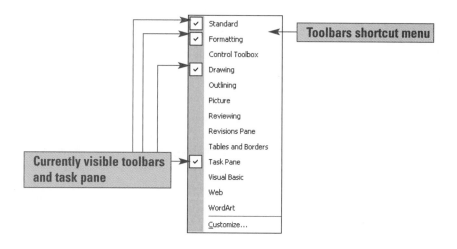

| Step 3 | *Click* | Tables and Borders in the shortcut menu |
| Step 4 | *Observe* | that the Tables and Borders toolbar appears on your screen |

QUICK TIP

Some of the toolbars that appear on the toolbars shortcut menu vary from one Office application to another.

The Tables and Borders toolbar, unless a previous user repositioned it, is visible in its own window near the middle of your screen. When a toolbar is visible in its own window, it is called a **floating toolbar** and you can move and size it with the mouse pointer similar to any window. When a toolbar appears fixed at the screen boundaries, it is called a **docked toolbar**. The menu bar and Standard and Formatting toolbars are examples of docked toolbars because they are fixed below the title bar at the top of the screen. In PowerPoint, the Drawing toolbar is docked at the bottom of the screen above the status bar. You can dock a floating toolbar by dragging its title bar with the mouse pointer to a docking position below the title bar, above the status bar, or at the left and right boundaries of your screen.

To dock the Tables and Borders toolbar below the Standard and Formatting toolbars, if necessary:

| Step 1 | *Click & hold* | the title bar in the Tables and Borders toolbar window |

Step 2	*Observe*	that the mouse pointer becomes a move pointer
Step 3	*Drag*	the toolbar window up slowly until it docks below the Standard and Formatting toolbars
Step 4	*Release*	the mouse button

Similarly, you float a docked toolbar by dragging it away from its docked position toward the middle of the screen. To float the Tables and Borders toolbar, if necessary:

| Step 1 | *Position* | the mouse pointer on the Tables and Borders toolbar move handle until it becomes a move pointer |
| Step 2 | *Drag* | the Tables and Borders toolbar down toward the middle of the screen until it appears in its own window |

When you finish using a toolbar, you can hide it with a shortcut menu. To hide the Tables and Borders toolbar:

| Step 1 | *Right-click* | the Tables and Borders toolbar |
| Step 2 | *Click* | Tables and Borders to remove the check mark and hide the toolbar |

2.c Working with Task Panes

The task pane is a tool with many uses in the Office applications. For example, when you launch Word, Excel, PowerPoint, or Access a new file task pane appears on the right side of the application window. This task pane allows you to create new documents in a variety of ways or open existing documents and replaces the New dialog box found in earlier versions of the Office applications. For example, in the Word application, this task pane is called the New Document task pane and contains hyperlink shortcuts for creating a new document or opening an existing document, creating a blank Web page, sending an e-mail message, choosing an existing document to use as the basis for a new document, and other options. A **hyperlink** is text or a graphic image that you can click to view another page or item. The hyperlink shortcuts in the task pane are colored blue. When you place your mouse pointer on a blue hyperlink shortcut, the mouse pointer changes to a hand with a pointing finger. You can then click the hyperlink shortcut to view the page or option to which the shortcut is linked.

Another way to use a task pane in each of the Office applications is to display the Search task pane and use it to search your local computer

---

M O U S E   T I P

You can dock a floating toolbar by double-clicking its title bar. The toolbar returns to its previously docked position.

You can close a floating toolbar by clicking the Close button on the toolbar's title bar.

Q U I C K   T I P

In Excel, the new file task pane is called the New Workbook task pane; in PowerPoint, it is called the New Presentation task pane; in Access, it is called the New File task pane.

Each Office application also contains specific task panes: for example— you can format text in a Word document, copy and paste data in an Excel worksheet, and apply an attractive design and animation scheme to a PowerPoint presentation—all from special task panes.

chapter
two

system and network for files based on specific criteria such as keywords in the file text, the file's location, the file type, and the file's name. You can also search for Outlook items using the Search task pane.

To view a blank Word document and the Search task pane:

Step 1	*Start*	the Word application using the Start menu
Step 2	*Click*	File on the menu bar
Step 3	*Click*	Search

The Basic Search task pane is now visible. Your screen should look similar to Figure 2-8.

FIGURE 2-8
Basic Search Task
Pane in Word

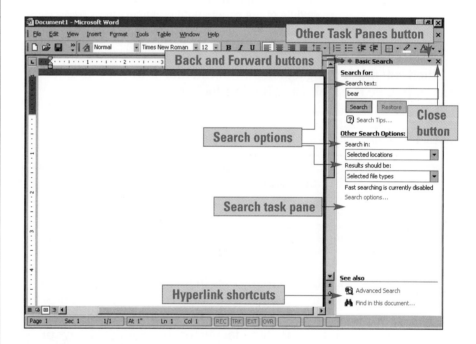

When you have multiple task panes open, you can use the Back and Forward buttons on the task pane title bar to switch between the task panes. To switch from the Basic Search task pane to the New Document task pane:

| Step 1 | *Click* | the Back button [icon] in the Basic Search task pane to view the New Document task pane |
| Step 2 | *Click* | the Forward button [icon] in the New Document task pane to view the Basic Search task pane |

MOUSE TIP

You also can view the Search task pane by clicking the Search button on the Standard toolbar.

You can key text in the Search text: text box to look for files containing specific text. You can use the Search in: list to select the locations in which to search, and use the Results should be: list to select the file types to search for. If your search criteria are more complex, you can click the Advanced Search link to view the Advanced Search task pane, where you can set additional search criteria such as file attributes called **properties**, or use operators such as "and" to set multiple criteria or "or" to set exclusive criteria.

A task pane appears docked on the right side of the application window by default. You can "float" the task pane in the application window or dock it on the left side of the application window, as you prefer. Like docking a floating toolbar, when you double-click a task pane title bar, it returns to its last docked or floating position. To float the docked task pane:

Step 1	*Double-click*	the Basic Search task pane title bar
Step 2	*Observe*	the task pane's new position, floating in the application window

Your screen should look similar to Figure 2-9.

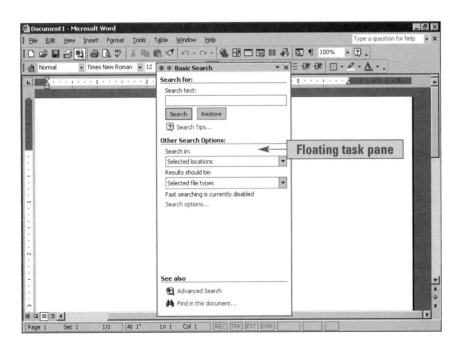

Step 3	*Double-click*	the Basic Search task pane title bar
Step 4	*Observe*	that the Basic Search task pane returns to its previous docked position

TASK PANE TIP

You can click the Other Task Panes list arrow on the task pane title bar to view a list of different task panes available in the application. Then, you can click one of the task panes in the list to open it. Additionally, some task panes appear automatically as you perform certain activities in an application.

You can also display the last previous visible task pane by using the Task Pane command on the View menu.

FIGURE 2-9
Floating Task Pane

MOUSE TIP

You can float a docked task pane by dragging the task pane away from its docked position using the mouse and the task pane title bar. Conversely, you can dock a floating task pane by dragging the task pane to the left or right side of the screen.

You can size a floating task pane by dragging the pane's top, bottom, left, or right borders with the mouse pointer.

chapter
two

You can close the current task pane by clicking the Close button on the task pane title bar. When you close the current task pane, all open task panes are also closed. For example, you currently have the New Document task pane and the Basic Search task pane open. When you close the Basic Search task pane, both task panes are closed. You can view the New Document task pane again with a menu command or toolbar button. To close the Basic Search and New Document task panes and then reopen the New Document task pane:

Step 1	*Click*	the Close button ☒ on the Basic Search task pane title bar
Step 2	*Observe*	that neither the Basic Search nor the New Document task pane is visible
Step 3	*Click*	File on the menu bar
Step 4	*Click*	New

The New Document task pane opens at the right side of the application window.

2.d Reviewing Smart Tags

Smart Tags are labels used to identify data as a specific type of data. You can use Smart Tags to perform an action in an open Office application instead of opening another application to perform that task. For example, a person's name is one kind of data that can be recognized and labeled with a Smart Tag. Suppose you key a person's name in a Word document and then want to create a contact item for that person in your Outlook Contacts folder. You can use a Smart Tag to create the contact item from Word without opening Outlook.

Smart Tags are represented by an action button and a purple dotted line underneath the text. The Smart Tag options are found in the AutoCorrect dialog box. To view the Smart Tag options in the Word application:

Step 1	*Click*	Tools on the menu bar
Step 2	*Click*	AutoCorrect Options
Step 3	*Click*	the Smart Tags tab in the AutoCorrect dialog box

The AutoCorrect dialog box on your screen should look similar to Figure 2-10.

QUICK TIP

The **Office Shortcut Bar** is a toolbar that you can open and position on your Windows desktop to provide shortcuts to Office applications and tasks. The Office Shortcut Bar can contain buttons for the New Office Document and Open Office Document commands you see on the Start menu, shortcut buttons to create various Outlook items, and buttons to open Office applications installed on your computer. You can access the Office Shortcut Bar with the Microsoft Office Tools command on the Programs menu.

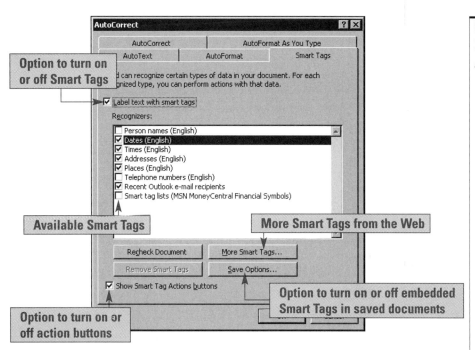

Option to turn on or off Smart Tags

Available Smart Tags

More Smart Tags from the Web

Option to turn on or off embedded Smart Tags in saved documents

Option to turn on or off action buttons

FIGURE 2-10
Smart Tags Tab in the
AutoCorrect Dialog Box

You can turn on or off the Smart Tag feature with the Label text with smart tags check box. You can use the Show Smart Tag Actions buttons check box to turn on or off the Smart Tag action buttons. By default, Smart Tags are embedded in a document when it is saved. You can turn off this feature with the Save Options button. You can also remove the Smart Tags or recheck the document using the Remove Smart Tags or Recheck Document buttons. The use of specific Smart Tags and action buttons is covered in more detail in later chapters.

Step 4	*Click*	the Cancel button to close the AutoCorrect dialog box without making any changes
Step 5	*Click*	the Close button ☒ on the title bar to close Word
Step 6	*Close*	tho PowerPoint application

QUICK TIP

A limited number of Smart Tags are installed with the Office applications. You can access more Smart Tags from the Microsoft Web site by clicking the More Smart Tags button in the Smart Tags tab of the AutoCorrect dialog box.

chapter
two

Summary

▶ The first time you launch an Office application after installing Office, you see personalized menus that contain basic commands. As you use different commands, they are automatically added to the personalized menu. Commands that are not used for some time are removed from the personalized menus.

▶ The first time you launch an Office application after installing Office, the Standard and Formatting toolbars share a single row below the menu bar. You can reposition the Formatting toolbar to view more or fewer toolbar buttons. The remaining default toolbar buttons that are not visible on the toolbars can be added from the Toolbar Options list. You can turn off or reset the personalized menus and toolbars in the Options tab of the Customize dialog box.

▶ You can hide or view toolbars as you need them by using a shortcut menu. Toolbars can be docked at the top, bottom, or side of the screen, or they can be floating on screen in their own window.

▶ You can open task panes that contain shortcuts to perform various activities; these task panes can be docked at the left or right side of the application window, or they can be floating in the application window. Two examples of a task pane are the New Document and Basic Search task panes.

▶ Smart Tags are labels that identify text or data as a certain type and provide shortcuts to taking certain actions with the text or data.

Commands Review

Action	Menu Bar	Shortcut Menu	Toolbar	Task Pane	Keyboard
Display or hide toolbars	View, Toolbars	Right-click a toolbar, click the desired toolbar to add or remove the check mark	[X] on the toolbar title bar		ALT + V, T
View the New Document task pane	File, New				ALT + F, N
View the Search task pane	File, Search		[icon]		ALT + F, H
View the last visible task pane	View, Task Pane	Right-click a toolbar, click Task Pane			ALT + V, K
View the available Smart Tag options	Tools, AutoCorrect Options, Smart Tags tab				ALT + T, A

Concepts Review

Circle the correct answer.

1. A menu is:
- [a] a set of icons.
- [b] a list of commands.
- [c] impossible to customize.
- [d] never personalized.

2. A toolbar is:
- [a] a list of commands.
- [b] always floating on your screen.
- [c] a set of icons.
- [d] never docked on your screen.

3. Which of the following is not an option in the Options tab in the Customize dialog box?
- [a] turning on or off ScreenTips for toolbar buttons
- [b] turning on or off Large icons for toolbar buttons
- [c] adding animation to menus
- [d] docking all toolbars

4. Right-clicking an item on screen displays:
- [a] the Right-Click toolbar.
- [b] animated menus.
- [c] expanded menus.
- [d] a shortcut menu.

5. Double-clicking the menu name on the menu bar:
- [a] resets your usage data.

- [b] floats the menu bar.
- [c] turns off the personalized menus.
- [d] expands a personalized menu.

6. A Smart Tag is:
- [a] a personalized menu.
- [b] displayed by double-clicking an item on your screen.
- [c] automatically expanded when you pause briefly.
- [d] a label used to identify text or data items for shortcut actions.

7. To view all the default buttons on both the Standard and Formatting toolbars at once, you should:
- [a] view the toolbar with a shortcut menu.
- [b] add the View All button to the toolbar.
- [c] reposition the Formatting toolbar on another row below the Standard toolbar.
- [d] drag the Formatting toolbar to the left.

8. The Advanced Search task pane cannot be viewed by clicking a:
- [a] command on a shortcut menu.
- [b] command on the File menu.
- [c] button on the Standard toolbar.
- [d] link on the Basic Search task pane.

Circle **T** if the statement is true or **F** if the statement is false.

T   F   1. The Standard and Formatting toolbars must remain on the same row.

T   F   2. When updating docked personalized toolbars, some buttons may be automatically removed from view to make room for the new buttons.

T   F   3. One way to use a Smart Tag is to create an Outlook contact from a name in a Word document.

T   F   4. You cannot add animation to menus.

T   F   5. A floating toolbar window can be resized and repositioned using techniques that are similar to those used for any other window.

chapter two

T   F   6. When you open an Office application, the Search task pane is docked at the right side of the application window.

T   F   7. You cannot use keyboard shortcuts to run commands in Office applications.

T   F   8. You cannot turn off the personalized menus and toolbars options.

Skills Review

Exercise 1

1. Open the Word application.

2. Open the Options tab in the Customize dialog box and reset the usage data; show the Standard and Formatting toolbars on one row, and show full menus after a short delay.

3. If necessary, drag the Formatting toolbar to the right until you can see approximately half of the Standard and half of the Formatting toolbar.

4. Add the Show/Hide button to the personalized Standard toolbar using the Toolbar Options list.

5. Add the Font Color button to the personalized Formatting toolbar using the Toolbar Options list.

6. Open the Customize dialog box and reset your usage data in the Options tab.

7. Close the Word application and click No if asked whether you want to save changes to the blank Word document.

Exercise 2

1. Open the Excel application.

2. Open the Options tab in the Customize dialog box and reset the usage data; show the Standard and Formatting toolbars on one row, and show full menus after a short delay.

3. View the personalized Tools menu.

4. Add the AutoCorrect Options command to the personalized Tools menu.

5. Reset your usage data.

6. Close the Excel application.

Exercise 3

1. Open the PowerPoint application.

2. Display the Basic Search task pane using a menu command.

3. Display the advanced search options.

4. Close the Advanced Search task pane.

5. Close the PowerPoint application.

Exercise 4

1. Open an Office application and verify that the New Document, New Presentation, or New Workbook task pane is docked at the right side of the application window.

2. Float the task pane by dragging it to the center of the application window.

3. Drag the left border of the floating task pane to resize it.

4. Double-click the task pane title bar to dock it in its previous position.

5. Close the task pane.

6. Open the Basic Search task pane using the Search button on the Standard toolbar.

7. Open the New Document task pane using the File menu.

8. Switch between task panes using the Back and Forward buttons on the task pane title bar.

9. Close the task pane.

10. Close the application.

Exercise 5

1. Open the Excel application.

2. View the Drawing, Picture, and WordArt toolbars using a shortcut menu.

3. Dock the Picture toolbar below the Standard and Formatting toolbars.

4. Dock the WordArt toolbar at the left boundary of the screen.

5. Close the Excel application from the taskbar.

6. Open the Excel with the New Office Document on the Start menu. (*Hint:* Use the Blank Workbook icon.)

7. Float the WordArt toolbar.

8. Float the Picture toolbar.

9. Hide the WordArt, Picture, and Drawing toolbars using a shortcut menu.

10. Close the Excel application.

Exercise 6

1. Open the Word application.

2. Turn off the personalized menus and toolbars.

3. Open the Options tab in the Customize dialog box and change the toolbar buttons to large icons and add random animation to the menus.

4. Observe the toolbar buttons and the menu animation.

5. Turn off the large buttons and remove the menu animation.

6. Turn on the personalized menus and toolbars and reset your usage data.

7. Close the Word application.

chapter two

Case Projects

SCANS

Project 1

As secretary to the placement director for the XYZ Employment Agency, you have been using an earlier version of Word—Word 97. After you install Office XP, you decide you want the Word menus and toolbars to appear on two rows the way they did in the Word 97 application. Use the Ask A Question Box to search for help on "personalized menus." Review the Help topics and write down all the ways to make the personalized menus and toolbars appear on two rows.

Project 2

You are the administrative assistant to the controller of the Plush Pets, Inc., a stuffed toy manufacturing company. The controller recently installed Excel 2002. She is confused about how to use the task panes and asks for your help. Use the Ask A Question Box to search for help on "task panes." Review the topics and write down an explanation of how task panes are used. Give at least three examples of task panes.

Project 3

As administrative assistant to the art director of MediaWiz Advertising, Inc. you just installed PowerPoint 2002. Now you decide you would rather view the complete Standard and Formatting toolbars rather than the personalized toolbars and want to learn a quick way to do this. Use the Ask A Question Box to search for help on "show all buttons." Review the topic and write down the instructions for showing all buttons using the mouse pointer. Open an Office application and use the mouse method to show the complete Standard and Formatting toolbars. Turn the personalized toolbars back on from the Customize dialog box.

Introduction to the Internet and the World Wide Web

Chapter Overview

Millions of people use the Internet to shop for goods and services, listen to music, view artwork, conduct research, get stock quotes, keep up to date with current events, and send e-mail. More and more people are using the Internet at work and at home to view and download multimedia computer files that contain graphics, sound, video, and text. In this chapter, you learn about the Internet, how to connect to the Internet, how to use the Internet Explorer Web browser, and how to access pages on the World Wide Web.

LEARNING OBJECTIVES

- ▶ Describe the Internet
- ▶ Connect to the Internet
- ▶ Use Internet Explorer
- ▶ Use directories and search engines

chapter
three

3.a What Is the Internet?

To understand the Internet, you must understand networks. A **network** is simply a group of two or more computers linked by cable or telephone lines. The linked computers also include a special computer called a **server** that is used to store files and programs that everyone on the network can use. In addition to the shared files and programs, networks enable users to share equipment, such as a common network printer.

The **Internet** is a worldwide public network of private networks, where users view and transfer information between computers. For example, an Internet user in California can retrieve (or **download**) files from a computer in Canada quickly and easily. In the same way, an Internet user in Australia can send (or **upload**) files to another Internet user in England. The Internet is not a single organization, but rather a cooperative effort by multiple organizations managing a variety of different kinds of computers.

You find a wide variety of services on the Internet. You can communicate with others via e-mail, electronic bulletin boards called newsgroups, real-time online chat, and online telephony. You can also download files from servers to your computer and search the World Wide Web for information. In this chapter, you learn about using a Web browser and accessing pages on the World Wide Web. Your instructor may provide additional information on other Internet services.

3.b Connecting to the Internet

To connect to the Internet you need some physical communication medium connected to your computer, such as network cable or a modem. You also need a special communication program called a Web browser program (such as Microsoft Internet Explorer) that allows your computer to communicate with computers on the Internet. The Web browser allows you to access Internet resources such as Web pages.

After setting up your computer hardware (the network cable or modem) and installing the Internet Explorer Web browser, you must make arrangements to connect to a computer on the Internet. The computer you connect to is called a **host**. Usually, you connect to a host computer via a commercial Internet Service Provider, such as America Online or another company who sells access to the Internet. An **Internet Service Provider (ISP)** maintains the host computer, provides a gateway or entrance to the Internet, and provides an electronic "mail box" with facilities for sending and receiving e-mail. Commercial ISPs usually charge a flat monthly fee for unlimited access to the Internet and e-mail services.

3.c Using Internet Explorer

A **Web browser** is a software application that helps you access Internet resources, including Web pages stored on computers called Web servers. A **Web page** is a document that contains hyperlinks (often called links) to other pages; it can also contain audio and video clips.

notes The activities in this chapter assume you are using the Internet Explorer Web browser version 5.0 or higher. If you are using an earlier version of Internet Explorer or a different Web browser, your instructor may modify the following activities.

To open the Internet Explorer Web browser:

Step 1	*Connect*	to your ISP, if necessary
Step 2	*Double-click*	the Internet Explorer icon 🌐 on the desktop to open the Web browser

When the Web browser opens, a Web page, called a **start page** or **home page**, loads automatically. The start page used by the Internet Explorer Web browser can be the Microsoft default start page, a blank page, or any designated Web page. Figure 3-1 shows the home page for the publisher of this book as the start page.

CAUTION TIP

During peak day and evening hours, millions of people are connecting to the Internet, and you may have difficulty connecting to your host computer or to other sites on the Internet.

QUICK TIP

Challenges to using the Internet include the amount of available information, communication speed, the dynamic environment, lack of presentation standards, and privacy/security issues. Evaluate the source and author of information from the Internet and confirm business-critical information from another source.

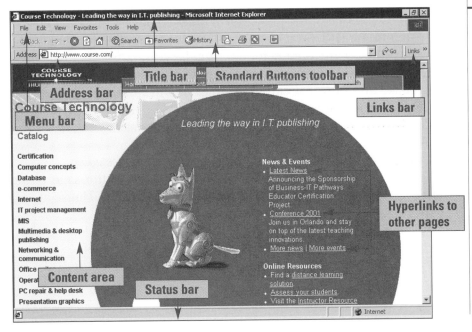

FIGURE 3-1
Internet Explorer Web Browser

chapter
three

MENU TIP

You can create a favorite by clicking the Favorites command on the menu bar and then clicking Add to Favorites, by right-clicking the background (not a link) on the current Web page and clicking Add to Favorites, or by right-clicking a link on the current Web page and clicking Add to Favorites.

MOUSE TIP

You can click the Stop button on the Standard Buttons toolbar to stop downloading a Web page.

QUICK TIP

Another way to load a favorite is to use the Favorites button on the toolbar to open the Favorites list in the Explorer bar. The **Explorer bar** is a pane that opens at the left side of the Web browser screen.

The **title bar** contains the Internet Explorer Web browser Control-menu icon and application name, the title of the current Web page, and the Internet Explorer Web browser Minimize, Restore, and Close buttons. The **menu bar** contains the menu commands you can use to perform specific tasks when viewing the Internet Explorer Web browser window—such as opening a file from your hard disk or printing the current Web page. The **Standard toolbar** contains buttons that provide shortcuts to frequently performed tasks. The **Address bar** contains a text box in which you key the path and filename of the Web page you want to load and a drop-down list of recently loaded Web pages and files. You can click the Go button to load the Web page after keying the page's address in the Address Bar. The **Links bar** is a customizable bar to which you can add shortcuts Web pages you load frequently. The **status bar** displays information about the current Web page. The security zone indicator on the right side of the status bar identifies the security zone you have assigned to the current Web page.

As a Web page loads, the progress bar illustrates the progress of the downloading process. When you place the mouse pointer on a link in the current Web page, its URL appears in the left side of the status bar. The **content area** contains the current Web page. Vertical and horizontal scroll bars appear as necessary so that you can scroll to view the entire Web page after it is loaded.

Loading a Web Page

Loading a Web page means that the Web browser sends a message requesting a copy of the Web page to the Web server where the Web page is stored. The Web server responds by sending a copy of the Web page to your computer. In order to load a Web page, you must either know or find the page's **URL** (Uniform Resource Locator)—the path and filename of the page that is the Web page's address. One way to find the URL for a Web page is to use a search engine or directory. If you are looking for a particular company's Web page, you might find its URL in one of the company's advertisements or on its letterhead and business card. Examples of URLs based on an organization's name are:

Course Technology	*www.course.com*
National Public Radio	*www.npr.org*
The White House	*www.whitehouse.gov*

You can try to "guess" the URL based on the organization's name and top-level domain. For example, a good guess for the U.S. House of Representatives Web page is *www.house.gov*.

You can key a URL directly in the Address bar by first selecting all or part of the current URL and keying the new URL to replace the selection. Internet Explorer adds the "http://" portion of the URL for you. To select the contents of the Address bar and key the URL for the U.S. House of Representatives:

Step 1	Click	the contents of the Address bar
Step 2	Key	www.house.gov
Step 3	Click	the Go button ⟲Go or press the ENTER key
Step 4	Observe	that the home page of the U.S. House of Representatives' Web site opens in your Web browser

Creating Favorites

Web pages are constantly being updated with new information. If you like a certain Web page or find a Web page contains useful information and plan to revisit it, you may want to save a shortcut to the page's URL in the Favorites folder. Such shortcuts are simply called **favorites**. Suppose you want to load the U.S. House of Representatives home page frequently. You can create a favorite that saves the URL in a file on your hard disk. Then at any time, you can quickly load this Web page by clicking it in a list of favorites maintained on the Favorites menu.

The URLs you choose to save as favorites are stored in the Favorites folder on your hard disk. You can specify a new or different subfolder within the Favorites folder and you can change the name of the Web page as it appears in your list of favorites in the Add Favorite dialog box. To create a favorite for the U.S. House of Representatives Web page:

Step 1	Click	Favorites
Step 2	Click	Add to Favorites
Step 3	Click	OK
Step 4	Click	the Home button 🏠 to return to the default start page

One way to load a Web page from a favorite is to click the name of the favorite in the list of favorites on the Favorites menu. To load the U.S. House of Representatives home page from the Favorites menu:

Step 1	Click	Favorites
Step 2	Click	the United States House of Representatives favorite to load the page

chapter
three

| Step 3 | **Click** | the Home button 🏠 to return to the default start page |

The Back and Forward buttons allow you to review recently loaded Web pages without keying the URL or using the Favorites list. To reload the U.S. House of Representatives home page from the Back button list:

| Step 1 | **Click** | the Back button list arrow ⇦▾ on the toolbar |
| Step 2 | **Click** | United States House of Representatives |

3.d Using Directories and Search Engines

Because the Web is so large, you often need to take advantage of special search tools, called search engines and directories, to find the information you need. To use some of the Web's numerous search engines and directories, you can click the Search button on the Standard toolbar to open the Search list in the Explorer bar. To view the Search list:

| Step 1 | **Click** | the Search button 🔍 Search on the Standard toolbar |
| Step 2 | **Observe** | the search list options |

Search engines maintain an index of keywords used in Web pages that you can search. Search engine indexes are updated automatically by software called **spiders** (or **robots**). Spiders follow links between pages throughout the entire Web, adding any new Web pages to the search engine's index. You should use a search engine when you want to find specific Web pages. Some of the most popular search engines include AltaVista, HotBot, and Northern Light.

Directories use a subject-type format similar to a library card catalog. A directory provides a list of links to broad general categories of Web sites such as "Entertainment" or "Business." When you click these links, a subcategory list of links appears. For example, if you click the Entertainment link, you might then see "Movies," "Television," and "Video Games" links. To find links to Web sites containing information about "Movies," you would click the "Movies" link. Unlike a search engine, whose index is updated automatically, Web sites are added to directories only when an individual or a company asks that a particular Web site be included. Some directories also provide review comments and ratings for the Web sites in their index. Most directories also provide an internal search engine that can only be used to search the directory's index, not the entire Web. You use a directory when you are looking for information on broad general topics. Popular directories include Yahoo and Magellan Internet Guide.

To search for Web pages containing "movie guides":

Step 1	*Key*	movie guides in the Find a Web page containing text box
Step 2	*Click*	the Search button or press the ENTER key
Step 3	*Observe*	the search results (a list of Web pages in the search list)

The search results list consists of Web page titles displayed as hyperlinks. You can click any hyperlink to load that page from the list. To close the Explorer bar and search list:

| Step 1 | *Click* | the Search button 🔍Search on the Standard toolbar |
| Step 2 | *Close* | Internet Explorer |

The Web's many search tools are all constructed differently. That means you get varying results when using several search engines or directories to search for information on the same topic. Also, search tools operate according to varying rules. For example, some search engines allow only a simple search on one keyword. Others allow you to refine your search by finding phrases keyed within quotation marks, by indicating proper names, or by using special operators such as "and," "or," and "not" to include or exclude search words. To save time, always begin by clicking the search tool's online Help link. Study the directions for using that particular search engine or directory, and then proceed with your search.

QUICK TIP

You can reload pages from the History folder, which stores the Web pages you load for a specific period of time. You set the number of days to store pages on the General tab in the Options dialog box. The default number of days to store pages in the History folder is 20 days. Click the History button on the toolbar to open the History list in the Explorer bar.

CAUTION TIP

After you find the desired information, "let the user beware!" Because the Web is largely unregulated, anyone can put anything on a Web page. Evaluate carefully the credibility of all the information you find. Try to find out something about the author and his or her credentials. Many college or university library Web sites have good tips on how to evaluate online information.

chapter
three

Summary

▶ A network is a group of two or more computers linked by cable or telephone lines, and the Internet is a worldwide "network of networks."

▶ The World Wide Web is a subset of the Internet from which you can download files and search for information.

▶ Other external networks related to the Internet are large commercial networks like America Online, CompuServe, Prodigy, the Microsoft Network and USENET.

▶ To access the Internet, your computer must have some physical communication medium such as cable or dial-up modem, and a special communication program such as Internet Explorer.

▶ An Internet Service Provider (or ISP) maintains a host computer on the Internet. In order to connect to the Internet, you need to connect to the host computer.

▶ You use a Web browser, such as Internet Explorer, to load Web pages. Web pages are connected by hyperlinks that are text or pictures associated with the path to another page.

▶ Directories and search engines are tools to help you find files and Web sites on the Internet.

Commands Review

Action	Menu Bar	Shortcut Menu	Toolbar	Task Pane	Keyboard
Load a Web page	File, Open		[Go]		ALT + F, O Key URL in the Address bar and press the ENTER key
Save a favorite	Favorites, Add to Favorites	Right-click hyperlink, click Add to Favorites	Drag URL icon to Links bar or Favorites command		ALT + A, A Ctrl + D
Manage the Standard toolbar, Address bar, and Links bar	View, Toolbars	Right-click the Standard toolbar, click desired command	Drag the Standard toolbar, Address bar, or Links bar to the new location		ALT + V, T
Load the search, history, or favorites list in the Explorer bar	View, Explorer Bar		[Search] [Favorites] [History]		ALT + V, E

Concepts Review

SCANS

Circle the correct answer.

1. A network is:
[a] the Internet.
[b] two or more computers linked by cable or telephone wire.
[c] two or more computer networks linked by cable or telephone lines.
[d] a computer that stores Web pages.

2. Which of the following is not a challenge to using the Internet?
[a] light usage
[b] dynamic environment
[c] volume of information
[d] security and privacy

3. The Address bar:
[a] is a customizable shortcut bar.
[b] contains the search list.
[c] contains your personal list of favorite URLs.
[d] contains the URL of the Web page in the content area.

4. The content area contains the:
[a] Standard toolbar.
[b] status bar.
[c] list of favorites.
[d] current Web page.

5. You can view a list of recently loaded Web pages in the:
[a] Channel bar.
[b] Explorer bar.
[c] Address bar.
[d] Links bar.

6. Search engines update their indexes of keywords by using software called:
[a] Webcrawler.
[b] HTTP.
[c] HotBot.
[d] spiders.

Circle **T** if the statement is true or **F** if the statement is false.

T   F   1. Commercial networks that provide specially formatted features are the same as the Internet.

T   F   2. USENET is the name of the military Internet.

T   F   3. All search engines use the same rules for locating Web pages.

T   F   4. Internet users in Boston or New York can access computer files on computers located in the United States only.

T   F   5. Spiders are programs that help you locate pages on the Web.

T   F   6. A Web page URL identifies its location (path and filename).

chapter three

Skills Review

Exercise 1

1. Open the Internet Explorer Web browser.

2. Open the Internet Options dialog box by clicking the Internet Options command on the Tools menu.

3. Review the options on the General tab in the dialog box.

4. Write down the steps to change the default start page to a blank page.

5. Close the dialog box and close the Web browser.

Exercise 2

1. Connect to the Internet and open the Internet Explorer Web browser.

2. Open the search list in the Explorer bar.

3. Search for Web pages about "dog shows."

4. Load one of the Web pages in the search results list.

5. Close the Explorer bar.

6. Print the Web page by clicking the Print command on the File menu and close the Web browser.

Exercise 3

1. Connect to the Internet and open the Internet Explorer Web browser.

2. Load the National Public radio Web page by keying the URL, *www.npr.org*, in the Address bar.

3. Print the Web page by clicking the Print command on the File menu and close the Web browser.

Exercise 4

1. Connect to the Internet and open the Internet Explorer Web browser.

2. Load the AltaVista search engine by keying the URL, *www.altavista.com*, in the Address bar.

3. Save the Web page as a favorite.

4. Search for Web pages about your city.

5. Print at least two Web pages by clicking the Print command on the File menu and close your Web browser.

Exercise 5

1. Connect to the Internet and open the Internet Explorer Web browser.

2. Load the HotBot search engine by keying the URL, *www.hotbot.com*, in the Address bar.

3. Save the Web page as a favorite.

4. Locate the hyperlink text or picture that loads the online Help page. Review the search rules for using HotBot.

5. Print the HotBot Help page by clicking the Print command on the File menu and close your Web browser.

Exercise 6

1. Connect to the Internet and open the Internet Explorer Web browser.

2. Load the Yahoo directory by keying the URL, *www.yahoo.com*, in the Address bar.

3. Save the Web page as a favorite.

4. Search for Web sites that contain information about restaurants in your city.

5. Print at least two Web pages by clicking the <u>P</u>rint command on the <u>F</u>ile menu and close your Web browser.

Exercise 7

1. Connect to the Internet and open the Internet Explorer Web browser.

2. View the Links bar by dragging the bar to the left using the mouse pointer.

3. Click each shortcut on the Links bar and review the Web page that loads.

4. Drag the Links bar back to its original position with the mouse pointer.

Exercise 8

1. Connect to the Internet and open the Internet Explorer Web browser.

2. Click the History button on the Standard toolbar to load the History list in the Explorer bar.

3. Review the History list and click a hyperlink to a page loaded yesterday.

4. Print the page by clicking the <u>P</u>rint command on the <u>F</u>ile menu, close the Explorer bar, and close the Web browser.

Case Projects

Project 1

Your organization recently started browsing the Web with the Internet Explorer Web browser and everyone wants to know how to use the toolbar buttons in the browser. Your supervisor asks you to prepare a fifteen-minute presentation, to be delivered at the next staff meeting, that describes the Internet Explorer Standard Buttons toolbar buttons. Review the Standard Buttons toolbar buttons and practice using them. Write an outline for your presentation that lists each button and describes how it is used.

Project 2

You are working for a book publisher who is creating a series of books about popular movie actors and actresses from the 1940s and 1950s, including Humphrey Bogart and Tyrone Power. The research director asks you to use the Web to locate a list of movies that the actors starred in. Use the Explorer bar search list and the Yahoo directory search tool to find links to "Entertainment." Click the Entertainment link and close the Explorer bar. Working from the Yahoo Web page, click the Actors and Actresses link. Search for Humphrey Bogart in

chapter three

the Actors and Actresses portion of the database. Link to the Web page that shows the filmography for Humphrey Bogart. Print the Web page that shows all the movies he acted in. Use the History list to return to the Actors and Actresses search page. Search for Tyrone Power, then link to and print his filmography. Close the Internet Explorer Web browser.

Project 3

You are the new secretary for the Business Women's Forum, a professional association. The association's president asked you to compile a list of Internet resources, which she will distribute at next month's lunch meeting. Connect to the Internet, open Internet Explorer, and search for Web pages containing the keywords "women in business" (including the quotation marks) using the AltaVista search engine. To load the AltaVista search engine key the URL, *www.altavista.com*, in the Address bar. From the search results, click the Web page title link of your choice to load the Web page. Review the new Web page and its links. Create a favorite for that page. Use the Back button list to reload the AltaVista home page and click a different Web page title from the list. Review the Web page and its links. Create a favorite for the Web page. Continue loading and reviewing pages until you have loaded and reviewed at least five pages. Return to the default home page. Use the Go To command on the View menu and the History bar to reload at least three of the pages. Print two of the pages. Delete all the favorites you added in this chapter, and then close Internet Explorer.

Microsoft
PowerPoint 2002
Introductory

Quick Start for PowerPoint

Chapter Overview

This chapter introduces you to the components of your working environment—the PowerPoint application window. First, you create a presentation using the AutoContent Wizard. Then, you navigate through the presentation and among the various view options of PowerPoint. Next, you create a new presentation using a design template. This simple presentation consists of a title slide and a bullet slide. You save, check spelling, change the design template, print, and finally close the presentation.

LEARNING OBJECTIVES

- ► Explore the PowerPoint window
- ► Create a presentation from the AutoContent Wizard
- ► Navigate in PowerPoint
- ► Close a presentation
- ► Create a presentation from a design template
- ► Save a presentation
- ► Check spelling
- ► Apply a design template
- ► Print slides
- ► Exit PowerPoint

Case profile

Teddy Toys, a toy manufacturing company located in Boise, Idaho, manufactures toys for all ages, from infants to grandparents, for distribution internationally as well as within the United States. Although it manufactures a wide range of toys, Teddy Toys is proudest of its line of quality teddy bears.

You are the administrative assistant to Sandra Hill, the new products manager at Teddy Toys. Ms. Hill has asked you to prepare a presentation that will be given to key personnel within the company in the next couple of weeks.

chapter one

notes This text assumes that you have little or no knowledge of the PowerPoint application. However, it is assumed that you have read Office Chapters 1–3 of this book and that you are familiar with Windows 98, Windows 2000 or Windows ME concepts.

The figures in this book were created using Windows 98. If you are using the PowerPoint application installed on Windows 2000 or Windows ME, you may notice a few minor differences in some figures. These differences do not affect your work in this book.

1.a Exploring the PowerPoint Window

When you start PowerPoint, a new document window opens with a blank slide displayed. You can begin creating a new presentation by keying text on the slide, or you can create a presentation based on a template or wizard. You also have the option of opening an existing presentation. To start the PowerPoint application and explore the PowerPoint window:

Step 1	*Click*	the Start button 🏁Start on the taskbar
Step 2	*Point to*	Programs
Step 3	*Click*	Microsoft PowerPoint

The application opens with the PowerPoint window displayed. Your screen should look similar to Figure 1-1.

The Microsoft PowerPoint application **title bar** at the top of the window indicates the application you are using and the name of the presentation file currently on the screen. Once you save a presentation file, the actual filename replaces the word "Presentation1" in the title bar. At the extreme left of the title bar are the application icon and name, and at the extreme right are the Minimize, Maximize or Restore, and Close buttons for the PowerPoint application window.

The **menu bar**, located below the title bar, contains the majority of commands you use to work on your presentation, organized into menus.

At the extreme left of the menu bar is the Document Control-menu icon, and at the extreme right is the document Close Window button.

chapter
one

FIGURE 1-1
PowerPoint Window

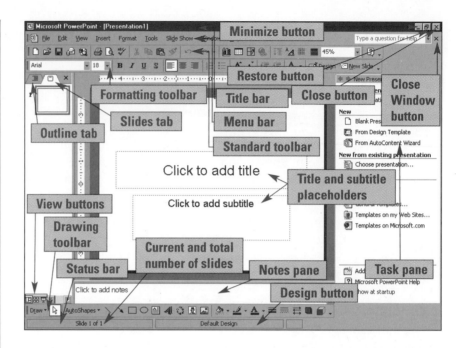

Below the menu bar are the **Standard toolbar** and the **Formatting toolbar**, which contain buttons for easy access to the most commonly used commands of the application. If you do not know what a toolbar button does, simply point to it; a yellow rectangular box called a **ScreenTip** appears with the name or a brief description of the button.

Below the Formatting toolbar, the current presentation is displayed in Normal view. A **task pane** at the right contains hyperlink shortcuts to common actions, such as creating a new presentation or choosing a design template. A **hyperlink** is text or a graphic that you click to view another page or item.

At the bottom of the window is the **status bar**, which, depending on the view, contains the current slide number and the total number of slides (Slide 1 of 1), the current presentation design template (*Default Design*), and the Spelling Status button (book icon with a check mark or an x mark) when PowerPoint is or has completed spell checking your presentation.

Just above the status bar is the **Drawing toolbar**, which contains buttons and list boxes you can use to create and manipulate text and shapes.

Located below the Outline tab and Slides tab, just above the Drawing toolbar, are the three **view buttons**: Normal View, Slide Sorter View, and Slide Show. You can switch between views by clicking the appropriate view button or by choosing the appropriate command on the View menu. Normal view is the PowerPoint default view. It combines four working areas of your presentation: a slide pane in the middle, an outline/slides pane at the left that includes both an Outline tab (where text is displayed in outline format) and a Slides tab (where miniature slides are displayed), a notes pane (where speaker notes are displayed) directly below the slide pane (where text and graphics are displayed on the slide), and a task pane (that provides easy access to many PowerPoint options) at the right.

When PowerPoint starts, it opens a new, blank PowerPoint presentation, which defaults to a blank title slide. A title slide is a slide based on one of many **layouts** (predesigned combinations of placeholders), available in PowerPoint to save you time in creating a presentation. Usually the first slide you create in a new presentation is one that contains a title and subtitle to introduce your topic. The Slides tab displays a miniature of the slide, and the slide pane displays a larger, more detailed version.

Because this is a new presentation, the slide does not yet contain any text or graphics, but the title slide layout does contain two placeholders. **Placeholders** are objects on a slide that hold text, charts, tables, organization charts, clip art, or other objects. They indicate what information is to be keyed in that location on the slide. Each PowerPoint layout contains a different combination of placeholders to make it easier to position and key information. Placeholders display eight sizing handles (four corner handles and four middle handles).

1.b Creating a Presentation from the AutoContent Wizard

The AutoContent Wizard is a welcome guide to anyone who is asked to plan, prepare, and give a presentation, especially for the first time. The wizard asks you questions and then provides an appropriate "look" for a particular type of presentation, along with starter text and suggestions on content and organization. The AutoContent Wizard lets you create a presentation in any of the following categories: General, Corporate, Project, Sales/Marketing, or the Carnegie Coach. Each category provides several presentation ideas and suggestions related to that category. To access the AutoContent Wizard:

| Step 1 | *Click* | the From AutoContent Wizard link in the New Presentation task pane |

The AutoContent Wizard dialog box opens, displaying a description of the wizard and a diagram illustrating the steps it guides you through.

| Step 2 | *Click* | Next > |

chapter
one

QUICK TIP

The Office Assistant (a Help feature that can answer your questions) is hidden unless you need it for a specific activity. The Office Assistant may pop up at various times, indicating presentation design tips as well as software shortcuts. If that happens, just hide it by right-clicking the Office Assistant, and then clicking Hide.

Step 3	*Click*	Projects
Step 4	*Click*	Project Overview in the list box, if necessary
Step 5	*Click*	Next >
Step 6	*Verify*	that the On-screen presentation is selected
Step 7	*Click*	Next >
Step 8	*Key*	Welcome to PowerPoint in the Presentation title: text box
Step 9	*Remove*	the check marks from Date last updated and Slide number check boxes, if necessary
Step 10	*Click*	Next >
Step 11	*Click*	Finish

The Project Overview presentation displays in Normal view. The Outline tab displays the text for each slide in outline format. Your screen should look similar to Figure 1-2.

FIGURE 1-2
Project Overview
Presentation in Normal View

CAUTION TIP

Based on the user information in the Options dialog box, the text on your slide may be different.

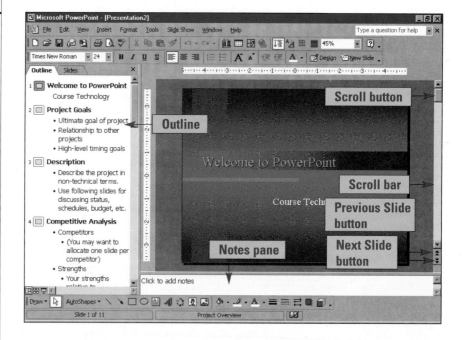

When you create a presentation using a template or wizard, the slides often contain sample text that you can customize for your own purposes.

1.c Navigating in PowerPoint

To work in PowerPoint, you need to move among various slides in a presentation so that you can add and edit text, make formatting changes, and review your work. You also need to switch among different views in the PowerPoint application so you can work effectively on various aspects of your presentation, such as organizing ideas or adding text and graphics.

Navigating Through a Presentation

To view the slides in a presentation in Normal view, you can click the Previous Slide and Next Slide buttons, drag the scroll box located at the right of the slide pane, or press the PAGE UP and PAGE DOWN keys. You can also check the status bar to tell which slide you are viewing and how many slides are in your presentation (such as Slide 1 of 11).

To view slides in Normal view:

Step 1	Press	the HOME key to display Slide 1, if necessary
Step 2	Click	the Next Slide button ⬇ below the vertical scroll bar to view Slide 2
Step 3	Press	the PAGE DOWN key to view Slide 3
Step 4	Drag	the scroll box down on the vertical scroll bar to the right of the slide to view Slide: 6 of 11
Step 5	Press	the HOME key to return to the first slide in the presentation

Navigating Among PowerPoint Views

You can view a presentation using one of three main PowerPoint views: Normal view, Slide Sorter view, Slide Show; and also in Notes Page view. **Normal view**, the default view that opens when you start PowerPoint, provides a combined look at your presentation: the slide pane in the center shows the currently selected slide in detail, the outline/slides pane at the left gives you a bird's-eye view of several slides in outline text and thumbnail slide formats, the notes pane below the slide pane displays speaker notes for the current slide, and the task pane at the right displays links to PowerPoint tasks. Normal view is good for creating a presentation because you can see the actual slide as you create it. The Normal View button is outlined in blue because that is the current view.

Slide Sorter view displays miniature representation of all the slides in a presentation on screen at one time. This view is excellent for rearranging, copying, or deleting slides, as well as for changing the

MOUSE TIP

When you drag the scroll box up or down the vertical scroll bar, a ScreenTip displays the slide number and the slide title.

You can click the up or down arrow on the vertical scroll bar to navigate from slide to slide.

QUICK TIP

You also can navigate easily through the presentation using the Outline tab (which displays text in outline format) and the Slides tab (which displays slide thumbnails) located at the left of the slide pane.

chapter one

FIGURE 1-3
Slide Sorter View

way slides appear on the screen and the speed at which they appear during a visual display of the presentation on the computer screen. To switch to Slide Sorter view:

| Step 1 | *Click* | the Slide Sorter View button ⬜ to the left of the horizontal scroll bar in the outline/slides pane |
| Step 2 | *Click* | Slide 7 to select it |

A selection border appears around the slide you selected. Your screen should look similar to Figure 1-3.

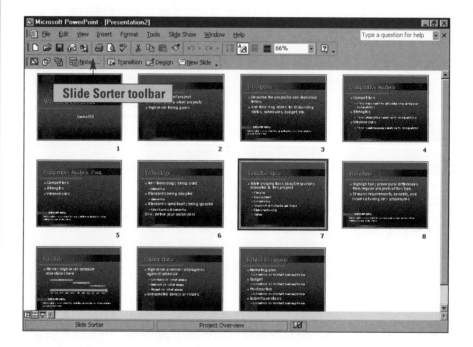

Notes Page view displays a miniature version of the current slide with a pane for keying speaker notes that can be printed and used by the presenter during a presentation. A small notes pane is displayed below the slide pane in Normal view for keying speaker notes. There is no Notes Page View button. To access Notes Page view, click the Notes Page command on the View menu. To switch to Notes Page view:

| Step 1 | *Click* | View |
| Step 2 | *Click* | Notes Page |

Notes Page view opens. Your screen should look similar to Figure 1-4.

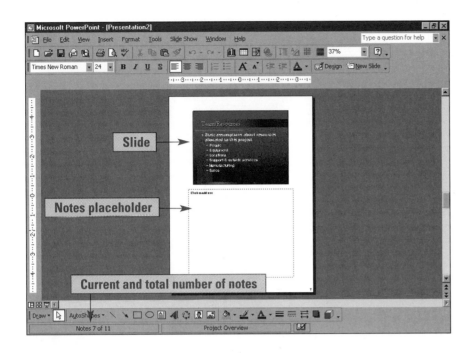

FIGURE 1-4
Notes Page View

MOUSE TIP

Double-clicking any slide in Notes Page view quickly returns you to Normal view.

Step 3	*Click*	the Next Slide button ⬇ below the vertical scroll bar to view the notes pane for a different slide
Step 4	*Click*	the Zoom button list arrow 50% on the Standard toolbar
Step 5	*Click*	66% to zoom in to read the speaker notes more easily

Slide Show displays all the slides in a presentation, sized to fill your screen, one after another at the speed you choose. The process is similar to projecting your own slides, assembled in a slide carousel, on a screen and moving to the next slide by clicking a button. When you switch to Slide Show view using the Slide Show button, the slide show runs, beginning with the currently selected slide. To start the slide show, beginning with Slide 6:

Step 1	*Display*	Slide 6 (Technology)
Step 2	*Click*	the Slide Show (from current slide) button 🖥 to the left of the horizontal scroll bar

Your slide should look similar to Figure 1-5.

MENU TIP

You can display a slide show by clicking the Slide Show command on the View menu or by clicking the View Show command on the Slide Show menu. These commands start the slide show from Slide 1, regardless of which slide is currently selected.

**chapter
one**

FIGURE 1-5
Technology Slide in Slide Show

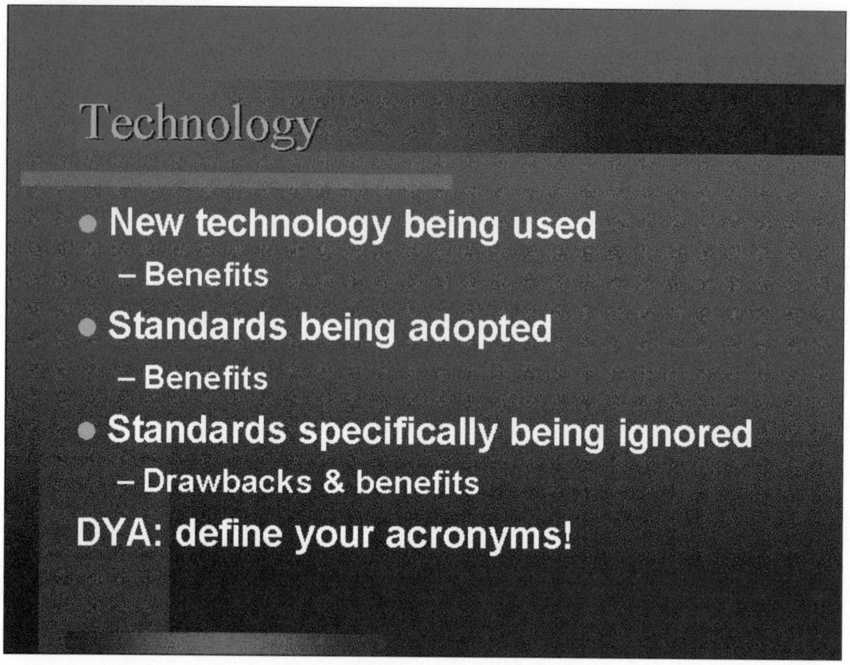

Technology
New technology being used
– Benefits
Standards being adopted
– Benefits
Standards specifically being ignored
– Drawbacks & benefits
DYA: define your acronyms!

QUICK TIP

You can start a slide show from Normal view by pressing the F5 key; no matter which slide is selected, the slide show starts from Slide 1.

CAUTION TIP

If you click the application Close button instead of the Close Window button, you exit PowerPoint.

Step 3	***Click***	the left mouse button to progress through the rest of the slides until you return to your previous view

1.d Closing a Presentation

PowerPoint allows you to have as many presentations open as your computer resources can handle. Each open presentation displays a separate presentation button on the taskbar. However, it is a good idea to close any presentations you are not using to free memory and allow the computer to run more efficiently. To close the *Project Overview* presentation:

Step 1	***Click***	the Close Window button on the menu bar
Step 2	***Click***	No if you are prompted to save the presentation

notes

The presentation design templates used in this book include the PowerPoint 2002 design templates. If the designs do not appear immediately, you need to install them from the Office XP CD-ROM before continuing this chapter.

1.e Creating a Presentation from a Design Template

PowerPoint provides many templates of presentation designs to help you set up a particular, consistent look for a presentation. **Design templates**, like blueprints, contain a master design that determines the overall look of a presentation—the color scheme that coordinates the colors on the slide so they complement each other; coordinating fonts, font styles, and font sizes; graphical elements to enhance the presentation; and the placeholder arrangement and alignment for various slide layouts within the presentation. You can create a presentation using a design template, or you can apply a design template to an existing presentation. To create a new presentation using a design template:

Step 1	*Click*	<u>F</u>ile
Step 2	*Click*	<u>N</u>ew

The New Presentation task pane displays shortcuts to creating a new presentation.

Step 3	*Click*	the From Design Template link under New in the New Presentation task pane

The Slide Design task pane opens. It displays design template previews organized as follows: Used in This Presentation (any previously used design templates for the existing presentation), Recently Used (any design templates recently selected for use in any presentation), and Available For Use (all available design templates). To see the name of a template, you point to the preview until a ScreenTip appears. When you point to a preview, a selection frame surrounds it and it displays a list arrow. If you click a preview, you automatically apply the design template to all slides. If you click the list arrow, you can elect to apply the template to all slides, only to selected slides, or to change the size of the previews so they are easier to view.

Step 4	*Point to*	each design template until its name appears in a ScreenTip
Step 5	*Scroll*	through the previews until you see the Crayons preview
Step 6	*Click*	the Crayons preview

TASK PANE TIP

If you click the <u>N</u>ew command on the <u>F</u>ile menu, the New Presentation task pane opens, displaying options for creating a Blank Presentation, creating a presentation from a Design Template, or creating a presentation from the AutoContent Wizard.

MOUSE TIP

If you click the New button on the Standard toolbar, PowerPoint opens a new, blank presentation, and the Slide Layout task pane appears with various slide layouts from which you can choose.

chapter
one

The Crayons design template is applied to the presentation. By default, PowerPoint assigns a title slide layout to the first slide in any new presentation. Your screen should look similar to Figure 1-6.

FIGURE 1-6
Title Slide with Slide
Design Task Pane

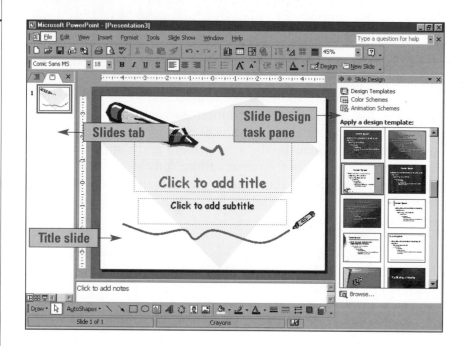

MENU TIP

You can insert a new slide by clicking the New Slide command on the Insert menu.

Title Slides

The **title slide**, usually the first slide in a presentation, introduces the topic of the presentation. The goal of a title slide is to grab the audience's attention, set the tone, and prepare the audience for what is to follow. Title slides can also be used to differentiate between sections of a presentation. To enter text on a title slide:

QUICK TIP

Because the first placeholder is automatically activated for data entry, you can also simply key the title in the title placeholder without first clicking it. You can move from the title placeholder to the subtitle placeholder by pressing the CTRL + ENTER keys. If you press the CTRL + ENTER keys in the last text box on a slide, you add a new text slide that contains a bulleted list.

Step 1	*Click*	the "Click to add title" placeholder
Step 2	*Key*	Teddy Toys
Step 3	*Click*	the "Click to add subtitle" placeholder
Step 4	*Key*	Focusing on the Future
Step 5	*Click*	outside the slide area to deselect the placeholder
Step 6	*Click*	the Slide Show button 🖵 to view the title slide on a full screen
Step 7	*Click*	on the screen until you return to Normal view

Bullet Slides

Bullet slides or **Text slides** are used to group related topics or items together, list items, emphasize important information, or summarize key points. In the Teddy Toys presentation, for example, you can use a bullet slide to list the sales meeting agenda. **Bullets** are symbols that guide the reader's eye to the start of each item in a list, helping to emphasize important material. To add a new bullet slide:

| Step 1 | *Click* | the New Slide button New Slide on the Formatting toolbar |

 The text assumes you have checked the Show when inserting new slides check box at the bottom of Slide Layout task pane.

The Title and Text slide layout, which is formatted for bullets, is automatically selected for the new slide. The Slide Layout task pane opens, in case you want to choose a different layout. A bulleted list or text slide appears in Normal view. The Slide Layout task pane displays 31 layouts in the Apply slide layout: section arranged in the following categories: Text Layouts, Content Layouts, Text and Content Layouts, and Other Layouts. **Layouts** are predesigned slide layouts that contain placement for titles, bulleted lists, text, charts, objects, clip art, and media clips. Instead of designing each slide manually, you can simply choose a layout that fits your needs.

Step 2	*Click*	the "Click to add title" placeholder
Step 3	*Key*	Agenda
Step 4	*Click*	the "Click to add text" placeholder
Step 5	*Key*	Mission statement
Step 6	*Press*	the ENTER key
Step 7	*Key*	the remaining bullets, including the intentional errors, pressing the ENTER key after each bullet except the last: Current products New products Future opportunities Current marrket status Projected marrket share
Step 8	*Click*	outside the slide area

DESIGN TIP

Using too many bullets lessens their effectiveness because the audience cannot quickly isolate the topics being discussed. Limit the number of bullets on any one slide to six or fewer, with each line containing no more than six to eight words.

Be sure to use parallel syntax when starting each bullet item to provide consistency throughout the slide. If the first bullet begins with an action verb, such as *highlight*, then all succeeding bullets should begin with an action verb, such as *discuss, introduce, compare,* and so forth.

TASK PANE TIP

You can insert a specific new slide from the Slide Design task pane by clicking the list arrow for the slide layout you desire, and then clicking Insert New Slide.

chapter one

Your screen should look similar to Figure 1-7.

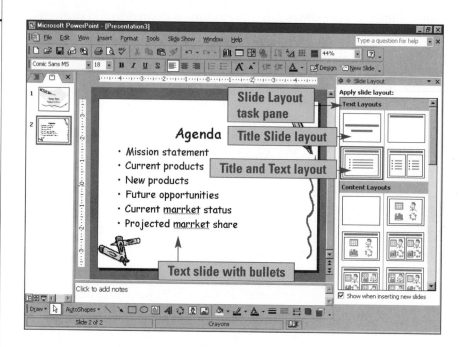

1.f Saving a Presentation

The first time you save a presentation, you can use either the Save command or the Save As command on the File menu. Both commands open the Save As dialog box. After you have saved a presentation, use the Save command to save the presentation with the same name to the same location, or use the Save As command to give the same presentation a different name or to specify a new disk drive and folder location. To save the *Teddy Toys* presentation:

notes Be sure to check with your instructor if you do not know on which disk drive and in which folder to save your presentations.

Step 1	*Click*	the Save button 💾 on the Standard toolbar

The Save As dialog box on your screen should look similar to Figure 1-8.

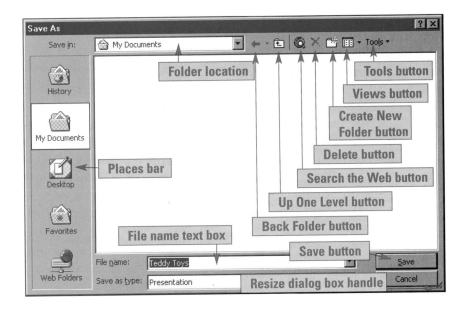

FIGURE 1-8
Save As Dialog Box

QUICK TIP

You can save a slide as a graphic so you can insert it as an image in any software program. In the Save As dialog box, click the Save as type: list arrow and select the graphic format of your choice.

In the Save As dialog box, the File name: text box suggests a filename based on the first text that appears in the presentation. You can use this name or key a different name of up to 255 characters, including the drive and path. Characters can include letters, numbers, spaces, and some special characters in any combination.

Step 2	*Key*	Teddy Toys in the File name: text box, if necessary
Step 3	*Verify*	that Presentation appears in the Save as type: list box
Step 4	*Switch to*	the appropriate disk drive and folder
Step 5	*Click*	Save

MOUSE TIP

The Save As dialog box can be resized to display more files at one time by dragging the lower-right corner of the dialog box (or any border). You can customize the Places bar to change the order of the folders by right-clicking the desired folder and then clicking either Move Up or Move Down. You can also remove or rename a folder and display folders as large or small icons.

Your presentation is saved and the filename, *Teddy Toys*, appears in the title bar. PowerPoint adds a .ppt extension to the presentation filename. This extension may also appear in the title bar. The *Teddy Toys* presentation is used throughout the PowerPoint chapters to introduce new slide types and concepts.

1.g Checking Spelling

After you create or edit a presentation, you should save the presentation, check spelling in the presentation, and then resave the presentation with the corrections. Even after you spell check a presentation, it is still necessary to proofread it because the spell

chapter
one

MOUSE TIP

You can right-click a word that displays a wavy red line to display a list of suggested spellings and then click the spelling you want.

INTERNET TIP

You can click the Save as Web Page command on the File menu to save your presentation as an .htm or .html file to be used on the Internet.

CAUTION TIP

As you work, periodically save your presentation by clicking the Save button on the Standard toolbar or by pressing the CTRL + S keys. Saving frequently ensures that you do not lose your work if there is a power outage, computer error, or human error.

checker does not correct grammatical errors, the use of the wrong word (for example, *from* instead of *form*), or know the spelling of proper names.

PowerPoint actively checks your spelling as you key text, while the Spelling Status button in the status bar indicates that action. If you make an error as you key, PowerPoint underscores the error with a wavy red line once you press SPACEBAR, and a red x mark replaces the red check mark on the Spelling Status button. To correct an error, you can manually correct it by selecting and keying the correct spelling, by right-clicking the error and selecting the correct spelling, or by double-clicking the Spelling Status button and selecting the correct spelling. To check the spelling of a presentation and save the changes:

Step 1	*Click*	the Spelling button [ABC✓] on the Standard toolbar

When spell-checking a presentation, you can click the Ignore button if the spelling is correct in the Not in Dictionary: text box, or select the correct word in the Suggestions: list box and click the Change button. If the spell checker stops at a word that is spelled incorrectly but offers no suggestions for replacement, key the correct word in the Change to: text box and then click the Change button.

Step 2	*Correct*	the text as needed
Step 3	*Click*	OK when PowerPoint has completed spell checking the entire presentation

Saving Changes to a Presentation

Once you save a presentation, you can make changes to it by editing, formatting, and adding slides. You then resave the presentation and all the changes automatically save. To save changes to a presentation:

Step 1	*Click*	the Save button [💾] on the Standard toolbar to save your changes to the presentation

1.h Applying a Design Template

After you have created a presentation with a design template, you have the option of changing the design template to one that better fits the needs of your presentation. Because design templates change the color, background, font, and formatting of all slides in a presentation, you can easily change the look of your presentation by changing the design template as often as you like. You can use more than one design template in a presentation by applying a design template only to selected slides.

To apply a design template to an entire presentation:

Step 1	*Click*	the Slide Design button button on the Formatting toolbar
Step 2	*Scroll*	through the design previews in the Available For Use section of the Slide Design task pane
Step 3	*Click*	the Quadrant design
Step 4	*View*	Slides 1 and 2 and observe the changes in the slides
Step 5	*Save*	the *Teddy Toys* presentation

1.i Printing Slides

C

PowerPoint provides different options for printing slides in a presentation. At this time, you want to print the presentation as slides and then as a handout. Printing all the slides in a presentation, one per page, is the default printing option, with each slide printing on a separate sheet of paper. By clicking the Print button on the Standard toolbar, your presentation automatically prints without displaying the Print dialog box.

To print all slides in the presentation:

| Step 1 | *Click* | the Print button 🖶 on the Standard toolbar |

A **handout** displays multiple slides per page at a reduced size, to provide a convenient copy of your presentation for audience members. To print as a handout with two slides per page:

| Step 1 | *Click* | File |
| Step 2 | *Click* | Print |

chapter
one

The Print dialog box opens with various printing options. The dialog box on your screen should look similar to Figure 1-9.

FIGURE 1-9
Print Dialog Box

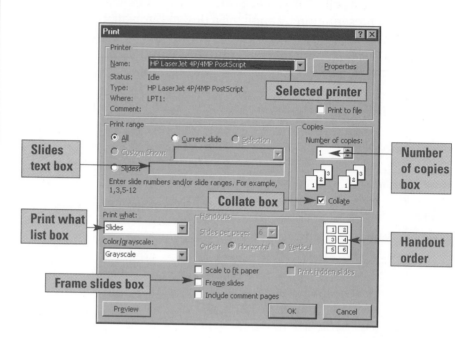

Step 3	*Click*	Handouts in the Print what: list box
Step 4	*Click*	the Slides per page: list arrow in the Handouts box
Step 5	*Click*	2 as the number of slides per page
Step 6	*Click*	OK

1.j Exiting PowerPoint

When you have completed all work in PowerPoint, you should exit the application. Any open documents close when you exit PowerPoint. If you haven't saved, you are prompted to save your changes. To exit PowerPoint and close any open documents:

Step 1	*Click*	the application Close button ☒ on the PowerPoint title bar

Because you didn't make any changes since you last saved *Teddy Toys*, the presentation closes, the PowerPoint application exits, and the Windows desktop appears.

Summary

► The PowerPoint default window includes the menu bar, Standard toolbar, Formatting toolbar, view buttons, scroll bars, Drawing toolbar, status bar, outline/slides pane, slide pane, notes pane, and task pane.

► You can work on a presentation in Normal view, Slide Sorter view, Notes Page view, and Slide Show. Normal view, the default view, combines an outline/slides pane, a slide pane, and a task pane.

► The task pane provides hyperlink shortcuts to common tasks, such as creating a new presentation, changing the design template, or changing slide layout.

► The AutoContent Wizard provides templates with text and suggestions on content and organization to help you start creating a presentation.

► Presentation design templates enable you to enhance your presentation by including a professionally designed background, color scheme, font appearance, and graphic elements.

► PowerPoint provides 31 layouts for help in creating different slide layouts, such as title slides and bulleted lists.

► For the first slide of a new presentation, PowerPoint uses the Title Slide Layout.

► Title slides are used as the first slide or as section dividers within a presentation.

► For the second slide of a presentation, PowerPoint uses the Title and Text Layout.

► Bullet slides include a title and a list of numbered or bulleted items. Bullets are symbols used to emphasize text that is listed.

► After creating a presentation, you should save it for future use.

► The Spelling feature displays errors as you key text and enables you to spell check a presentation for typographical errors.

► Proofreading is an essential part of preparing any presentation because spell checking does not find all types of errors.

► You can change the presentation design template of a presentation after it has been created.

► You can print one slide per page or print a handout page with two slides per page.

► Closing a presentation frees computer resources and enables the computer to run more efficiently.

► When you finish working in PowerPoint, you should exit the application.

chapter one

Commands Review

Action	Menu Bar	Shortcut Menu	Toolbar	Task Pane	Keyboard
Display the task pane	View, Task Pane	Right-click any toolbar, click Task Pane			ALT + V, K
Create a new presentation	File, New			Blank Presentation, From Design Template, or From AutoContent Wizard links in New Presentation task pane	CTRL + N ALT + F, N
Display the New Presentation task pane	File, New	Right-click any toolbar, click Task Pane		Other Task Panes list arrow, click New from Existing Presentation	ALT + F, N
View the next slide			Drag scroll box down one slide		PAGE DOWN
View the previous slide			Drag scroll box up one slide		PAGE UP
Display the first slide					HOME
Display the last slide					END
Display Normal view	View, Normal				ALT + V, N
Display Slide Sorter view	View, Slide Sorter				ALT + V, D
Display Notes Page view	View, Notes Page				ALT + V, P
Display Slide Show	View, Slide Show Slide Show, View Show				ALT + V, W ALT + D, V F5
Add a new slide	Insert, New Slide	Right-click slide layout, click Insert New Slide	New Slide	Click list arrow on slide layout in Slide Layout task pane, click Insert New Slide	CTRL + M ALT + I, N ALT + N
Display the Slide Layout task pane	Format, Slide Layout	Right-click empty area on slide, click Slide Layout		Click Other Task Panes list arrow, click Slide Layout	ALT + O, L
Apply a layout				Click a slide layout in Apply slide layout: section in Slide Layout task pane	
Display the Slide Design task pane	Format, Slide Design	Right-click empty area on slide, click Slide Design	Design	Click Other Task Panes list arrow, click Slide Design-Design Templates	ALT + O, D
Apply a design template			Double-click design template button in status bar	Click a design template in Apply a design template: section in Slide Design task pane	
Save a presentation	File, Save File, Save As				CTRL + S ALT + F, S F12
Check the spelling in a presentation	Tools, Spelling	Right-click word with wavy red line	, Double-click Spelling Status icon in status bar		F7 ALT + T, S
Print a presentation	File, Print				CTRL + P ALT + F, P
Close a presentation	File, Close		X		CTRL + F4 ALT + F, C
Exit PowerPoint	File, Exit	Right-click PowerPoint button on the taskbar, click Close	X		ALT + F, X ALT + F4

Concepts Review

Circle the correct answer.

1. **Most commands can be found on the:**
   [a] menu bar.
   [b] Standard toolbar.
   [c] Formatting toolbar.
   [d] Drawing toolbar.

2. **The PowerPoint window displays which of the following toolbars by default?**
   [a] Outlining toolbar, Standard toolbar, and Clipboard toolbar
   [b] Standard toolbar, Formatting toolbar, and Drawing toolbar
   [c] Picture toolbar, Formatting toolbar, Drawing toolbar
   [d] Standard toolbar, Formatting toolbar, and WordArt toolbar

3. **You cannot navigate through a PowerPoint presentation in Normal view by:**
   [a] pressing the PAGE UP and PAGE DOWN keys.
   [b] dragging the scroll box.
   [c] clicking the Previous Slide and Next Slide buttons.
   [d] pressing the F5 key.

4. **A combination view consisting of an outline pane, a slide pane, and a task pane is the:**
   [a] Slide Sorter view.
   [b] Notes Page view.
   [c] Normal view.
   [d] Slide Show.

5. **Presentation designs that regulate the formatting and layout for the slide are called:**
   [a] blueprints.
   [b] placeholders.
   [c] design templates.
   [d] design plates.

6. **You can create a new presentation by doing any of the following *except*:**
   [a] pressing the Ctrl + N keys.
   [b] clicking File, Open.
   [c] clicking File, New.
   [d] clicking the New button on the Standard toolbar.

7. **Objects on a slide that hold text are called:**
   [a] textholders.
   [b] layouts.
   [c] object holders.
   [d] placeholders.

8. **The type of slide used to introduce a topic and set the tone for a presentation is called a:**
   [a] title slide.
   [b] bullet slide.
   [c] graph slide.
   [d] table slide.

9. **What type of symbols are used to identify items in a list?**
   [a] graphics
   [b] bullets
   [c] markers
   [d] icons

10. **To exit the PowerPoint application, you can:**
    [a] double click the document Control-menu icon.
    [b] click the application Close button.
    [c] click the Close Window button.
    [d] click the application Minimize button.

chapter one

Circle **T** if the statement is true or **F** if the statement is false.

T F   1. You can create a presentation from within PowerPoint or use the New Office Document command on the Start menu.

T F   2. The title bar of PowerPoint contains the name of the application—Microsoft PowerPoint—as well as the name of the active presentation.

T F   3. To begin a new presentation, you must close all current presentations.

T F   4. When you add a new slide, PowerPoint provides 51 layout designs from which to choose.

T F   5. A title slide can be used only as the first slide in any presentation.

T F   6. A bullet slide should include as many bullets as necessary to fill the slide.

T F   7. After initially saving a presentation, you should use the Save command to give your presentation a new name.

T F   8. As you work in PowerPoint, you should save periodically to avoid losing your work.

T F   9. *Midwest Sales Report** is a valid filename for saving a PowerPoint presentation.

T F   10. Clicking the Print button automatically prints the presentation.

notes
In subsequent chapters, you build on the presentations you create below. Therefore, it is advisable to complete all Skills Review exercises and Case Projects and to use the filenames suggested before going on to the next chapter. It is a good idea to save three presentations per one disk so that you do not run out of disk space.

Skills Review

SCANS

Exercise 1

1. Create a new presentation using the Layers design template.

2. Use the Title Slide layout for the first slide. The title should read "PowerPoint"; the subtitle should read your name.

3. Add a new slide using the Title and Text layout. The slide title should read "PowerPoint Defined." The bullet should read "PowerPoint is an easy-to-use presentation graphics application that allows you to create slides that entertain, motivate, convey, persuade, sell, or inform."

4. Save the presentation as *PowerPoint*.

5. Spell check, proofread, and resave the presentation, and then print the presentation as a two-slides-per-page handout and close it.

Exercise 2 ⏵🄲

1. Create a new, blank presentation.

2. Use the Title Slide layout for the first slide. The title should read "Why Microsoft Office Professional?"; the subtitle should read "Are You Ready?"

3. Apply the Shimmer design template to the presentation.

4. Add a new slide using the Title and Text layout. The slide title should read "What is Office Professional?" Key the following as separate bullets: "Word," "Excel," "PowerPoint," "Access," and "Outlook."

5. Save the presentation as *Office*.

6. Spell check, proofread, and resave the presentation, and then print and close it.

Exercise 3 ⏵🄲

1. Create a new presentation using the Curtain Call design template.

2. Use the Title Slide layout for the first slide. The title should read "Designing a Presentation"; the subtitle should read your name.

3. Add a new slide using the Title and Text layout. The slide title should read "Dale Carnegie Presentation Tips." Key the following as separate bullets: "Plan," "Prepare," "Practice," and "Present."

4. Save the presentation as *Design*.

5. Spell check, proofread, and resave the presentation, and then print the presentation as a two-slides-per-page handout and close it.

Exercise 4 ⏵🄲

1. Create a new, blank presentation.

2. Use the Title Slide layout for the first slide. The title should read "Precision Builders"; the subtitle should read "Builders of Distinction."

3. Apply the Cliff design template to the presentation.

4. Add a new slide using the Title and Text layout. The slide title should read "Why Precision Builders?" Key the following as separate bullet items: "Quality craftsmanship," "Quality materials," "Dedicated personnel," and "Excellent reputation."

5. Save the presentation as *Precision Builders*.

6. Spell check, proofread, and resave the presentation, and then print and close it.

Exercise 5 ⏵🄲

1. Create a new presentation using the Maple design template.

2. Add a Title slide with the title "S & L Nature Tours" and the subtitle "Enjoying the Outdoors While Promoting Good Health."

3. Add a Title and Text slide with the title "National Park Tours" and the following bullets: "Glacier National Park," "Yellowstone National Park," "Rocky Mountain National Park," and "Teton National Park."

4. Save the presentation as *Nature Tours*.

5. Spell check, proofread, and resave the presentation, and then print the presentation as a two-slides-per-page handout and close it.

chapter one

Exercise 6

1. Create a new presentation using the Eclipse design template.

2. Add a Title slide with the title "Health in the New Millennium" and the subtitle "Are You Ready to Reduce Stress in Your Life?"

3. Add a Title and Text slide with the title "Good Health Helps Everyone." Add the following bullets: "Eat a balanced diet," "Drink plenty of water," "Exercise regularly," "Visit your doctor periodically," "Reduce the level of stress," and "Enjoy life."

4. Save the presentation as *A Healthier You*.

5. Spell check, proofread, and resave the presentation, and then print and close it.

Exercise 7

1. Create a new presentation using the Satellite Dish design template.

2. Add a Title slide with the title "Buying A Computer" and the subtitle "A Guide to Selecting the Perfect Computer for Your Needs."

3. Add a Title and Text slide with the title "Getting Started."

4. Add the following bullets: "What do I need to do on the computer?"; "How much can I afford?"; "Where should I purchase the computer?"; and "Where can I find information about computers?"

5. Save the presentation as *Buying A Computer*.

6. Spell check, proofread, and resave the presentation, and then print the presentation as a two-slides-per-page handout and close it.

Exercise 8

1. Create a new presentation using the Ocean design template.

2. Add a Title slide with the title "Leisure Travel" and the subtitle "You Deserve a Great Vacation."

3. Add a Title and Text slide with the title "Vacation Packages for Everyone." Add the following bullets: "Spring Rafting Package," "Summer Hiking Package," "Fall Get-A-Way Package," "Winter Ski Package," "Canada's Splendor Package," and "Land Down Under Package."

4. Save the presentation as *Leisure Travel*.

5. Spell check, proofread, and resave the presentation, and then print and close it.

Case Projects

Project 1

You have been asked to explain to your fellow assistants how to create a presentation using Web templates. Using online Help, review information on creating presentations using templates from the Web. Print the "Select from templates on a web site" and the "Select from templates on Office Update" topics.

Project 2

You work in the Human Resources Department of Communicate Corporation. You have been selected to give a presentation to train employees on proper telephone usage. Apply a presentation design template of your choice to create a title slide introducing the topic and a Title and Text slide defining the subject matter and topics to be covered. Save the presentation as *Communicate*. Spell check and proofread the presentation, and then print the presentation as a two-slides-per-page handout.

Project 3

You work for Souner & Associates, a software training company. You are to give a sales presentation to a group of office managers that contains information about why they should hire your organization. Apply a presentation design template of your choice to create a Title slide introducing your company and a Title and Text slide displaying training classes offered. Spell check the presentation, and then save it as *Souner*. Print the presentation as a two-slides-per-page handout.

Project 4

Create a realistic presentation about the company you work for or an organization with which you are familiar. Choose an occasion on which it might be appropriate to create a PowerPoint presentation for this company or organization. Consider what your message will be, who your audience will be, and what medium you will use to present your topic. To help you accomplish this, you can use the Office Assistant to access Presentation tips from Dale Carnegie Training®. Apply a presentation design template of your choice and begin with a Title slide and a Title and Text slide. Use your company or organization name and any other information that pertains to the presentation. Save the presentation as *My Presentation*. Spell check and then print the presentation.

Project 5

You have just accepted a full-time summer job at your local zoo. One of your job responsibilities is to create a presentation that entices grammar school children to visit the zoo during the summer as well as the regular school season. Decide what areas of the zoo, and possibly any special attractions, that would be of interest. Apply a presentation design template of your choice and begin with a Title and a Title and Text slide. Save the presentation as *Zoo*. Print the presentation as a two-slides-per-page handout.

Project 6

Your employer has asked whether or not you think your department should upgrade from your existing PowerPoint software to PowerPoint 2002. Connect to the Internet and visit the Microsoft PowerPoint page at *http://www.microsoft.com/office/powerpoint*. Search for new features in PowerPoint 2002. Use the presentation design of your choice to create a PowerPoint Title and Text slide itemizing some of the new features you found. Print the slide and close the presentation without saving it.

Project 7

As a consumer education instructor, part of your curriculum is to educate students on how to purchase a new car. Decide how you plan to introduce this topic to a class of 15- and 16-year-old students. Connect to the Internet and search the Web to find out current information on the best-selling new cars this past year. Based on your research, create a new presentation consisting of a Title slide and a Title and Text slide. Save the presentation as *Cars*, and print it.

Project 8

You are a teaching assistant at Millennium University. Your lead professor is teaching an Introduction to the Internet class for college freshmen. You and another teaching assistant (choose a member of your PowerPoint class to work with) must gather the information and create a PowerPoint presentation for the professor to use in his class. Decide on the topics to be covered in this eight-week course. Connect to the Internet to search the Web for new Internet topics that you feel should be covered. Download and use a presentation design template that you find on the Internet. Save the presentation as *Internet*, and print it.

chapter one

Editing and Formatting Slides

Chapter Overview

The process of creating a presentation usually spans more than one work session and involves modifying slide text so it conveys information effectively and captures viewer attention. In this chapter, you learn about opening an existing presentation, adding a slide, working with next-level bullets, editing and formatting text, using the slide master, and printing an individual slide.

LEARNING OBJECTIVES

- ▶ Open a presentation and add a slide
- ▶ Work with bulleted text
- ▶ Work with slides in the outline/slides pane
- ▶ Edit and format text on slides
- ▶ Modify the slide master
- ▶ Print an individual slide

Case profile

Today you are asked to continue working on the *Teddy Toys* presentation. Ms. Hill would like you to list the current products produced by Teddy Toys to help the personnel at the meeting understand how the new product she plans to introduce fits in the Teddy Toys family.

chapter
two

2.a Opening a Presentation and Adding a Slide

When you complete a presentation, you save and close it. If you want to edit or add to that presentation at a later time, you open it from the location where it was saved. When you add a slide to a presentation, the slide is inserted after the current slide. To open an existing presentation and add a slide:

Step 1	*Click*	the Open button 📂 on the Standard toolbar
Step 2	*Display*	the folder or drive containing your work
Step 3	*Double-click*	the *Teddy Toys* presentation
Step 4	*Display*	the last slide in the presentation in the slide pane
Step 5	*Click*	the New Slide button [🗐 New Slide] on the Formatting toolbar

A Title and Text slide displays in Normal view, and the Slide Layout task pane opens. PowerPoint automatically applies this slide layout to the new slide. The Slide Layout task pane opens to facilitate changing the slide layout.

Step 6	*Click*	the "Click to add title" placeholder
Step 7	*Key*	Mission Statement
Step 8	*Click*	the "Click to add text" placeholder
Step 9	*Key*	Teddy Toys strives to manufacture toys that are developmentally appropriate, safe, guaranteed to last, and fun for the youth market.
Step 10	*Save*	the *Teddy Toys* presentation

2.b Working with Bulleted Text

Much of the text in a PowerPoint presentation is formatted in bullets rather than paragraphs. Bulleted text is easy to scan, so viewers can grasp the main points on a slide while the speaker elaborates as necessary. You can format slide text in up to five available bullet levels. Each level is indented further than the previous bullet level, uses a smaller font size, and displays a different bullet symbol. First-level or major

---

TASK PANE TIP

You can open an existing presentation by clicking the Presentations or More presentations link in the New Presentation task pane.

MOUSE TIP

You can open an existing presentation by clicking the Search button on the Standard toolbar, which opens the Search task pane and allows you to locate a presentation by having the computer search Everywhere, in My Computer, Web Folders, or Outlook.

chapter
two

MENU TIP

You can open a PowerPoint presentation by clicking the Open command on the File menu.

TASK PANE TIP

You can add a new slide to a presentation by clicking the list arrow on the desired layout in the Slide Layout task pane, and then clicking Insert New Slide.

MOUSE TIP

You can indent (demote) bullet text in a level by clicking the Increase Indent button on the Formatting toolbar or the Demote button on the Outlining toolbar. You can remove an indent (promote) by clicking the Decrease Indent button on the Formatting toolbar or clicking the Promote button on the Outlining toolbar.

bullets introduce an idea. Second-level or minor bullets support or provide additional information about the first-level bullet. Third-, fourth-, and fifth-level bullets provide additional information about each previous bullet level. Second-level through fifth-level bullets are also known as **next-level** bullets because they are demoted one or more levels. A first-level bullet, or any bullet that is at a higher level than another existing bullet, is also known as a **previous-level** bullet. To avoid filling a slide with overly detailed information at several font sizes, you should avoid using too many bullet levels.

When you create a new supporting bullet level, you demote the bullet by moving the selected paragraph to the next (lower) bullet level. **Demoting** (indenting) moves the bullet down one level to the right. When you want to create a higher bullet level, you promote the bullet by moving the selected paragraph to the previous (higher) bullet level. **Promoting** moves the bullet up one level to the left. To add first- and second-level bullets:

Step 1	*Click*	the New Slide button ⬚ New Slide on the Formatting toolbar
Step 2	*Click*	the "Click to add title" placeholder
Step 3	*Key*	Introducing Baby Teddy
Step 4	*Click*	the "Click to add text" placeholder
Step 5	*Key*	Great new addition to the family
Step 6	*Press*	the ENTER key
Step 7	*Press*	the TAB key to demote the text to the second-level bullet position
Step 8	*Key*	Targeted for the infant market
Step 9	*Press*	the ENTER key
Step 10	*Key*	Safest & softest Teddy available
Step 11	*Press*	the ENTER key

On this line, you plan to key a first-level bullet, so you need to move this bullet position to the first-level position. Pressing the SHIFT + TAB keys or clicking the Decrease Indent button moves a bullet from its existing level to the previous level.

Step 12	*Press & hold*	the SHIFT key as you press the TAB key
Step 13	*Key*	Potential for a teen bear
Step 14	*Save*	the *Teddy Toys* presentation

Your screen should look similar to Figure 2-1.

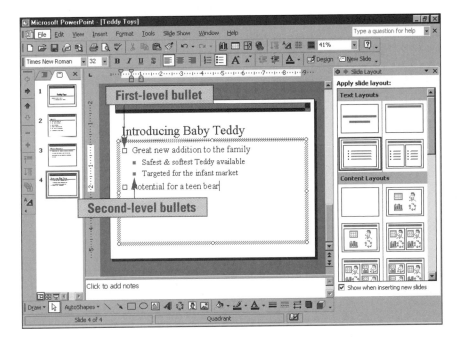

FIGURE 2-1
Introducing Baby
Teddy Slide

2.c Working with Slides in the Outline/Slides Pane

The outline/slides pane is useful for working with text and organizing slides in a presentation. You can add slides in either tab of this pane, and you can edit and format slide text in the Outline tab. The Slides tab is excellent for rearranging slides (though you can also rearrange slide order in the Outline tab), and the Outline tab lets you expand or collapse your view of a slide to see more or less of the text it contains. These choices make it easier to concentrate on organizing the ideas in your presentation rather than focusing on details like graphics and formatting. To add a slide in the Outline tab:

Step 1	*Click*	the Outline tab in the Outline/Slides pane
Step 2	*Click*	after the Introducing Baby Teddy text
Step 3	*Click*	the New Slide button [New Slide] on the Formatting toolbar
Step 4	*Key*	Current Products and press the ENTER key
Step 5	*Press*	the TAB key and key Family bears

QUICK TIP

The current bullet level is retained when you press the ENTER key until you promote or demote the level by pressing the TAB key or the SHIFT + TAB keys, clicking the Increase Indent or Decrease Indent button on the Formatting toolbar, or clicking the Demote or Promote button on the Outlining toolbar.

Pressing the CTRL + ENTER keys moves you from the first text placeholder on a slide to the next. When you press the CTRL + ENTER keys from the last text placeholder on the slide, you add a text slide to your presentation.

chapter
two

MOUSE TIP

You can move a selected slide in the Outline tab by clicking the Move Up or Move Down buttons on the Outlining toolbar until the slide is at a new location.

QUICK TIP

You can add a slide from the outline/slides pane by clicking immediately to the right of the slide title text on the Outline tab and then pressing the ENTER key, or by clicking on or between thumbnail images on the Slides tab and then pressing the ENTER key.

You can double-click a slide icon in the Outline tab to collapse a single bullet family, and double-click it again to expand a single bullet family.

MENU TIP

If the Outlining toolbar is not displayed, right-click any toolbar, and then click Outlining.

Step 6	*Press*	the ENTER key and then the TAB key to create a second-level bullet
Step 7	*Key*	Papa Teddy and press the ENTER key
Step 8	*Key*	Mama Teddy and press the ENTER key
Step 9	*Press & hold*	the SHIFT key as you press the TAB key
Step 10	*Key*	Action bears and press the ENTER key
Step 11	*Press*	the TAB key
Step 12	*Key*	the following second-level bullets under Action bears: Dancing Teddy Sport Teddy Rock & Roll Teddy
Step 13	*Save*	the *Teddy Toys* presentation

You decide to rearrange the slides in your presentation to improve the flow of information. To move slides in the outlines/slides pane:

Step 1	*Click*	the Slides tab located on the outline/slides pane
Step 2	*Point to*	Slide 5 until the ScreenTip displays: Current Products
Step 3	*Drag*	the Current Products slide to above Slide 4, the Introducing Baby Teddy slide
Step 4	*Release*	the mouse button when a horizontal line representing the slide appears above Slide 4
Step 5	*Click*	the Outline tab located on the outline/slides pane
Step 6	*Scroll*	to view the Teddy Toys title slide icon
Step 7	*Click*	the Expand All button ⬇️ on the Standard toolbar

The Expand All button is a toggle that expands to show slide titles and bullet text, and also collapses to show only slide numbers and titles.

Step 8	*Click*	the Expand All button ⬇️ to display the bullets

Rearranging Bullets in the Outline Tab

You may often need to rearrange bullets after keying them so that they follow a more logical sequencing of topics. Moving bullets is easy in the Outline tab. You can also use the Outlining toolbar in Normal view. To move a bullet:

Step 1	*Display*	the Outlining toolbar if necessary
Step 2	*Click*	the Introducing Baby Teddy slide icon in the Outline tab
Step 3	*Click*	the bullet symbol to the left of the "Targeted for the infant market" bullet in the Outline tab
Step 4	*Click*	the Move Down button once on the Outlining toolbar

Your screen should look similar to Figure 2-2.

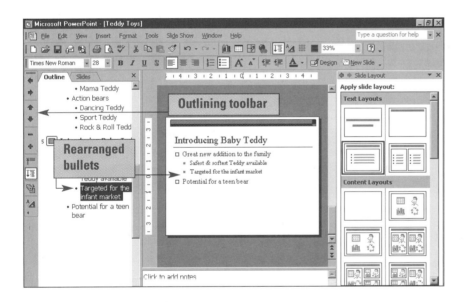

FIGURE 2-2
Slide with
Rearranged Bullets

2.d Editing and Formatting Text on Slides

While working on a presentation, you often want to change the look of text on a slide. You can change the spacing between lines and paragraphs, alignment of text, indents, and type of bullets. Although you can edit and format a slide on the Outline tab of the outline/slides pane, it may be more convenient to make these changes in the slide pane, where your view of the slide is larger.

chapter
two

CAUTION TIP

As you work, periodically save your presentation by clicking the Save button on the Standard toolbar or by pressing the CTRL + S keys. Saving frequently ensures that you do not lose your work if there is a power outage, computer error, or human error.

To switch to the Slides tab and edit and format text on an existing slide:

Step 1	*Click*	the Slides tab
Step 2	*Click*	Slide 1 in the Slides tab
Step 3	*Click*	at the end of the "Focusing on the Future" subtitle on the title slide

A hatch-marked border with eight sizing handles appears around the subtitle text placeholder, and the insertion point appears, indicating that the placeholder is active. The insertion point is positioned just to the right of the text and is blinking to indicate that new text will be keyed here. Your slide should look similar to Figure 2-3.

FIGURE 2-3
Selected Text Placeholder

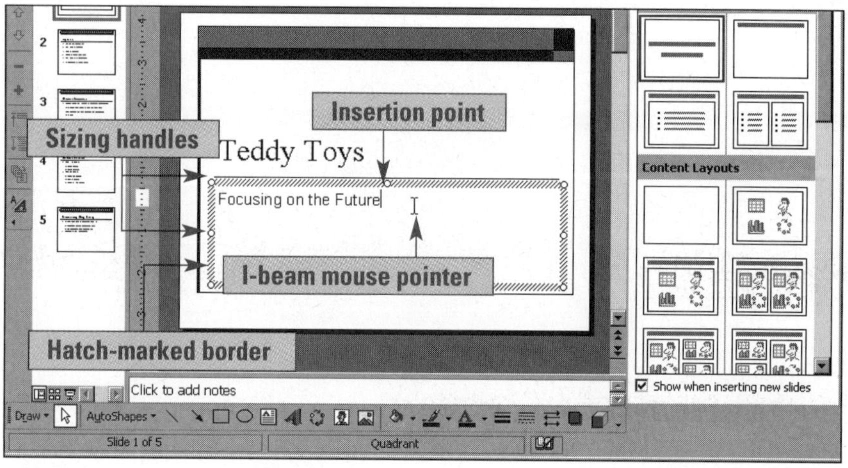

Step 4	*Press*	the ENTER key
Step 5	*Press*	the TAB key
Step 6	*Key*	Great Ideas, Great Products

Before you can edit text in a text placeholder, the placeholder must be active or selected. A hatch-marked border with eight sizing handles around a placeholder indicates it is selected. To edit or format some of the text in a placeholder, you select just the text to which you want to apply changes. To select an entire placeholder, you can hold down the SHIFT key and click anywhere in an inactive placeholder including the existing text, or you can click any border of an active placeholder.

QUICK TIP

You can further increase your view by switching to the Slides tab in the outline/slides pane; this makes more room for the slide pane and also lets you use the Slides tab to quickly navigate through your presentation. To make even more room for the slide pane, you can close the outline/slides pane by clicking the Close button. You can click the Normal View (Restore Panes) button to the left of the horizontal scroll bar to restore the outline/slides pane.

| Step 7 | *Drag* | to select "Great Ideas, Great Products" |
| Step 8 | *Click* | the Decrease Font Size button on the Formatting toolbar to reduce the size of the text to the next size smaller |

Changing Text Alignment

Changing **alignment** adjusts the horizontal position of text on a slide. For example, the title and subtitle text placeholders on the Quadrant design template use left alignment. Four types of alignment options—left, center, right, and justify—are available.

If the insertion point appears in the placeholder, you must click in the paragraph or select the paragraphs you want to align. To change the alignment of the title and subtitle text:

Step 1	*Click*	the Teddy Toys title text placeholder
Step 2	*Click*	the Center button on the Formatting toolbar
Step 3	*Click*	outside the placeholder to deselect it
Step 4	*Press & hold*	the SHIFT key
Step 5	*Click*	the subtitle text placeholder

The placeholder is selected, but the insertion point does not appear. When you change the alignment, both paragraphs in the subtitle change.

| Step 6 | *Click* | the Align Right button on the Formatting toolbar |
| Step 7 | *Click* | the Undo button to change back to left alignment |

Changing Line Spacing

Depending on the number of lines on a slide, you may want to either increase or decrease the line spacing to fit more lines on a slide, make the lines stand out more, or fill more of the slide. **Line spacing** is a measurement of space between lines of text on a slide. **Paragraph spacing** refers to the spacing between paragraphs. Changes to the line spacing on a slide affect the amount of white space between the lines of a paragraph. **White space** is the empty space on a slide between

You can select individual lines of text or you can select the entire placeholder. To select individual lines of text or individual characters, you drag the mouse pointer across the desired text in an active placeholder; the text you selected is then highlighted.

CAUTION TIP

If an insertion point appears within a text placeholder when you attempt to change alignment, you only change the alignment for the line containing the insertion point. If the placeholder is selected but the insertion point does not appear, any alignment changes you make affect all the paragraphs in the placeholder.

chapter two

QUICK TIP

If you want to change the line spacing or paragraph spacing of all the bulleted text on a slide, you must first select the bulleted text placeholder or select the text within the box. If you see the blinking insertion point, you are changing the line spacing between only two bullets instead of between all the bullets.

lines or surrounding lines of text and is intended to aid the readability of the text. To change the line spacing of bulleted text on a slide:

Step 1	*Display*	the Mission Statement slide
Step 2	*Press & hold*	the SHIFT key
Step 3	*Click*	anywhere in the bullet text placeholder to select the entire placeholder
Step 4	*Click*	Format
Step 5	*Click*	Line Spacing

The Line Spacing dialog box opens, with options for changing the line spacing and spacing before and after paragraphs. Line spacing increases or decreases the amount of space between all lines of text. The Before and After paragraph spacing options increase or decrease the amount of space before or after paragraphs only, not between the lines within a paragraph.

Step 6	*Drag*	the Line Spacing dialog box to the right so you can see the bullet on the Mission Statement slide
Step 7	*Key*	1.25 in the Line spacing box
Step 8	*Click*	Preview

If the Line Spacing dialog box obscures your view of the slide, drag the title bar so you can see the effect these line spacing changes have on the text.

Step 9	*Click*	OK

The AutoFit Options button may appear on your slide and display the following options: AutoFit Text to Placeholder, Stop Fitting Text to This Placeholder, Split Text Between Two Slides, Continue on a New Slide, Change to Two-Column Layout, and Control AutoCorrect Options. When the AutoFit Text to Placeholder option is activated, you can set the text size to change automatically to fit the placeholder.

Step 10	*Display*	the Introducing Baby Teddy slide

QUICK TIP

The AutoFit Options button is a Smart Tag, an Office feature that appears when you complete certain actions, such as autofitting text to a placeholder, to enable you to make further modifications if desired. Other Smart Tags include the AutoCorrect Options button, the Paste Options button, and the Automatic Layout Options button.

Step 11	*Press & hold*	the SHIFT key
Step 12	*Click*	anywhere in the bullet text placeholder to select the entire bullet placeholder
Step 13	*Open*	the Line Spacing dialog box
Step 14	*Key*	0.4 in the Before paragraph box
Step 15	*Click*	Preview to view the changes
Step 16	*Click*	OK
Step 17	*Save*	the *Teddy Toys* presentation

Changing Bullet Symbols

A **bullet symbol** is a design element that sets off each bullet point in a list. PowerPoint enables you to use symbols, pictures, font characters, numbers, and letters as bullet symbols. You can keep the bullet symbol styles determined by the presentation design, or change their color and size, or even select a different bullet symbol. The Formatting toolbar provides a quick method for displaying or hiding bullet symbols and numbers. The Format menu provides additional symbols and bullet customization. To change the bullets from symbols to numbers:

Step 1	*Display*	the Agenda slide
Step 2	*Select*	the entire bullet text placeholder
Step 3	*Click*	the Numbering button ▤ on the Formatting toolbar
Step 4	*Display*	the Introducing Baby Teddy slide
Step 5	*Select*	the entire bullet text placeholder
Step 6	*Click*	Format
Step 7	*Click*	Bullets and Numbering
Step 8	*Click*	the Numbered tab in the Bullets and Numbering dialog box, if necessary
Step 9	*Double-click*	the first example in row 2 to display capital letters A. B. C.
Step 10	*Save*	the *Teddy Toys* presentation

DESIGN TIP

Increasing the line spacing between lines of text opens up a slide by making it appear lighter (because there is more white space between the lines). Decreasing the line spacing between the lines of text may make it appear darker.

CAUTION TIP

If the insertion point is positioned in one bullet line, the bullet changes on that line only.

chapter
two

2.e Modifying the Slide Master

The **slide master** is an element of a template that controls the formatting, color, and graphic elements for all the slides in a presentation based on that template. Making changes to a slide master enables you to make formatting changes—such as font style, placeholder positions, bullet styles, background design, and color scheme—to all slides (except title slides) in a presentation automatically, instead of manually changing each one. Global title slide formatting is controlled by a **title master**, to guarantee consistent formatting across multiple title slides in a presentation. The information stored in the title and slide masters is based on the design template. You work with the title master in a future chapter. For now, you want to use the slide master to make some simple formatting changes. To change the bullets on the slide master:

Step 1	*Point to*	the Normal View button located to the left of the horizontal scroll bar
Step 2	*Press & hold*	the SHIFT key until the ScreenTip displays: Slide Master View
Step 3	*Click*	the Slide Master View button

Your screen should look similar to Figure 2-4.

FIGURE 2-4
Slide Master View

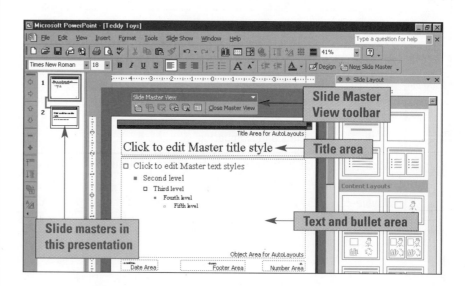

The slide master template displays placeholders for the title, bullet, date, footer, and slide number areas. It displays existing formats in terms of font, point size, alignment, color scheme, graphic elements, and bullet symbols dependent on the design template used. The Slide

Master View toolbar is displayed in the slide master, with options for inserting a new slide master, inserting a new title master, deleting a master, preserving a master, renaming a master, accessing the Master Layout dialog box, and closing the master view.

Adding Graphical Bullets to the Slide Master

You can add graphical bullets to your presentation to enhance the look of your text slides. Graphical bullets are more colorful and more interesting in shape than the default bullet symbols. When you change bullets on the slide master, bullet symbols change on all text slides in the presentation. To add a graphical bullets to the slide master:

Step 1	*Right-click*	in the first-level bullet text
Step 2	*Click*	Bullets and Numbering
Step 3	*Click*	the Bulleted tab, if necessary
Step 4	*Click*	Picture
Step 5	*Double-click*	the bullet example that is a brown split circular shape (ScreenTip displays: bullets, global marketing)
Step 6	*Right-click*	in the second-level bullet text
Step 7	*Click*	Bullets and Numbering
Step 8	*Click*	Customize
Step 9	*Click*	Wingdings in the Font: list box
Step 10	*Double-click*	the star bullet in the ninth row, twelfth column
Step 11	*Click*	the first brown color in the Color: list
Step 12	*Click*	OK
Step 13	*Click*	the Slide Show button located to the left of the horizontal scroll bar and progress through the slide show
Step 14	*View*	the bullet symbols on each slide until you return to the slide master

The changes you've made to the slide master are applied throughout the presentation. The bullet symbols change only on the text slides that follow the slide master. If you make individual changes to bullets on a slide, that slide follows the individual changes and does not follow the slide master.

MENU TIP

You can display the slide master by pointing to the Master command on the View menu, and then clicking the Slide Master command on the submenu.

MOUSE TIP

You can close the slide master by clicking the Close Master View button on the Slide Master View toolbar; you then return to the previous view.

chapter two

Your changes to the slide master are saved and you return to Normal view. As you observed during the slide show, when you change bullets on an individual slide, you override the slide master. You can reapply the slide master formatting to any slide. To close the slide master and reapply the current master styles:

Step 1	*Click*	the Close Master View button Close Master View on the Slide Master View toolbar
Step 2	*Display*	the Agenda slide
Step 3	*Right-click*	a blank area of the slide (not on a placeholder)
Step 4	*Click*	Slide Layout
Step 5	*Click*	the Title and Text layout list arrow in the Slide Layout task pane
Step 6	*Click*	Reapply Layout
Step 7	*Display*	the Introducing Baby Teddy slide
Step 8	*Click*	the Title and Text layout list arrow
Step 9	*Click*	Reapply Layout
Step 10	*Save*	the *Teddy Toys* presentation

2.f Printing an Individual Slide

PowerPoint provides different options for printing a presentation. If you want to print only a single slide, you can use the Print command on the File menu. In addition, you can print a range of slides using the Slides: text box in the Print dialog box by clicking the Slides: option button, and then keying the range of slides, such as 2-3. You also can print a slide as an overhead transparency by placing a transparency in your printer when you print your slides. To print an individual slide:

Step 1	*Display*	the Current Products slide
Step 2	*Click*	File
Step 3	*Click*	Print to open the Print dialog box
Step 4	*Click*	the Current slide option button
Step 5	*Click*	OK
Step 6	*Save*	the *Teddy Toys* presentation and close it

Summary

▶ PowerPoint enables you to add slides at any point in the presentation.

▶ First-level bullets introduce a topic and second-level bullets provide additional information regarding first-level bullets.

▶ The Outline tab in the outline/slides pane allows you to create, edit, rearrange, and add slides easily.

▶ The Slides tab in the outline/slides pane allows you to add and rearrange slides.

▶ The sequence or order of slides in a presentation can be changed in the outline/slides pane.

▶ Changes may be made to any presentation design to personalize the look of the presentation.

▶ Alignment changes the position of text within a text placeholder.

▶ Left, center, right, and justify are four types of alignment for positioning text.

▶ Increasing or decreasing line spacing changes the space between lines of text on a slide.

▶ White space is the empty space on a slide that aids readability.

▶ The slide master controls settings for the formatting, color, and graphic elements such as bullets on all slides in a presentation.

▶ You can move indents by dragging the first-line indent marker, bullet text marker, or left indent marker on the horizontal ruler.

▶ You reapply the formatting of the slide master to any slide by reapplying the current master styles of the slide layout.

▶ You can print a single slide or selected slides by clicking Print on the File menu.

Commands Review

Action	Menu Bar	Shortcut Menu	Toolbar	Task Pane	Keyboard
Open an existing presentation	File, Open		🗁	Click desired presentation in the Open a presentation section in New Presentation task pane	CTRL + O ALT + F, O
Add a slide from outline/slides pane					Click after slide title on Outline tab, press ENTER Click between thumbnail images on Slides tab, press ENTER

chapter two

Action	Menu Bar	Shortcut Menu	Toolbar	Task Pane	Keyboard
Create a next-level bullet			⇨		TAB
Return to a previous-level bullet			⇦		SHIFT + TAB
Change line spacing on a slide	Format, Line Spacing				ALT + O, S
Display the ruler	View, Ruler				ALT + V, R
Undo a previous action	Edit, Undo		↺		CTRL + Z ALT + E, U
Redo previous Undo	Edit, Redo		↻		CTRL + Y ALT + E, R
Access the slide master	View, Master, Slide Master		SHIFT + ⊞		ALT + V, M, S
Display the Slide Layout task pane	Format, Slide Layout	Right-click empty area on slide, click Slide Layout		Other task panes list arrow, click Slide Layout in Slide Layout task pane	ALT + O, L
Reapply the master styles		Click the slide layout list arrow, then click Reapply Layout		Click list arrow on slide layout, click Apply to Selected Slides or Apply Layout in Slide Layout task pane	
Print an individual slide	File, Print, Current slide				ALT + F, P, C CTRL + P

Concepts Review

Circle the correct answer.

1. To open an existing presentation, click:
[a] File, New.
[b] File, Open.
[c] Insert, New Presentation.
[d] File, Add a New Presentation.

2. To promote a bullet up one previous level, press the:
[a] TAB key.
[b] ENTER key.
[c] SHIFT key.
[d] SHIFT + TAB KEYS.

3. Which of the following is not a Smart Tag?
[a] AutoCorrect Options button
[b] AutoFit Options button
[c] Automatic Layout Options button
[d] AutoDelete Options button

4. The bullets order can be changed in the Outline tab by:
[a] clicking the Move Up or Move Down buttons.
[b] dragging the tab marker to its new location.
[c] dragging the indent markers to their new location.
[d] clicking the Collapse or Expand buttons.

5. You can tell that a text placeholder is selected when:
[a] a dotted border with eight selection handles appears surrounding the text.
[b] a hatch-marked border with eight small sizing handles appear surrounding the text.
[c] the text placeholder is shaded.
[d] a solid black border with eight selection handles appears surrounds the text.

6. **Line spacing is the amount of white space:**
   [a] between lines of text.
   [b] before and after paragraphs.
   [c] between the characters of a line.
   [d] between words of a line.

7. **Alignment refers to the:**
   [a] length of the line.
   [b] horizontal position of a line on the page.
   [c] vertical space between the lines of text.
   [d] size of the characters in a line.

8. **Which of the following is *not* used to position text on a slide?**
   [a] tabs
   [b] alignment
   [c] line spacing
   [d] font color

9. **If you want all the slides in the presentation to be formatted with the same new bullet symbol, use:**
   [a] a presentation design template.
   [b] the slide master.
   [c] the add a slide option.
   [d] the slide layout option.

10. **Reapplying the current master styles to a slide:**
   [a] changes the formatting on all slides.
   [b] reverts formatting changes to the styles on the slide master.
   [c] adds an identical slide.
   [d] removes any inserted or drawn objects on a slide.

Circle **T** if the statement is true or **F** if the statement is false.

T F 1. Second-level bullets are the exact same size as first-level bullets.

T F 2. Much of the text in a PowerPoint presentation is formatted in paragraphs.

T F 3. Bullets can be moved by clicking the Move Up or Move Down button on the Outlining toolbar.

T F 4. When applying a particular presentation design, you must apply this design to each slide individually.

T F 5. You can add a slide from the Outline/Slides pane by clicking immediately to the right of the slide title text, on the Outline tab and then pressing the TAB key.

T F 6. You can select an entire placeholder by holding down the CTRL key and then clicking anywhere in the placeholder.

T F 7. Increasing or decreasing line spacing aids in readability.

T F 8. Paragraph and line spacing change the spacing between lines of type within a paragraph.

T F 9. The slide master displays placeholders and formatting for titles and text on all slides in a presentation except the title slide.

T F 10. PowerPoint does not allow you to print an individual slide.

Skills Review

Exercise 1   Ⓒ

1. Open the *PowerPoint* presentation you created in Chapter 1, and add a Title and Text slide at the end of the presentation.

2. The title of the new slide should read "The Views of PowerPoint" and the bullets should read "Normal View," "Slide Sorter View," "Notes Page View," and "Slide Show."

chapter two

3. Move the Slide Show bullet up two levels in the Outline tab so that it appears as the second bullet.

4. Use the slide master to change the first-level bullet to a Picture bullet using any bullet symbol with the following ScreenTip: bullets, romanesque, web bullets.

5. Save, spell check, and proofread the presentation, then resave if necessary.

6. Print only the new slide, and then close the presentation.

Exercise 2   ⓒ

1. Open the *Office* presentation you created in Chapter 1, and add a Title and Text slide at the end of the presentation.

2. The title should read "Why Use Office Professional?" The bullets should read "Share files on the Internet," "Use speech recognition technology," "Use IntelliSense™ technology," and "Use e-mail based collaboration." Use the Symbol command on the Insert menu to insert the trademark symbol in the third bullet.

3. Using the slide master, change the bullet symbol of the first-level bullet to the Microsoft Windows symbol (last Wingdings symbol) from the Wingdings font list under the Customize section in the Bullets and Numbering dialog box.

4. Using the slide master, change the size of the new bullet to 75%.

5. Using the Line Spacing dialog box, change the paragraph spacing on the bullet text of the Why Use Office Professional? slide to 0.5 lines before the paragraph.

6. Save, spell check, and proofread the presentation, then resave if necessary.

7. Print the presentation as a three-slides-per-page handout, and then close the presentation.

Exercise 3   ⓒ

1. Open the *Design* presentation you created in Chapter 1, and add a Title and 2 Column Text slide at the end of the presentation.

2. The title should read "Presentation Fonts." The first-level bullet item in the first text placeholder on the left should read "Serif Fonts." Key the following next-level bullets: "Serious messages," "Ease of reading," and "Large amounts of text." The first-level bullet in the second text placeholder on the right should read "Sans Serif Fonts." Key the following next-level bullets: "Lighthearted messages," "Cleaner look," and "Titles and headlines."

3. Change the line spacing of the bullets in each text placeholder to 1.5.

4. Display the Dale Carnegie Presentation Tips slide.

5. Edit the text slide in the Outline tab by adding the following next-level bullets under each of the first-level bullets: Under the first-level bullet "Plan" add the next-level bullet "Define audience, purpose, and medium"; under the first-level bullet "Prepare" add the next-level bullet "Establish positive mindset and prepare structure of presentation"; under the first-level bullet "Practice" add the next-level bullet "Review, rehearse, get feedback"; under the first-level bullet "Present" add the next-level bullet "Build rapport with audience."

6. Change the first-level bullet on the slide master to a Picture bullet. Adjust bullet size as necessary.

7. Change the next-level bullet on the slide master to a Customized bullet. Adjust bullet size as necessary.

8. View the presentation as a slide show.

9. Save, spell check, and proofread the presentation, then resave if necessary.

10. Print only slides two and three, and then close the presentation.

Exercise 4

1. Open the *Precision Builders* presentation you created in Chapter 1, and add a Title and Text slide at the end of the presentation.

2. The title should read "Our Motto" and the bullet should read "Precision Builders wants to work with you to build the home of your dreams at a price that will not shatter your dreams."

3. Change the line spacing of the bullet to 1.25 lines on the Our Motto slide.

4. Display the Precision Builders title slide and change the alignment of the subtitle to align right.

5. Reapply the layout of the current master of a Title and Text slide to the Our Motto slide.

6. Save, spell check, and proofread the presentation, then resave if necessary.

7. Print the presentation as a three-slides-per-page handout, and then close the presentation.

Exercise 5

1. Open the *Nature Tours* presentation you created in Chapter 1, and add a Title and Text slide at the end of the presentation.

2. The title should read "Available Tours." The first-level bullet should read "Each tour is available at beginning, intermediate, and expert levels." The next-level bullets should read "Hiking," "Biking," "Rafting," and "Horseback riding."

3. Using the slide master, change the bullet symbol for the first- and next-level bullet using a Picture bullet.

4. Using the slide master, change the line spacing of the bullet text to 1.1; 0.0 spacing before and after paragraphs.

5. If necessary, change the size of the bullet and/or increase or decrease the size of the text on the master.

6. Save, spell check, and proofread the presentation, then resave if necessary.

7. Print only the new slide, and then close the presentation.

Exercise 6

1. Open the *A Healthier You* presentation you created in Chapter 1, and add a Title and Text slide at the end of the presentation.

2. The title should read "Balanced Diet at a Glance" and the bullets should read "Carbohydrates," "Proteins," "Fats," "Minerals," "Vitamins," and "Fiber."

3. Using the Outline tab or the Normal View, move the Fats bullet to the end of the bullet list.

4. Using the slide master, change the paragraph spacing of the bullet text to increase the spacing before the paragraphs.

5. Display the Good Health Helps Everyone slide.

6. Add the following first-level bullet as the first bullet: "Basic common sense rules."

7. Demote the remaining bullets to next-level bullets.

8. Save, spell check, and proofread the presentation, then resave if necessary.

9. Print the presentation as a three-slides-per-page handout, and then close the presentation.

chapter two

Exercise 7

1. Open the *Buying A Computer* presentation you created in Chapter 1, and add a Title and 2 Column Text slide at the end of the presentation.

2. The title should read "Reasons to Buy a Computer." The first-level bullet item in the first text placeholder on the left should read "Family essentials." Key the following next-level bullets: "Family budgets," "Address book," "School homework," and "Personal e-mail." The first-level bullet in the second text placeholder on the right should read "Family enjoyment." Key the following next-level bullets: "Internet surfing," "Computer games," "Web page design," and "Holiday cards."

3. Change the bullet symbols on the slide master.

4. Rearrange the order of the bullets in order of your priority.

5. Display the Getting Started slide. Add the following first-level bullet as the first bullet: "Ask yourself the following:"

6. Demote the remaining bullets to next-level bullets.

7. Save, spell check, and proofread the presentation, then resave if necessary.

8. Print Slides 2 and 3 as a two-slides-per-page handout, and then close the presentation.

Exercise 8

1. Open the *Leisure Travel* presentation you created in Chapter 1, and add a Title and Text slide at the end of the presentation.

2. The title should read "Leave Everything to Us." The first-level bullet should read "We do all the work." The next-level bullets should read "Travel arrangements," "Hotel accommodations," "Restaurant reservations," "Golf tee times," and "Sight-seeing tours." Add another first-level bullet that reads "You will be pampered and relaxed."

3. Change the bullet size on the Leave Everything to Us slide.

4. Change the alignment of the title on the slide master.

5. Change the bullet symbols on the Vacation Packages for Everyone Slide to a lettering style, and change the lettering color.

6. Save the presentation, print only the slides with changes, and then close the presentation.

Case Projects

Project 1

An administrative assistant in the next department has asked you how to remove the bullets in front of the bullet text. Using online Help, review information on removing bullets or numbering from text on a text slide. Create a simple text slide to summarize the information you find so your coworker can refer to it again. Print the new slide, remembering to spell check and proofread your work first.

Project 2

You have been asked to add a Title and Text slide to the *Communicate* presentation you created in the previous chapter. This slide should provide information about the first bullet on the previous text slide. Make any formatting decisions with regard to alignment, line spacing, and bullet symbols. Save the presentation, and print the new slide.

Project 3

As you work toward your goal of selling your Souner & Associates training program to prospective clients, you need to begin "selling them" early in the presentation. Add a Title and Text slide to the *Souner* presentation you created in the previous chapter, detailing what your organization can provide. Make any formatting decisions with regard to alignment, line spacing, and bullet symbols. Make some of the changes to the slide master. Save the *Souner* presentation, and print the presentation as a four-slides-per-page handout.

Project 4

Open the *My Presentation* presentation you created in the previous chapter. As this is the project on which you are working independently, all decisions are entirely up to you. You should edit your previous slides and add another slide to your presentation. Keep in mind your message, audience, and medium as you work. Make any formatting decisions with regard to alignment, line spacing, and bullet symbols. Make some of the changes to the slide master. It may be necessary to change your presentation design template to set the tone of your topic. Save *My Presentation*, and print the new slide.

Project 5

Open the *Zoo* presentation you created in the previous chapter, and add a Title and 2 Column Text slide that can be added to the presentation concerning possible zoo events, occasions, important dates, or animal facts. Make any formatting decisions with regard to alignment, line spacing, and bullet symbols. Make some of the changes to the slide master. Save and print the presentation as a three-slides-per-page handout.

Project 6

You cannot find an appropriate design template for your presentation. So, you decide to connect to the Internet and visit the Microsoft Home Page at *http://www.microsoft.com* to search for information on downloading new presentation design templates. Print the Web pages.

Project 7

As you continue building the *Cars* presentation you created in the previous chapter, add a Title and Text slide on how to purchase a new car. This slide should summarize the locations to use for finding out as much as you can about your particular car choice. Connect to the Internet to search the Web for current information about the car you plan to buy. Make any formatting decisions with regard to alignment, line spacing, and bullet symbols. Make some of the changes to the slide master. Save *Cars,* and print the presentation as a three-slides-per-page handout.

Project 8

You and your partner continue to work on the *Internet* presentation you created in the last chapter. Add a Title and Text slide at the end of the presentation that highlights one of the topics you chose earlier. Connect to the Internet to search the Web for your research. Make any formatting decisions with regard to alignment, line spacing, and bullet symbols. Make some of the changes to the slide master. Save and print the new slide.

chapter two

Working with Clip Art, Pictures, and WordArt

Chapter Overview

Y ou can enhance the slides in your presentation by adding clips and WordArt and by changing the layout of individual slides. You also can insert a variety of pictures and other art files from Clip Organizer, a floppy or Zip disk, a network drive, or the Internet. WordArt is a feature you can use to create special text effects, such as unusual alignment, stretching, and 3-D. In this chapter, you also learn to change the layout of a slide, so that it best suits your purposes as you develop a presentation.

LEARNING OBJECTIVES

- ▶ Add clip art images to slides
- ▶ Move and resize an image
- ▶ Edit clip art images
- ▶ Insert images from another source
- ▶ Change the layout of individual slides
- ▶ Add animated clip images
- ▶ Add an image to the slide background
- ▶ Add WordArt to a slide

Case profile

Ms. Hill has sent you to a workshop on creating effective presentations. At that workshop, you learn that adding graphic images to slides in a presentation supports the text or data on the slide. In addition, you learn that images should be added only if they add value to the message; they should not overwhelm the message. You decide to add images and WordArt to your *Teddy Toys* presentation and to change the layout of some slides to present information more effectively.

chapter
three

3.a Adding Clip Art Images to Slides

You can add clip art images to the slides in your presentation to enhance, emphasize, or convey an idea graphically. You can obtain clip art images in the Microsoft Clip Organizer or from a disk, hard drive, network folder, CD-ROM, or the Internet. Methods for adding clip art images from all these sources are presented throughout this chapter.

Images can be categorized as drawn or bitmapped. **Drawn pictures** (also known as **vector drawings**) are created using a sequence of mathematical statements that create lines, curves, rectangles, and other shapes. Windows Metafile images, which end with the .wmf extension, are one example of drawn pictures that can be edited extensively in PowerPoint. Most images in the Microsoft Clip Organizer Gallery are drawn pictures. **Bitmap pictures** (also known as **raster images**) are comprised of a series of small dots. Bitmap pictures can be flipped or rotated, but they cannot be ungrouped to isolate and modify individual parts of the image. Editing of bitmaps must be accomplished by using a paint or graphics editing program. Examples of bitmap pictures are those that end with .bmp, .png, .jpg, or .gif.

notes Depending on your installation of Microsoft Office, the Microsoft Clip Organizer may display different categories and clip art images than displayed in this text. All images used within this chapter can be found on the Data Disk. If you don't see an image used in this chapter in the Clip Organizer, obtain it from the Data Disk.

Inserting Clip Images from the Microsoft Clip Organizer

The Microsoft Clip Organizer contains a wide variety of pictures, photographs, sounds, and video clips that improve the appearance of your slides. Images in the Clip Organizer are organized by category so they are easy to access. You can find an image by using the Search text: text box in the Insert Clip Art task pane or browsing the Microsoft Clip Organizer. The Clip Organizer also lets you import clips from other sources, as well as search the Web for online clips. Microsoft provides a site on the Internet, Microsoft Design Gallery Live, which provides new clips to review and download to your Clip Organizer.

You can add a clip to a slide that contains a Clip Art placeholder or a Content placeholder, or to any slide. Depending on your settings in the AutoFormat As You Type tab in the AutoCorrect dialog box, inserting an

chapter
three

FIGURE 3-1
Insert Clip Art Task Pane

image in a slide containing text or content placeholders, rather than on a blank slide, results in the layout of that slide automatically changing to accommodate the clip art image. If this happens, the Smart Tag, the Automatic Layout Options button, appears at the bottom right on the inserted image. Click the button to Undo Automatic Layout, Stop Automatic Layout of Inserted Objects, or Control AutoCorrect Options. To add a blank slide and then add a clip image:

Step 1	*Open*	the *Teddy Toys* presentation you modified in Chapter 2, and display the last slide in the presentation
Step 2	*Close*	the Outlining toolbar, if necessary
Step 3	*Display*	the Slide Layout task pane
Step 4	*Click*	the list arrow on the Blank layout in the Content Layouts section of the Slide Layout task pane
Step 5	*Click*	Insert New Slide
Step 6	*Click*	the Insert Clip Art button ⬛ on the Drawing toolbar
Step 7	*Click*	Later, if a dialog box opens, asking if you want to organize and catalog all media files

The Insert Clip Art task pane opens, providing you with options for searching for clip art by topic, searching for clip art within folders, searching different media types, accessing the Clip Organizer, Clips Online, and Tips for Finding Clips. Your screen should look similar to Figure 3-1.

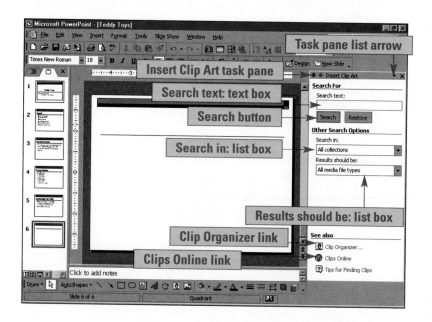

Step 8	*Click*	the Clip Organizer link at the bottom of the Insert Clip Art task pane and click Later, if necessary

The Microsoft Clip Organizer dialog box opens with a Collection List task pane that includes My Collections, Office Collections, and Web Collections folders. These folders organize your clip images.

Step 9	*Click*	the plus sign to the left of the Office Collections folder
Step 10	*Click*	the Sports folder

The Microsoft Clip Organizer window on your screen should look similar to Figure 3-2.

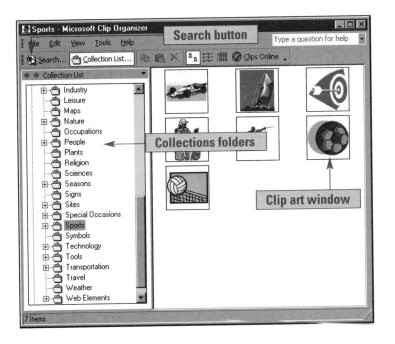

FIGURE 3-2
Microsoft Clip
Organizer Window

Step 11	*Point to*	the soccer ball image (ScreenTip displays: soccer, soccer balls)
Step 12	*Click*	the list arrow on the soccer ball image
Step 13	*Click*	Copy
Step 14	*Click*	the Close button ☒ on the Clip Organizer window title bar
Step 15	*Click*	Yes to the Would you like these to remain on the clip-board after Clip Organizer shuts down? question
Step 16	*Click*	the Paste button 📋 on the Standard toolbar

QUICK TIP

You can insert an image from another source, such as the Data Disk, by clicking the Insert Picture button on the Drawing toolbar, switching to the folder that contains the image, and then double-clicking the image.

MOUSE TIP

To see a preview (larger size image), you click the list arrow of the clip, and then click Preview/Properties.
  If the Picture toolbar is not displayed, right-click any toolbar and click Picture. If the toolbar is in the way of the image, drag its title bar to move it out of the way.

chapter
three

DESIGN TIP

Every slide in a presentation may not require an image. Add images only when they relate to or enhance the message of the presentation. Remember to limit the number of images so they do not distract the audience.

The clip art image is automatically aligned at the center of the slide. If you know what type of clip art you want to find in the Clip Organizer, you can speed the search by defining a specific category and media type. To add images using the Search text: text box in the Insert Clip Art task pane:

Step 1	Key	bear in the Search text: text box on the Insert Clip Art task pane
Step 2	Click	All media file types in the Results should be: list box, if necessary
Step 3	Click	Search
Step 4	Scroll	through the Results: list box
Step 5	Click	the panda bear identified by the ScreenTip as animals, bears, cartoons, leisure

3.b Moving and Resizing an Image

Images are graphic objects that can be moved, resized, edited, and copied. You can **move** an image by pointing anywhere inside the image's border and sizing handles (the mouse pointer changes to a four-directional arrow) and dragging. In order to work with an image, it must be selected. When an image is selected, eight sizing handles surround it, a rotate handle appears at the top center of the picture, and the Picture toolbar is displayed. To move the bear image:

Step 1	Click	the bear image to select it, if necessary
Step 2	Observe	that the image displays sizing handles, indicating that it is selected
Step 3	Point to	the middle of the image or anywhere inside the image's borders and sizing handles
Step 4	Drag	the bear image to the lower-right corner of the slide
Step 5	Drag	the soccer ball image to the lower-left corner of the slide

Your screen should look similar to Figure 3-3.

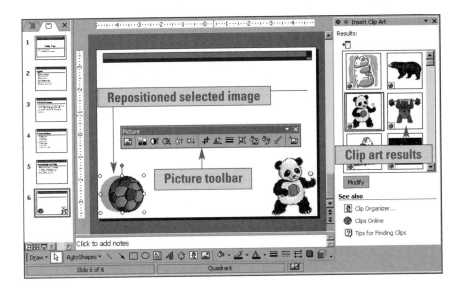

FIGURE 3-3
Clip Art Placement

INTERNET TIP

You can click the Clips Online link in the Insert Clip Art task pane to access more images on the Web. You can insert images from the Internet into a slide by right-clicking the image, clicking Copy, right clicking an area on the PowerPoint slide, and then clicking Paste.

You can **resize** (change the size of) an image by using the Format Picture dialog box or by dragging any sizing handle (pointer becomes a double-headed arrow). If you drag a middle handle, you resize only in one direction, changing the proportions of the image. If you drag a corner handle, you maintain the image's original proportions. You can resize to exact measurements by accessing the Format Picture dialog box, where you specify the width, height, and scale of the image. To resize an image using the Format Picture dialog box:

Step 1	*Right-click*	the bear image
Step 2	*Click*	Format Picture
Step 3	*Click*	the Size tab of the Format Picture dialog box
Step 4	*Key*	1.75 in the Height: text box

TASK PANE TIP

You can insert an image in a specific location on the slide by dragging the image from the Insert Clip Art task pane search results area to the desired location.

You decide to lock the aspect ratio of a picture and set resizing to be relative to the original picture size. The **aspect ratio** is the relationship between the height and the width of an object. When you maintain the aspect ratio while resizing an object, you change the height and width simultaneously; if the height changes, the width changes automatically in proportion to the height.

Step 5	*Verify*	that the Lock aspect ratio and Relative to original picture size check boxes contain check marks
Step 6	*Click*	OK and position the bear in the lower-right corner

chapter
three

3.c Editing Clip Art Images

Clip art images can be customized to fit your presentation design, slides, and words. Suppose you want to use a clip art image, but the colors within the image clash with those colors used on the presentation design. Or, suppose you want to use part of the clip art image, not the entire image; or the image directs the eye away from the words you want to reinforce, instead of toward them. To remedy such situations, you can edit or modify the image.

Recoloring an Image

Recoloring an image changes its original colors. When you edit a clip art image, you can recolor selected parts of the image, so you have a great degree of control over its appearance. To add and recolor an image:

| Step 1 | Click | Modify in the Insert Clip Art task pane |

The Results: box closes and the Search text: text box and Other Search Options section appear.

Step 2	Key	tops in the Search text: text box
Step 3	Click	Search
Step 4	Scroll	down to the image of a spinning top with a purple background (ScreenTip displays: households, playthings)
Step 5	Click	the spinning top image in the Results: list box
Step 6	Click	the Recolor Picture button on the Picture toolbar
Step 7	Drag	the Recolor Picture dialog box if it obscures the image you are recoloring
Step 8	Click	the turquoise color list arrow in the New: list box
Step 9	Click	the darker green color (sixth from left)
Step 10	Click	the reddish-brown color list arrow below the turquoise color
Step 11	Click	the white color
Step 12	Click	the red color list arrow
Step 13	Click	the white color
Step 14	Scroll	down to the purple color
Step 15	Change	the purple color to the lighter green color (fifth from left)

The Recolor Picture dialog box on your screen should look similar to Figure 3-4.

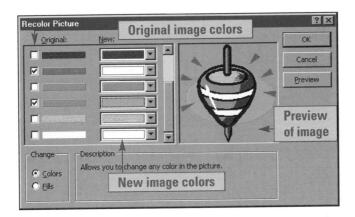

FIGURE 3-4
Recolor Picture Dialog Box

> **QUICK TIP**
>
> You can use the arrow keys on the keyboard to **nudge** (move slightly) an image in any direction.

Step 16	*Change*	the pink color to black
Step 17	*Click*	Preview to view the effect of the intended changes
Step 18	*Remove*	the check mark from the pink color check box in the Original: column to return to the original color
Step 19	*Click*	OK
Step 20	*Resize*	the spinning top image to approximately 1 inch high and 1 inch wide using the Format Picture dialog box
Step 21	*Reposition*	the spinning top image to the upper-right corner of the slide

> **MOUSE TIP**
>
> You can recolor a picture by right-clicking the object, clicking Format Picture, clicking the Picture tab, and then clicking Recolor.

Cropping an Image

Cropping an image trims or cuts part of an image or object so that you can use only part of it. Cropping an image enables you to trim or cut off a portion of that image along its vertical and/or horizontal edges so that you can see only a portion of it. You can also **outcrop** an image by increasing the size of the padding around the picture, giving it more white space around the image. You decide to add another image to this slide and crop the image so that you only use the portion of the image you need for this slide. To insert and crop an image:

Step 1	*Click*	Modify in the Insert Clip Art task pane
Step 2	*Key*	puzzles in the Search text: text box
Step 3	*Click*	Search

chapter
three

MENU TIP

You can also recolor an image by selecting the image, clicking the Picture command on the Format menu, and then clicking Recolor.

CAUTION TIP

The recolor option is available only for image files that end in .bmp, .png, .jpg, or .gif.

FIGURE 3-5
Cropped Puzzle Piece Image

Step 4	*Scroll*	to the puzzle pieces image (ScreenTip displays: games, households, jigsaws, puzzles)
Step 5	*Click*	the puzzles image
Step 6	*Click*	the Crop button on the Picture toolbar
Step 7	*Move*	the mouse pointer to the lower-left corner of the puzzle piece image until the mouse pointer shape changes
Step 8	*Drag*	the lower-left corner of the puzzle piece image to the right until only the yellow puzzle piece is displayed in the dotted rectangle
Step 9	*Release*	the mouse button
Step 10	*Crop*	the puzzle piece image to just above and just below the yellow puzzle piece
Step 11	*Click*	outside the image area

The image on your screen should look similar to Figure 3-5.

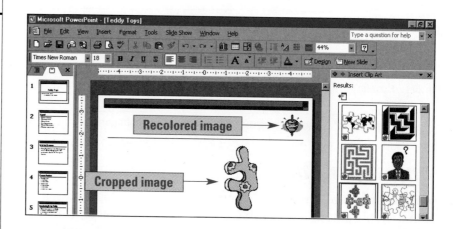

Step 12	*Move*	the puzzle piece image to the upper-left corner of the slide
Step 13	*Save*	the *Teddy Toys* presentation

Flipping and Rotating an Image

When viewing a presentation, the eye goes to the top of the slide first, then works from left to the right and down in a Z pattern. When an image points off the slide, the eye follows the direction of the image off the slide. To avoid having the audience work to bring their eyes back to the rest of the slide once they have been guided off, it is best to flip the image so that it points into the slide. You realize that the bike image points away from the text, so you need to adjust it. You can **flip** an image to change its vertical or horizontal direction. You can also **rotate** an image to change its angle.

To flip and rotate an image:

Step 1	Select	the puzzle piece image, if necessary
Step 2	Click	the Draw button [Draw ▾] on the Drawing toolbar
Step 3	Point to	Rotate or Flip
Step 4	Click	Flip Horizontal
Step 5	Point to	the rotate handle above the center of the picture
Step 6	Drag	the rotate handle to the right slightly
Step 7	Resize	the puzzle piece image to approximately 2 inches high and 1 inch wide
Step 8	Resize	the soccer ball image to approximately 1.2 inches high and 1.4 inches wide
Step 9	Save	the *Teddy Toys* presentation

3.d Inserting Images from Another Source

You can insert images of any graphics format, such as .bmp, .gif, .png, or .jpg, on a slide. The images can be stored on other folders on your computer's hard drive, diskettes, a network server, or the Internet. You can add more than one image at a time if the images are located in the same path location. To add multiple images from another source:

Step 1	Add	a new slide with the blank layout at the end of the presentation
Step 2	Click	the Insert Picture button [icon] on the Drawing toolbar
Step 3	Click	the Look in: list arrow, and switch to the drive or folder where the Data Files are stored
Step 4	Select	the *blocks.wmf* graphics file
Step 5	Press & hold	the CTRL key
Step 6	Select	the *lightbulb.wmf* graphics file
Step 7	Click	Insert
Step 8	Move	the light bulb image to the upper-right corner of the slide
Step 9	Resize	the light bulb image to approximately 1.5 inches high and 1.3 inches wide

QUICK TIP

You can restore a cropped picture to its original dimensions by clicking the Reset button on the Picture tab in the Format Picture dialog box.

DESIGN TIP

When possible, rotate or flip an image so that it points or leads the eye to the text message. Images should not face off the page, because they draw attention away from your message.

chapter
three

Step 10	*Rotate*	the light bulb image down and to the right
Step 11	*Resize*	the blocks image to approximately 3.0 inches high and approximately 3.75 inches wide
Step 12	*Reposition*	the blocks image to the center of the slide, if necessary
Step 13	*Save*	the *Teddy Toys* presentation

3.e Changing the Layout of Individual Slides

Once you have inserted a slide using a particular layout, you are not tied forever to that layout. You can change the layout of a slide at any time using the Slide Layout task pane. To change the slide layout:

Step 1	*Verify*	that the last slide in the presentation is active
Step 2	*Display*	the Slide Layout task pane, if necessary
Step 3	*Click*	the Title Only layout slide under Text Layouts in the Apply slide layout: section
Step 4	*Key*	We Welcome New Ideas in the title placeholder

Your screen should look similar to Figure 3-6.

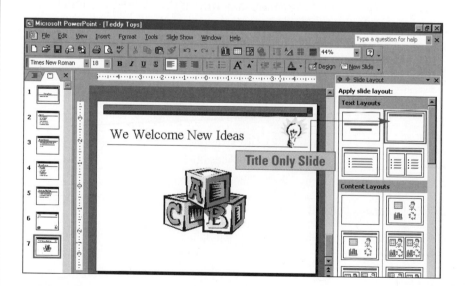

FIGURE 3-6
Slide with New Layout

Step 5	*Save*	the *Teddy Toys* presentation

3.f Adding Animated Clip Images

Animated clips or **motion clips** are clip images, usually in GIF format, that show movement or motion. The Clip Organizer includes motion clips, as does the Design Gallery Live on the Internet. In addition, you can search the Internet for animated clip images and insert the clips on your slide. You only see the animation during the slide show.

To add an animated clip image and position it on a slide:

Step 1	*Display*	the slide which contains the bear, top, puzzle piece and soccer ball
Step 2	*Delete*	the bear image in the lower-right corner of the slide
Step 3	*Click*	the Insert Picture button on the Picture or Drawing toolbar
Step 4	*Switch to*	the drive or folder where the Data Files are stored
Step 5	*Double-click*	the *horse.gif* image file
Step 6	*Resize*	the rocking horse image so that it is approximately 2 inches high and 2.6 inches wide
Step 7	*Reposition*	the rocking horse image to the center of the slide, if necessary
Step 8	*Click*	the Insert Picture button on the Picture or Drawing toolbar
Step 9	*Switch to*	the drive or folder where the Data Files are stored
Step 10	*Double-click*	the *present.gif* image file
Step 11	*Drag*	the present image to the lower-right corner of the slide
Step 12	*Resize*	the present image so that it is approximately 1.75 inches high and 2 inches wide
Step 13	*Flip*	the present image horizontally
Step 14	*Click*	the Slide Show button to view the animation
Step 15	*Save*	the *Teddy Toys* presentation

MENU TIP

You can add an image by clicking the Picture command on the Insert menu, and then clicking From File.

MOUSE TIP

You can add an image stored on disk, hard drive, or network drive, or an image you have scanned and saved, to a PowerPoint slide by clicking the Insert Picture button on the Picture toolbar or the Drawing toolbar.

chapter three

3.g Adding an Image to the Slide Background

Consistency throughout a presentation creates a sense of unity, a feeling among the audience that the slides belong together, and works to reinforce the intended goal of the presentation. To accomplish this, you can add an image to the slide master so that it appears on the background of all the slides for that slide master. As you have learned, a slide master controls the font, size, color, style, and alignment for the titles and main text on your slides. It also determines the location of placeholders, background colors, and objects. If you add an image to the slide master, the image appears on the backgrounds of all slides in a presentation except for the title slides (there is a separate title master for the title slides in a presentation). To add an image to the slide master:

Step 1	**Switch to**	Slide Master view
Step 2	**Click**	the Insert Picture button on the Picture or Drawing toolbar
Step 3	**Double-click**	the *teddybear.wmf* image file
Step 4	**Resize**	the teddy bear image until it is 1.5 inches high
Step 5	**Move**	the teddy bear image to the lower-right corner of the slide master
Step 6	**Flip**	the teddy bear image so it faces the center of the slide

Your screen should look similar to Figure 3-7.

FIGURE 3-7
Bear Image on
Slide Master

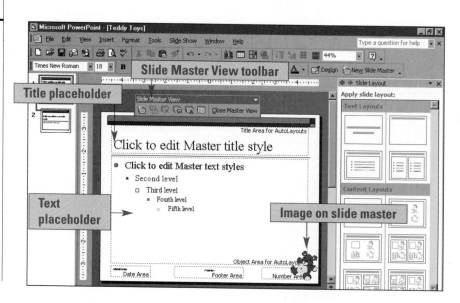

Step 7	*Run*	the slide show to verify that the teddy bear image does not overlap any object on the slides (ignore the placement of the teddy bear on the slide containing the animated present image)
Step 8	*Resize*	or move the teddy bear image as needed
Step 9	*Switch to*	Normal view
Step 10	*Save*	the *Teddy Toys* presentation

Omitting Background Graphics

A **background graphic** is any image or pattern in a background fill on a slide. PowerPoint provides an option that enables you to omit or hide a background graphic on an individual slide or selected slides. When you hide a background graphic on an individual slide, all graphics from the design template are also hidden. To hide the background graphics on a slide:

Step 1	*Display*	the slide that contains the animated clip images, if necessary
Step 2	*Right-click*	a blank area on the slide
Step 3	*Click*	Ba<u>c</u>kground
Step 4	*Click*	the Omit background <u>g</u>raphics from master check box in the Background dialog box
Step 5	*Click*	<u>A</u>pply

The teddy bear image, the horizontal line, and the bar object across the top are no longer displayed.

| Step 6 | *Save* | the *Teddy Toys* presentation |

3.h Adding WordArt to a Slide

WordArt enables you to enhance a string of text by using the Insert WordArt button on the Drawing toolbar. WordArt enhances text by shadowing, skewing, rotating, and stretching, as well as applying a predefined shape to the text. To add WordArt to a slide:

| Step 1 | *Click* | the Insert WordArt button  on the Drawing toolbar |

chapter
three

QUICK TIP

To add a custom background image to a slide, such as a picture you have saved to disk, click Background on the Format menu, click the Background fill color list arrow, click Fill Effects, click the Picture tab, click Select Picture, switch to the drive or folder that contains the file, select the file, and then click the Insert button.

The WordArt Gallery dialog box opens, with several styles of WordArt from which to choose.

| Step 2 | *Double-click* | the yellow and orange WordArt style in the third row, first column |

The Edit WordArt Text dialog box opens. Here you can key, edit, and format the text you want the WordArt object to display.

| Step 3 | *Key* | Our Toys Rock, Spin, and Amaze! in the Text: text box in the Edit WordArt Text dialog box |

The dialog box on your screen should look similar to Figure 3-8.

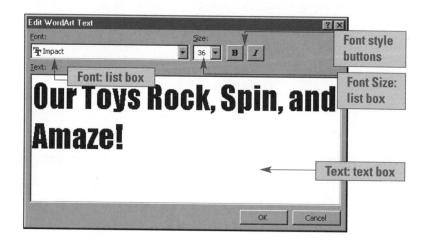

FIGURE 3-8
Edit WordArt Text
Dialog Box

| Step 4 | *Click* | OK |
| Step 5 | *Drag* | the rocking horse image to a position above the WordArt object |

Editing a WordArt Object

WordArt objects can be resized and moved just like other objects. You can edit WordArt text using the WordArt toolbar, which opens when a WordArt object is selected, or you can make your changes in the Edit WordArt dialog box. To edit the WordArt object using the Edit WordArt dialog box:

| Step 1 | *Double-click* | the Our Toys Rock, Spin, and Amaze! WordArt object |
| Step 2 | *Click* | immediately to the left of the letter S in Spin |

MENU TIP

You can insert a WordArt object by pointing to the Picture command on the Insert menu and then clicking WordArt.

Step 3	Press	the ENTER key
Step 4	Click	the Size: list arrow
Step 5	Click	48
Step 6	Click	the Font: list arrow
Step 7	Click	Times New Roman
Step 8	Click	the Bold button
Step 9	Click	OK
Step 10	Reposition	the WordArt object at the center of the slide

You can format WordArt using the WordArt toolbar, or you can make your changes in the Format WordArt dialog box. To format the WordArt object with different colors using the WordArt toolbar:

Step 1	Verify	that the WordArt object is selected and that the WordArt toolbar is displayed
Step 2	Click	the Format WordArt button 🖎 on the WordArt toolbar
Step 3	Click	the Colors and Lines tab, if necessary
Step 4	Click	the Fill Color: list arrow
Step 5	Click	Fill Effects
Step 6	Click	the Color 1: list arrow on the Gradient tab
Step 7	Click	the brown color (ScreenTip displays: Follow Shadows Scheme Color)
Step 8	Click	the From center option button in the Shading Styles box
Step 9	Click	the variant style at the right in the Variants box
Step 10	Click	OK twice to return to the slide

Changing the shape of a WordArt object adds interest to the artistic text. In addition, you can create different moods simply by changing the shape of the WordArt object. To change the WordArt shape:

Step 1	Select	the WordArt object, if necessary
Step 2	Click	the WordArt Shape button 🔲 on the WordArt toolbar
Step 3	Click	the Double Wave 2 shape in the third row, last column
Step 4	Run	the slide show

chapter
three

Your completed slide should look similar to Figure 3-9.

FIGURE 3-9
Completed Slide with
Edited WordArt

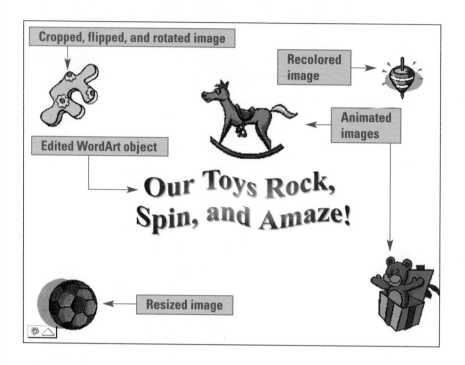

| Step 5 | *Save* | the *Teddy Toys* presentation and close it |

Summary

- ▶ The Microsoft Clip Organizer contains a wide variety of pictures, photographs, sounds, and video clips, organized by category.

- ▶ Images are objects that can be moved, resized, deleted, recolored, cropped, and copied.

- ▶ Images (with the exception of bitmap images) can be converted into Microsoft Office drawing objects that can be moved, resized, deleted, colored, flipped, rotated, and cropped.

- ▶ Limit the number of clip images per slide to eliminate the possibility of the audience being distracted.

- ▶ Resizing an image by dragging the corner handles maintains its original proportions.

- ▶ Resizing an image by dragging the middle handles distorts the image's original proportions.

- ▶ To resize an image to exact specifications, use the Format Picture dialog box.

- ▶ Recoloring an image changes the original colors.

- ▶ Recoloring of bitmap images is accomplished in a paint or picture editing program, not PowerPoint.

- ▶ Cropping an image is done when you want to use only a portion of the image.

- ▶ Outcropping an image is used when you want to add padding or white space around the image.

- ▶ Flipping an image changes its vertical and/or horizontal direction.

- ▶ Images can be added from other folders, clip art packages, and the Internet.

- ▶ Slide layouts can be changed at any time.

- ▶ Animated clip images show movement or motion in the slide show.

- ▶ Images that are placed on the slide master can be hidden on individual slides.

- ▶ Clip art images can be added to any slide in a presentation, as well as to the slide master.

- ▶ WordArt is used to shape, skew, and change the appearance of a string of text.

chapter three

Commands Review

Action	Menu Bar	Shortcut Menu	Toolbar	Task Pane	Keyboard
Display the Insert Clip Art task pane	Insert, Picture, Clip Art; Insert, Object, Microsoft Media Gallery		[icon]	Other Task Panes list arrow, and then click Slide Layout	ALT + I, P, C ALT + I, O
Insert an image from the Clip Organizer		Click the list arrow, click Insert; Drag the clip to the slide; Right-drag the clip, click Copy Here		Click the Clip Organizer on the Insert Clip Art task pane	
Insert an image from another source	Insert, Picture, From File		[icon]	Click the Clips Online link on the Insert Clip Art task pane	ALT + I, P, F
Move a selected image			Drag the middle of the image [icon]		
Resize a selected image	Format, Picture, Size; Format, Object, Size	Right-click image, Format Picture, Size; Format, Object, Size	Drag a sizing handle [icon]		ALT + O, I ALT + O, O
Delete a selected image					DELETE
Recolor a selected image	Format, Picture, Picture, Recolor	Right-click image, Format Picture, Picture, Recolor; Double-click the image, Picture, Recolor	[icon]		ALT + O, I, ALT + E
Crop a selected image	Format, Picture, Picture	Right-click image, Format Picture, Picture	[icon]		ALT + O, I
Rotate an image	Draw button on Drawing toolbar, Rotate or Flip	Drag rotate handle on object	[icon]		ALT + R, P, L or R
Flip an image	Draw button on Drawing toolbar, Rotate or Flip				ALT + R, P, H or V
Change slide layout		Click the slide layout list arrow, click Apply to Selected Slides or Apply Layout		Click a slide layout in the Apply slide layout: section	
Omit background graphics from slide master	Format, Background, Omit background graphics from master	Right-click slide background, click Background, click Omit background graphics from master check box			ALT + O, K, ALT + G
Insert a WordArt image	Insert, Picture, WordArt		[icon]		ALT + I, P, W
Edit text of a selected WordArt object	Edit, Text	Right-click WordArt object, Edit Text Double-click the WordArt image	Edit Text...		ALT + E, X ALT + X
Change the WordArt shape			[Abc icon]		
Format selected WordArt object	Format WordArt	Right-click WordArt object, Format Word Art	[icon]		ALT + O, O

Concepts Review

Circle the correct answer.

1. **The Microsoft Clip Organizer allows you to:**
   [a] add slides to a presentation.
   [b] add picture, sound, and motion clips to a slide.
   [c] spell check your presentation.
   [d] add WordArt images to a slide.

2. **When an image is selected, it displays:**
   [a] six boxes and a rotate handle.
   [b] eight sizing handles and a rotate handle.
   [c] six middle handles and a rotate handle.
   [d] two corner handles and a rotate handle.

3. **When you want to resize an image from the center and keep it proportioned, press the:**
   [a] SHIFT key.
   [b] CTRL key.
   [c] ALT key.
   [d] SPACEBAR.

4. **After moving a clip art image to a particular location on the slide, you can immediately reverse the action by doing all of the following *except*:**
   [a] clicking the Redo button.
   [b] clicking the Undo button.
   [c] clicking the Undo Move Object command on the Edit menu.
   [d] pressing the CTRL + Z keys.

5. **A good design practice when adding clip art images to your slides is to:**
   [a] add as many clip art images as you desire.
   [b] resize the image so it takes up as much space as your text.
   [c] be sure to place at least one clip art image per slide.
   [d] add clip art sparingly and only if it relates to your topic.

6. **To delete an image, you must first:**
   [a] move the image to a new location.
   [b] resize the image.
   [c] select the image.
   [d] double-click the image.

7. **What term describes dragging a handle of an image?**
   [a] copying
   [b] selecting
   [c] resizing
   [d] moving

8. **What term describes the separation of a clip art image into different parts so that it becomes a Microsoft Office drawing?**
   [a] grouping
   [b] ungrouping
   [c] regrouping
   [d] embedding

9. **What is the term for changing the direction in which a clip art image faces?**
   [a] crop
   [b] flip
   [c] group
   [d] align

10. **You can change the layout of a slide by:**
    [a] right-clicking the slide and then clicking Background.
    [b] clicking Edit, Change Layout.
    [c] clicking the desired layout on the Slide Layout task pane.
    [d] clicking Format and then clicking Slide Design.

chapter three

Circle **T** if the statement is true or **F** if the statement is false.

T F 1. Clip art and WordArt should be used only to enhance the goal of a presentation.

T F 2. Images in the Microsoft Clip Organizer are arranged by category so they are easy to access.

T F 3. The Picture toolbar may appear when you insert an image from the Microsoft Media Gallery.

T F 4. Selecting the image and dragging it to a new location is the same as moving an image.

T F 5. To resize an image from the center while maintaining its original proportions, you should press the ALT key when you drag to resize.

T F 6. Once an image is added to a slide, you cannot remove it.

T F 7. By design, images should face off the slide, away from the text.

T F 8. The slide master enables you to create consistency in your presentation by adding images so they appear on all slides in your presentation, except the title slide.

T F 9. The layout of a slide can never be changed once you have saved it in your presentation.

T F 10. WordArt contains only five styles to display your text.

Skills Review

Exercise 1

1. Open the *PowerPoint* presentation you modified in the previous chapter, and display a slide that could benefit from clip art images.

2. Access the Microsoft Clip Organizer, and select a category that pertains to the topic of the slide.

3. Add a clip art image to the slide, and then resize and move the image as needed. (When you add the image to the text slide, the layout of the slide may automatically change to a text and clip art layout, and the bullet text readjusts to fit the new text placeholder if the Automatic layout for inserted objects feature is activated.)

4. If necessary, flip the image so it faces the text.

5. Add a blank slide at the end of the presentation for a WordArt object.

6. Use the WordArt style in the fourth row, third column.

7. Add the following text: "PowerPoint Presentations," pressing the ENTER key between the words.

8. Change the WordArt font to Impact and the Font size to 48.

9. Resize the WordArt object to approximately 2.5 inches high and 6.5 inches wide, and position it at the center of the slide.

10. Run the slide show.

11. Save the presentation, print the slides containing images and WordArt only, and then close the presentation.

Exercise 2

1. Open the *Office* presentation you modified in Chapter 2.

2. Use the Search For clips feature to find an image for one of your text slides. Make sure the clip art image enhances and complements the text on the slide. You may want to consider searching for computers, software, or technology.

3. Recolor the clip art image to match the design template, if necessary.

4. Add a blank slide at the end of the presentation for a WordArt object.

5. Use the first WordArt style in the first row, first column. Add the following text: "Office XP Is Here"

6. Change the WordArt font to Times New Roman, Bold, and the font size to 60.

7. Change the shape of the WordArt object to Stop.

8. Change the WordArt fill color to Pale Blue and the WordArt line color to White or Dark Blue. Resize the WordArt object as needed.

9. Browse the Microsoft Clip Organizer, and then add an image from the People, Groups category of the Office Collections to the WordArt slide.

10. Reposition and resize the image as necessary to complement the WordArt image on the slide.

11. Run the slide show.

12. Save the presentation, print only the slides containing images and WordArt, and then close the presentation.

Exercise 3 C

1. Open the *Design* presentation you modified in Chapter 2.

2. Add a blank slide at the end of the presentation for a WordArt object.

3. Use the WordArt style in the third row, fifth column.

4. Add the following text: "Design and You"

5. Change the WordArt font to Comic Sans MS and the font size to 60, and then resize the WordArt object as needed.

6. Search for "ideas" in the Microsoft Clip Organizer, select the light bulb image (*lightbulb.wmf*), and add it to the slide master.

7. Resize the image and place it in the lower-right corner.

8. Save the presentation, print only the slides containing images and WordArt, and then close the presentation.

Exercise 4 C

1. Open the *Precision Builders* presentation you modified in Chapter 2.

2. Display the Why Precision Builders? slide, and change the layout to the Title, Text, and Clip Art layout.

3. Double-click the clip art placeholder, and search for an appropriate image that depicts carpentry and complements the presentation design template.

4. Resize, move, rotate, or flip the image as needed.

5. Resize the bullet placeholder to avoid word wrapping of any bullet text.

6. Add a blank slide at the end of the presentation for a WordArt object.

7. Use the WordArt style in the fourth row, first column.

8. Add the following text: "Distinctive Designs"

9. Change the WordArt font to Book Antiqua and the font size to 60.

10. Change the color of the fill to the Parchment texture in Fill Effects.

11. Resize the WordArt object as needed.

12. Save the presentation, print only the slides containing images and WordArt, and then close the presentation.

Exercise 5

1. Open the *Nature Tours* presentation you modified in Chapter 2.

chapter three

2. Using the Clip Organizer or the Design Gallery Live on the Internet, find photographic image of any park, and copy and paste it on one of the slides.

3. Resize, move, rotate, or flip the image as needed.

4. Add a clip art image to the slide master. Resize, move, rotate, or flip the image as needed.

5. Make any adjustments to bullet placeholders to aid readability.

6. Add a blank slide at the end of the presentation for the following WordArt object: "Are You Ready for a Great Tour?"

7. Change the WordArt font, size, and colors to match the design template.

8. Resize the WordArt object as needed.

9. Save the presentation, print only the slides containing images and WordArt, and then close the presentation.

Exercise 6

1. Open the *A Healthier You* presentation you modified in Chapter 2.

2. Use the Search feature to add an appropriate clip image or images to one of the slides.

3. Resize, move, recolor, crop, rotate, or flip the image as needed.

4. Add a blank slide at the end of the presentation for the following WordArt object: "A Healthy Body is a Happy Body"

5. Change the WordArt font, size, and colors to match the design template.

6. Add the exercise animated GIF image (*exercise.gif*) from the Data Disk to the WordArt slide.

7. Resize the WordArt object as needed.

8. Save the presentation, print only the slides containing images and WordArt, and then close the presentation.

Exercise 7

1. Open the *Buying A Computer* presentation you modified in Chapter 2.

2. Add a computer clip art image or an appropriate image to a slide of your choice.

3. Add an animated clip image to a different slide of your choice.

4. Resize, move, recolor, crop, rotate, or flip the images as appropriate.

5. Add a blank slide at the end of the presentation for the following WordArt object: "The World at Our Door"

6. Change the WordArt font, size, and colors to match the design template.

7. Resize the WordArt object as needed.

8. Save the presentation, print only the slides containing images and WordArt, and then close the presentation.

Exercise 8

1. Open the *Leisure Travel* presentation you modified in Chapter 2.

2. Add a blank slide at the end of the presentation for the following WordArt object: "Make the World Your Playground"

3. Change the WordArt font, size, and colors to match the design template. Resize the WordArt object as needed.

4. Add an image related to world travel to the WordArt slide.

5. Omit the background graphics from the master on the WordArt slide.

6. Use the Search for clips feature to find an image relating to world travel, and then add this image to the slide master.

7. Modify and move the images as appropriate.

8. Save the presentation, print only the slides containing images and WordArt, and then close the presentation.

Case Projects

Project 1

You have been asked by an assistant in the Personnel Department to explain how to connect to the Design Gallery Live Web site, where you can preview and download additional clips. Access the Microsoft Design Gallery Live Web site and download a few clips so you can explain the procedure correctly to the other assistant. Create a PowerPoint text slide listing the steps needed to access the Design Gallery Live. Print the slide.

Project 2 ⒸC

You decide to add Microsoft Clip Organizer images to the *Communicate* presentation you modified in Chapter 2. Use the Search for clips feature, and be selective with the clip images. Resize and move the images as needed. Recolor or crop as needed. Add a WordArt slide at the end of the presentation. Run the slide show and save the presentation. Print the slides with WordArt or clip images only.

Project 3 Ⓒ

As you look over the *Souner* presentation you modified in the previous chapter, you feel you need to incorporate an image of cooperation between clients and your company to strengthen your message. You decide to add an appropriate clip image to one of the existing slides. The image you portray should be positive and encourage the spirit of teamwork. You also decide to add a new slide at the end of the presentation consisting of a WordArt object. Be as creative as possible. Run the slide show and save the presentation. Print the slides with WordArt or clip images only.

Project 4 Ⓒ

You determine that there are several options you can pursue to enhance your independent presentation, *My Presentation,* that you modified in Chapter 2. You can let the software help you find appropriate images by using the Search for clips feature, you can ask coworkers if they have clip art images you can add, you can access the Internet and copy and paste clip images or animated clip images to enhance your slides, or you can create a WordArt object. Decide what option(s) to pursue and make whatever editing changes necessary to give your presentation a professional touch. Save and print the presentation.

Project 5 Ⓒ

Because you work for a zoo, the *Zoo* presentation you modified in Chapter 2 should definitely include appropriate clip images on several of the slides. Remember that the audience of this presentation is children. Be selective and remember not to overload the slides with clip images. Make all decisions regarding placement, size, color, and rotation of the images. If possible, change the layout of one of the slides with clip art to a Title, Text, and Clip Art layout. Add an image to the slide master. Save and print the new slides.

Project 6 Ⓒ

You are taking a class at the local community college and are assigned to a group that will be conducting a class discussion on multiculturalism in the workplace. Access the PowerPoint home page through the Office on the Web command on the Help menu. Search for clip images that best illustrate the term multicultural. Download one or more clip images, and add the clip images to a PowerPoint slide. Print the slide containing the clip art images.

chapter three

Project 7

You want to dress up the *Cars* presentation you modified in Chapter 2 by adding clip art images to a slide or slides of the presentation. Use the Microsoft Design Gallery Live on the Internet to download clip images. Access different automobile sites on the Web, and copy and paste photographic images to add to your slides. Search the Internet for animated clip images related to cars. Add one or two animated images to the slides. Make all formatting decisions regarding the images. If possible, make changes to the slide master. Add WordArt to a new slide or an existing slide. Save the presentation, and print only the slides with WordArt or clip art images.

Project 8

You and your partner want to use the most recent and high-tech images available for your presentation. Connect to the Internet and search the Web for clip images and animated images to download that relate to the *Internet* presentation you modified in Chapter 2. The two of you also investigate bringing in clip images from other sources such as different clip software and scanned images. Make all formatting decisions regarding the images. If possible, make changes to the slide master. Add WordArt to a new slide or an existing slide. Save the presentation, and print only the slides with WordArt or clip art images.

Using Drawing Tools

Chapter Overview

I n this chapter, you learn how to use the drawing tools in PowerPoint to create shapes. You learn to use the AutoShapes tool to create more sophisticated shapes, such as stars, squiggly lines, and arrows. By creating your own art elements on a slide, you can grab the audience's attention, control the focus of the audience on a word or a point, and enhance interest.

LEARNING OBJECTIVES

- ▶ Add AutoShapes to slides
- ▶ Use the Office Clipboard
- ▶ Work with multiple objects
- ▶ Format shapes
- ▶ Add text to shapes
- ▶ Order and group objects

Case profile

Reading through the material you received when you attended the workshop on design, you notice that several example slides include simple graphics, such as stars, rectangles, and arrows. Looking at your *Teddy Toys* presentation, you determine that adding shapes to some slides will help your audience follow the presentation and remember the important points.

chapter four

4.a Adding AutoShapes to Slides

Shapes are objects you create using the Drawing toolbar. You can add one or more shapes to a slide to add visual interest, direct the flow of information, or help the audience notice and retain important information. The Drawing toolbar contains tools for drawing and modifying shapes to create the greatest visual impact. **AutoShapes** are ready-made shapes—squares, rectangles, hearts, stars, callouts, flowchart symbols, lines, arrows, and so on—that are available in PowerPoint at the click of a button. These shapes are organized into submenus located on the AutoShapes menu. When you click the AutoShapes button, you see a list of commands, such as Lines or Connectors. Pointing to a command displays a submenu of related AutoShapes. These submenus can be dragged onto a slide as separate toolbars.

notes PowerPoint displays the Drawing toolbar by default. If the Drawing toolbar is not displayed, right-click any toolbar, and then click Drawing on the shortcut menu.

It is a good idea to display the ruler, grid, and guides to assist you in placing and drawing your shapes. The ruler helps you to draw or move an object to a precise location or size. The grid and guides are non-printing lines that help you draw, align, and move objects with a great degree of control. The **horizontal** and **vertical guides** divide the slide area into four equal parts, providing another visual reference when drawing and positioning shapes and other objects. To add a blank slide and display the ruler, grid, and guides:

Step 1	*Open*	the *Teddy Toys* presentation you modified in Chapter 3 and display the last slide
Step 2	*Add*	a new slide with the Blank layout
Step 3	*Display*	the ruler if necessary
Step 4	*Click*	View
Step 5	*Click*	Grid and Guides
Step 6	*Verify*	that the Snap objects to grid check box contains a check mark
Step 7	*Verify*	that the spacing is 0.083 in the Spacing text box under Grid settings
Step 8	*Click*	the Display grid on screen and Display drawing guides on screen check boxes to add check marks

| Step 9 | **Click** | OK |

Your screen should look similar to Figure 4-1.

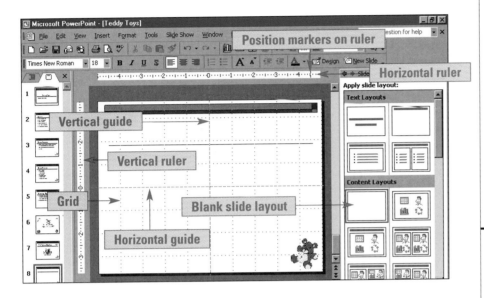

MENU TIP

To change the spacing between gridlines in the grid, click Grid and Guides on the View menu, then key a different number in the Spacing text box. The smaller the number, the closer the gridlines are set, allowing you more control when placing the objects or snapping them to the grid.

FIGURE 4-1
Blank Slide with Ruler, Guides, and Grid

MOUSE TIP

When moving any shape, you can hold down the ALT key to position the shape in a precise location.

You can show or hide the grid by clicking the Show/Hide Grid button on the Standard toolbar.

Drawing Shapes

To draw shapes, you click a shape button, position the mouse, and then drag to create the desired shape. If you click a shape button and then click the slide (instead of dragging), you insert a default-sized, proportionally shaped object at that location. If you click a shape button, position the mouse, and then drag, you determine the size of the object. To draw shapes using the grid and guides:

DESIGN TIP

The default color of a drawing shape is based on the color scheme of the Presentation design template.

Step 1	**Click**	the AutoShapes button AutoShapes ▾ on the Drawing toolbar
Step 2	**Point to**	Flowchart
Step 3	**Click**	the AutoShape in the first row, first column (ScreenTip displays: Flowchart: Process)
Step 4	**Position**	the mouse pointer at the center of the slide (intersection of guides)
Step 5	**Press & hold**	the CTRL + SHIFT keys
Step 6	**Drag**	to draw the AutoShape from the center of the slide to approximately the 1-inch mark on the horizontal ruler
Step 7	**Drag**	the process shape to the left side of the slide resting on the horizontal guide and to the right of the first vertical grid line (see Figure 4-2 for placement)

chapter
four

The process shape is filled with green (the default color based on the design template) and is selected displaying the eight sizing handles and the rotate handle. When an AutoShape is selected, it displays eight sizing handles, a rotate handle, and an adjustment handle that allows you to alter the shape of the AutoShape.

Step 8	*Click*	the AutoShapes button `AutoShapes ▾` on the Drawing toolbar
Step 9	*Point to*	Flowchart
Step 10	*Click*	the AutoShape in the second row, third column (Flowchart: Document)
Step 11	*Position*	the mouse pointer at the center of the slide (intersection of guides)
Step 12	*Press & hold*	the SHIFT key to draw the document shape from the center of the slide to the right approximately to the 2-inch mark on the horizontal ruler
Step 13	*Move*	the document shape to the center of the slide, with the lower middle handle of the shape resting on the vertical and horizontal guides (see Figure 4-2 for placement)
Step 14	*Add*	the Flowchart: Preparation shape in the third row, second column to the right side of the slide resting on the horizontal guide
Step 15	*Size*	the preparation shape to approximately 1.3 inches high and 2.3 inches wide using the Format AutoShape dialog box
Step 16	*Save*	the *Teddy Toys* presentation

Your screen should look similar to Figure 4-2.

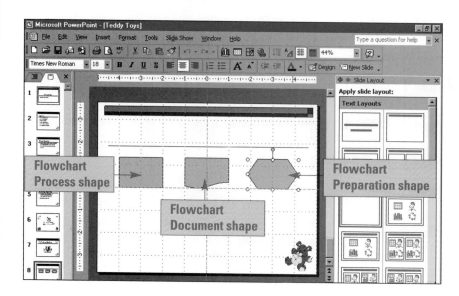

FIGURE 4-2
Slide with Flowchart
AutoShapes

4.b Using the Office Clipboard

The Office Clipboard enables you to copy up to 24 items so you can paste them to different locations. You can copy objects to a new place on a slide, to different slides, and between other Office XP applications.

Copying Objects

When you want the same object to appear in more than one place in your presentation, you copy that object. Copying is actually a two-step process that involves copying the object and then pasting it onto the slide. If you copy more than one object without pasting it, the objects are placed on the Office Clipboard so that you can choose which object you want to paste. To copy shapes:

Step 1	Select	the process shape (the flowchart shape at the left)
Step 2	Click	the Copy button on the Standard toolbar
Step 3	Click	the document shape (the flowchart shape at the center)
Step 4	Click	the Copy button on the Standard toolbar

The Office Clipboard task pane appears with the two copied flowchart shapes. Your task pane should look similar to Figure 4-3.

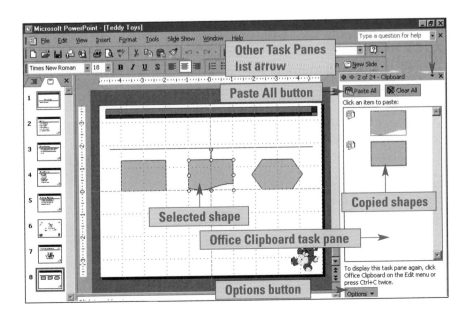

QUICK TIP

If you make an error while drawing, simply click the Undo button on the Standard toolbar, click the appropriate drawing tool, and start over.

You can use the CTRL key to draw a shape from the center to the outside. You can use the SHIFT and the CTRL keys to draw a perfect circle or square from the center to the outside.

You can use the SHIFT key when drawing a line if you want to constrain the line to draw at 15-degree increments from its starting point.

FIGURE 4-3
Office Clipboard Task Pane

TASK PANE TIP

You can display the Office Clipboard by clicking the Other Task Panes list arrow in the task pane, and then clicking Clipboard.

chapter four

The Office Clipboard icon may appear in the taskbar if that option has been activated. The icon in the taskbar displays the number of copied items in the Office Clipboard and enables you to access the Office Clipboard in any Office application.

Step 5	*Copy*	the preparation shape

The third shape is automatically placed in the Office Clipboard. When you point to each item on the Office Clipboard task pane, it displays a list arrow with options for pasting or deleting the item.

Pasting Objects

When you **paste** an object, you complete the copy process by placing the copied object in a different location. When a copy of an object is pasted on the same slide as the original object, it is positioned slightly below and to the right of the original object. If the copied object is pasted on a different slide, it is positioned at the location of the original copied object. Once you've pasted an object, you can move it to the desired location. To paste Clipboard objects:

Step 1	*Click*	the process shape on the Office Clipboard (third shape from the top)
Step 2	*Click*	each of the remaining shapes on the Office Clipboard

4.c Working with Multiple Objects

When working with multiple shapes and other objects on a slide, you often need to select more than one object at a time to delete, move, copy, arrange, or align them. You select multiple objects by clicking each object while pressing and holding the SHIFT key, by drawing a marquee box around the objects you want to select, or by using the menu or keyboard to select all the objects on a slide. To select and move multiple objects:

Step 1	*Select*	the copied process shape at the left
Step 2	*Press & hold*	the SHIFT key

Step 3	*Click*	each remaining copied shape on the slide
Step 4	*Drag*	the selected shapes down to a position directly above the last horizontal grid line and to the right of the first vertical grid line

Your screen should look similar to Figure 4-4.

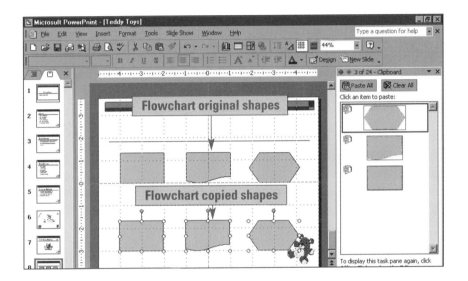

FIGURE 4-4
Slide with Repositioned Flowchart Shapes

MOUSE TIP

The Paste All button at the top of the Office Clipboard task pane pastes a copy of every object in the clipboard onto your slide or document. The Clear All button removes all objects from the Office Clipboard.

DESIGN TIP

Using Connector AutoShapes instead of simple lines to connect objects provides you with greater flexibility and control.

Connecting Shapes

PowerPoint includes AutoShapes that let you add connector lines between shapes on your slide. Connector AutoShapes move with the shape to which they are attached. You can change the color, style, shape, and thickness of any Connector AutoShape to achieve a particular visual effect. When you use Connector AutoShapes (straight, elbow, or curved) to connect AutoShapes, **connection sites** (nonprinting colored dots) appear on the shapes to help you connect them successfully. Once you click a Connector AutoShape tool and then point to an existing shape on a slide, the shape displays four blue connection sites. After a successful connection, the connection sites display in red indicating that you have locked or attached the connector line to the shape. If the connection is not successful, the connection sites remain blue and the end of the connector line displays a green circle, indicating that the site is unlocked.

chapter
four

To connect the flowchart shapes:

Step 1	*Click*	the AutoShapes button `AutoShapes ▾` on the Drawing toolbar
Step 2	*Point to*	Connectors
Step 3	*Click*	the Straight Arrow Connector in the first row, second column
Step 4	*Point to*	the middle-right handle of the first process shape
Step 5	*Drag*	from the rightmost middle blue connection site on the process shape to the leftmost middle blue connection site on the document shape to the right
Step 6	*Release*	the mouse

The connector arrow should be selected with the connection sites displayed in red. If either or both ends of the arrow display a green circle, then the shape is not connected to the arrow. You would then drag the green circle to the blue connection site on the shape.

Step 7	*Draw*	another Straight Arrow Connector from the rightmost middle connection site of the document shape in the center of the slide to the leftmost middle connection site of the preparation shape at the right
Step 8	*Click*	the Curved Arrow Connector AutoShape in the third row, second column of the Connectors category
Step 9	*Drag*	from the rightmost middle connection site on the preparation shape at the right of the slide to the top middle connection site on the process shape in the lower-left corner of the slide

Two yellow diamonds appear that enable you to reshape the curved line. The shaping diamonds or adjustment handles can be dragged to change the shape of the line.

Step 10	*Draw*	another Curved Arrow Connector AutoShape from the bottom middle connection site of the process shape in the lower-left corner of the slide to the bottom-middle connection site of the document shape in bottom center of the slide
Step 11	*Draw*	the Elbow Arrow Connector (second row, second column) AutoShape from the top-middle connection site of the document shape in bottom center of the slide to the rightmost connection site of the preparation shape in the lower-right corner of the slide

Step 12	**Save**	the *Teddy Toys* presentation

Your screen should look similar to Figure 4-5.

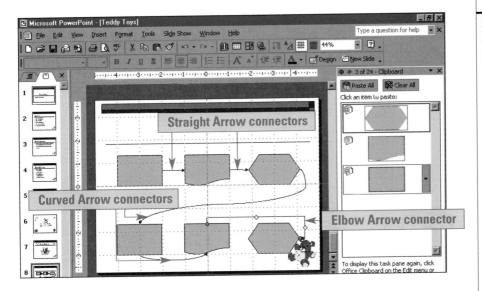

FIGURE 4-5
Shapes with Connector
Lines

FIGURE 4-5
Shapes with Connector
Lines

MOUSE TIP

You can select multiple
objects on a slide by
drawing a marquee box
encompassing the
objects.

You can size and scale
an AutoShape by right-
clicking the shape, clicking Format AutoShape,
and then clicking the
Size tab.

Aligning Objects with Other Objects

Even with the help of the grid and guides, it can be difficult to align
two or more objects by dragging them separately. When objects are
aligned, it is easier for the audience to follow the directional flow of the
slide. You can **align** objects on the same line at the left, right, center,
top, bottom, or middle. You also can distribute the shapes so that the
space between the shapes is even. To align objects:

Step 1	**Select**	the three flowchart shapes at the center of the slide
Step 2	**Click**	the Draw button Draw on the Drawing toolbar
Step 3	**Point to**	Align or Distribute
Step 4	**Click**	Align Middle
Step 5	**Select**	the three flowchart shapes at the bottom of the slide
Step 6	**Align**	the three shapes at the middle

QUICK TIP

Selected objects display
eight handles—four
middle handles and four
corner handles—and a
rotate handle. Lines and
arrows, however, dis-
play only two handles,
one at each end.

Objects can be aligned on a slide, but the spacing between the objects
may or may not be even. Depending on the message of the slide, you
can distribute the spacing between the objects to appear evenly both
horizontally and vertically. To distribute space between objects, you
need to have three or more objects. The space is distributed evenly

**chapter
four**

between objects based on the amount of space between the first and last objects. To distribute space evenly between objects:

Step 1	*Select*	the three flowchart shapes at the center of the slide
Step 2	*Click*	the Draw button Draw ▾ on the Drawing toolbar
Step 3	*Point to*	Align or Distribute
Step 4	*Click*	Distribute Horizontally to evenly distribute the space between the three shapes
Step 5	*Select*	the three flowchart shapes at the bottom of the slide
Step 6	*Distribute*	the space between the shapes horizontally
Step 7	*Save*	the *Teddy Toys* presentation

4.d Formatting Shapes

You can format shapes to improve their appearance by changing fill color, line color and style, shadow style, and 3-D effects. You can format shapes individually, or you can format one shape and use the Format Painter to apply those formats to any other shapes with the simple click of a button.

Changing Fill and Line Colors

By default, drawing shapes and basic AutoShapes use colors from the current design template. AutoShapes from the More AutoShapes dialog box, however, do not use the design template colors because they are predesigned shapes with predetermined colors similar to clip art images. You can change the fill color of shapes and AutoShapes to solid colors, gradients, textures, and patterns. You can even fill a shape with a picture. PowerPoint provides 24 preset gradients if you want to use a specific look instead of creating your own gradients. **Gradients** are shaded variations of a color or combination of colors. To change the fill colors of the flowchart shapes:

Step 1	*Select*	the first process shape at the left of the slide
Step 2	*Click*	the Fill Color button list arrow 🎨 ▾ on the Drawing toolbar
Step 3	*Click*	Fill Effects

The Fill Effects dialog box on your screen should look similar to Figure 4-6.

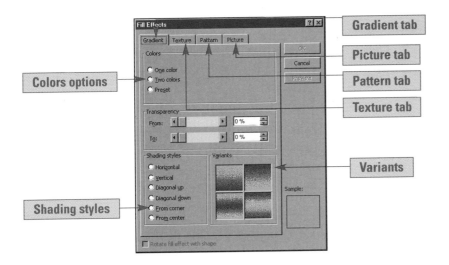

Gradient tab

Picture tab

Pattern tab

Texture tab

Colors options

Shading styles

Variants

QUICK TIP

When aligning objects, the object you select first is the anchor object. The other objects will be aligned to that first selected object.

FIGURE 4-6
Fill Effects Dialog Box

Step 4	*Click*	the Gradient tab if necessary
Step 5	*Click*	Preset in the Colors box
Step 6	*Click*	the Preset colors: list arrow
Step 7	*Click*	Parchment
Step 8	*Click*	From center in the Shading styles box
Step 9	*Click*	the leftmost Variants example
Step 10	*Click*	OK

Applying Special Effects

The Drawing toolbar makes it easy to add shadow and 3-D effects to images. When objects are formatted to be **three-dimensional (3-D)**, they appear raised instead of flat. The shadow effect casts a gray shadow near the shape just as a shadow appears when the sun shines on an object. Textures also add to a three-dimensional look. To add shadow and 3-D effects:

| Step 1 | *Click* | the Shadow Style button  on the Drawing toolbar |
| Step 2 | *Click* | the style in the first row, first column (ScreenTip displays: Shadow Style 1) |

MOUSE TIP

You can align objects at the same time you are copying them, by holding down the SHIFT and CTRL keys while you drag; in other words, if you copy to the left or right, the objects are aligned horizontally; if you copy up or down, the objects are aligned vertically.

MENU TIP

You can size and scale an AutoShape by clicking the Format AutoShape command on the Format menu, and then clicking the Size tab.

chapter
four

After applying a shadow effect, you decide to change to a 3-D effect. When you apply a 3-D effect to a shape, the shadow effect is automatically removed.

Step 3	*Click*	the 3-D Style button 🔲 on the Drawing toolbar
Step 4	*Click*	the style in the first row, second column (ScreenTip displays: 3-D Style 2)

You can change the thickness, color, and style of lines and arrows, and the style and shape of the arrowheads. You cannot change their fill colors, because these objects are comprised only of length and width of line. To change the thickness, color, and style of the line and arrow:

Step 1	*Select*	the first connector arrow
Step 2	*Click*	the Line Style button 🔲 on the Drawing toolbar
Step 3	*Click*	the 4½ pt example
Step 4	*Click*	the Line Color button list arrow 🖉▾ on the Drawing toolbar
Step 5	*Click*	the brown color (ScreenTip displays: Follow Shadows Scheme Color)
Step 6	*Click*	the Arrow Style button 🔳 on the Drawing toolbar
Step 7	*Click*	the double arrow style (ScreenTip displays: Arrow Style 7)
Step 8	*Click*	Undo to return to the single arrow style
Step 9	*Save*	the *Teddy Toys* presentation

Using the Format Painter

The **Format Painter** allows you to copy the formatting attributes of shapes and text boxes without going through the trouble of applying the same set of attributes to each. You can use the Format Painter to "paint" or copy any combination of fill color, line color, line thickness, font, font size, font style, and 3-D effects from one object to another. To use the Format Painter, you select the object whose formatting you want to copy, click or double-click the Format Painter button on the Standard toolbar, and then click the object to which you want to copy the formatting. If you click the Format Painter button one time, you can paint the formatting to one object. If you double-click the Format Painter button, you can paint until you turn off the feature by clicking the Format Painter button again or by clicking the slide background.

To use the Format Painter:

Step 1	*Select*	the first process shape at the left of the slide
Step 2	*Click*	the Format Painter button 🖌️ on the Standard toolbar
Step 3	*Click*	the document shape located to the right of the process shape
Step 4	*Verify*	that the document shape is still selected
Step 5	*Double-click*	the Format Painter button 🖌️ on the Standard toolbar
Step 6	*Click*	each of the remaining shapes
Step 7	*Click*	the Format Painter button 🖌️ to turn it off
Step 8	*Click*	the first connector arrow
Step 9	*Double-click*	the Format Painter button 🖌️ on the Standard toolbar
Step 10	*Click*	each of the remaining connector lines to paint their color and thickness
Step 11	*Click*	the Format Painter button 🖌️ to turn it off
Step 12	*Save*	the *Teddy Toys* presentation

QUICK TIP

To change line options, including line color, thickness, and arrow-head direction, select the object and then use the Line Color button list arrow, Line Style button, and Arrow Style button on the Drawing toolbar to make your changes.

Changing the Shape of an AutoShape

Once you have added an AutoShape to a slide, you may decide a different shape better fits your needs. You can change the shape of an AutoShape easily. Any formatting you have applied to the shape remains after you have changed the shape. You can change the shape of multiple shapes by selecting each shape and then applying the change to all at one time. To change the shape of selected AutoShapes:

Step 1	*Select*	the process shape in the lower-left corner of the slide and the document shape in the bottom center of the slide
Step 2	*Click*	the Draw button [Draw ▾] on the Drawing toolbar
Step 3	*Point to*	Change AutoShape
Step 4	*Point to*	Flowchart
Step 5	*Click*	the AutoShape in the first row, second column (ScreenTip displays: Change Shape to Flowchart: Alternate Process)

chapter
four

Step 6	*Select*	the process shape at the left of the slide and the preparation shape in the lower-right corner of the slide
Step 7	*Change*	the selected shapes to the shape in the third row, first column (ScreenTip displays Change Shape to Flowchart: Terminator)
Step 8	*Resize*	the terminator shapes to 1.3 inches high and 2 inches wide using the Format AutoShape dialog box
Step 9	*Save*	the *Teddy Toys* presentation

4.e Adding Text to Shapes

In addition to adding text to placeholders, you can add text to shapes, AutoShapes, and text boxes. You can format text on a shape just as you do text in a text placeholder, to modify its font, size, style, alignment, or color.

Adding Text to AutoShapes

Just as you can add text to a slide and format it, you can add text to a shape or an AutoShape. You do so by selecting the shape and then keying the text. To add text to an AutoShape:

Step 1	*Select*	the first terminator shape at the left of the slide
Step 2	*Key*	Discover What the Consumer Wants
Step 3	*Click*	outside the shape to deselect it

The text is too long for the shape, but you change that later in the chapter. Your screen should look similar to Figure 4-7.

CAUTION TIP

When selecting a shape that contains text, be sure to click when you see the four-directional arrow. If you select a shape when the insertion point is present, you are only placing the insertion point in that text area.

FIGURE 4-7
AutoShape with
Unwrapped Text

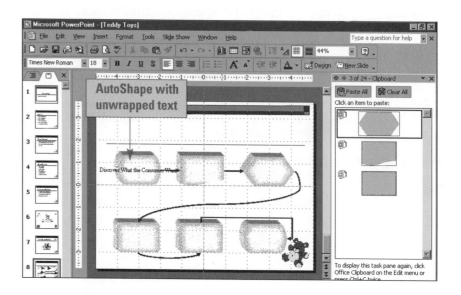

You can format the text within a shape by changing the font, size, and color. If you have text that is too large to fit a shape, you can change the size of the text to fit the AutoShape or you can change the size of the AutoShape to fit the size of the text. You also can word wrap the text within the AutoShape. **Word wrap** is the adjusting of text to fit horizontally in the AutoShape. If the text added to an AutoShape is too long to fit within the horizontal limits of the shape, it automatically wraps to continue to the next line. In addition, you can change the anchor point of the text within the AutoShape. An **anchor point** is the point in the AutoShape to which you want to anchor the text, relative to the selection border. Anchor points are Top, Middle, Bottom, Top Centered, Middle Centered, and Bottom Centered. To format and wrap the text:

Step 1	*Select*	the first terminator shape (do not click in the text area)
Step 2	*Click*	the Font Color button list arrow ◪ ▾ on the Drawing toolbar
Step 3	*Click*	the brown color (ScreenTip displays: Follow Shadows Scheme Color)
Step 4	*Click*	the Font button list arrow [Comic Sans MS ▾] on the Formatting toolbar
Step 5	*Click*	Comic Sans MS
Step 6	*Double-click*	the first terminator shape
Step 7	*Click*	the Text Box tab in the Format AutoShape dialog box
Step 8	*Verify*	that the Text anchor point: list box displays Middle
Step 9	*Click*	the Word wrap text in AutoShape check box to add a check mark
Step 10	*Click*	OK
Step 11	*Key*	one line of the following text in each box, starting with the second flowchart shape: Produce the Product Price Correctly Promote the Product as New or Improved Create a Page to Link with Home Page Sell the Product

You decide to use the Format Painter to format the remaining text boxes so that you don't have to manually change the font, size, color, and word wrap alignment of each.

chapter
four

| Step 12 | *Format* | all the AutoShapes using the Format Painter so that they match the formatting of the first terminator shape at the left of the slide |

Your screen should look similar to Figure 4-8.

FIGURE 4-8
Slide with Changed
Shapes and Wrapped Text

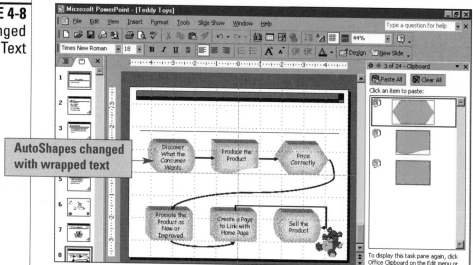

FIGURE 4-8
Slide with Changed
Shapes and Wrapped Text

AutoShapes changed
with wrapped text

Adding a Text Box

You can add additional text objects to a slide without keying text into a layout placeholder or AutoShape. To add text to a slide without using a placeholder, you use the Text Box button on the Drawing toolbar. You can use the Text Box button to draw a text box by dragging on top of a shape or other object or by dragging on the blank area of a slide. You can move, resize, edit, format, and rotate text boxes to help convey the message of your slide. To add and format a text box:

Step 1	*Click*	the Text Box button on the Drawing toolbar
Step 2	*Click*	at the vertical guide directly below the first horizontal grid line
Step 3	*Click*	the Center button ☰ on the Formatting toolbar
Step 4	*Key*	Marketing Strategies for Future Toys

Step 5	Click	the selection border of the text box to select the entire text box
Step 6	Click	the Increase Font Size button 𝐀 on the Formatting toolbar until the Font Size button list box displays 32
Step 7	Change	the color of the font to dark brown
Step 8	Change	the font to Comic Sans MS
Step 9	Run	the slide show from the beginning of the presentation
Step 10	Save	the *Teddy Toys* presentation

4.f Ordering and Grouping Objects

When a slide contains several shapes and other objects, you may find it easier to manipulate all the objects to achieve the look you want. A large image may obscure a smaller one, hiding it completely instead of providing the framing effect you hoped for. Or, you may find you have moved several objects into a perfect combination and then have to repeat your work one object at a time because you want to flip the objects so they face the other way. Ordering and grouping are two techniques that make it easier to work with multiple objects so they complement instead of compete with each other on a slide.

Ordering Objects

On a PowerPoint slide, each object resides on its own invisible plane. The **order**, or layering position, of each object is determined by the order that the objects were drawn or copied onto the slide. If three objects are added to the slide, there are three planes, each succeeding one placed atop the previous one. You can change the order of objects to create a layered effect, such as using a solid box as a background for a graphic. PowerPoint provides options for sending objects to the back, to the front, backward one layer, or forward one layer. To change the order of objects:

Step 1	Display	the We Welcome New Ideas slide
Step 2	Click	the Rectangle button ▢ on the Drawing toolbar
Step 3	Draw	a rectangle over the blocks clip art image

MOUSE TIP

If you want to rotate a text box, drag the green rotate handle of the text box; the text rotates with the text box.

If you want to rotate just the text within a text box, select the text box, right-click the text box, click Format Text Box, click the Text Box tab on the Format Text Box dialog box, and then click the Rotate text within AutoShape by 90° check box to add a check mark.

CAUTION TIP

When you click to draw a text box, the text box expands to accommodate the text. When you drag to draw the text box instead, the text box has a definite width and the keyed text wraps to fit the text box.

chapter
four

Step 4	*Resize*	the rectangle shape to 4 inches high and 6 inches wide
Step 5	*Click*	the Fill Color button list arrow on the Drawing toolbar
Step 6	*Click*	Fill Effects
Step 7	*Click*	the Two colors option button in the Colors box on the Gradient tab
Step 8	*Click*	the Color 1: list arrow
Step 9	*Click*	the brown color (ScreenTip displays: Follow Shadows Scheme Color)
Step 10	*Click*	the From center option button in the Shading styles box
Step 11	*Click*	the rightmost Variants example
Step 12	*Click*	OK
Step 13	*Click*	the Draw button Draw ▾ on the Drawing toolbar
Step 14	*Point to*	Order
Step 15	*Click*	Send to Back

The rectangle shape is placed behind the blocks image. It provides an attractive backdrop for the blocks.

Grouping Objects

Grouping is a feature that allows you to take two or more objects and group them so they behave as one. When you group objects, you can than manipulate that one object easier than the separate objects. For example, you can rotate, flip, resize, or scale a grouped object as if it were a single object. To align and group objects and make final positioning changes:

Step 1	*Select*	both the rectangle shape and the blocks image
Step 2	*Align*	both objects at the center and at the middle
Step 3	*Click*	the Draw button Draw ▾ on the Drawing toolbar
Step 4	*Click*	Group

| Step 5 | *Reposition* | the grouped shape so that it is centered horizontally below the ruled line using the grid and guides for placement |

When you are finished using the drawing tools, you may want to remove the grid and guides. You can hide or display the grid by clicking Show/Hide Grid button on the Standard toolbar. You decide to hide both the grid and guides before saving and closing the presentation. To hide the grid and guides:

Step 1	*Right-click*	the slide background
Step 2	*Click*	Grid and Guides
Step 3	*Click*	the Display grid on screen and the Display drawing guides on screen check boxes to remove the check marks
Step 4	*Click*	OK

Your screen should look similar to Figure 4-9.

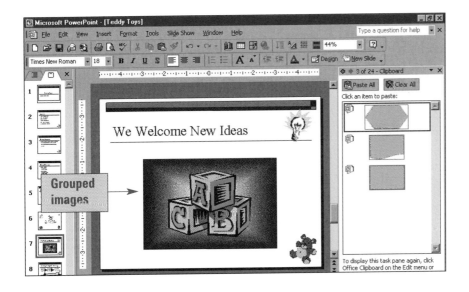

| Step 5 | *Save* | the *Teddy Toys* presentation and close it |

The drawing tools enable you to add visual appeal to any presentation.

FIGURE 4-9
Completed We Welcome New Ideas Slide

Summary

▶ You can draw shapes on a slide to grab the audience's attention, control the focus of the audience, and add visual appeal.

▶ Displaying the ruler, grid, and guides helps to position objects on slides more precisely.

▶ Using the SHIFT key in combination with drawing tools lets you draw straight lines, circles, and squares.

▶ AutoShapes are common shapes that you can draw for use in a slide.

▶ You can change fill and line colors of drawing shapes and line colors of lines and arrows.

▶ Shadow effects and 3-D effects may be added to drawing and AutoShape objects.

▶ The Office Clipboard allows you to copy up to 24 objects and paste them into different programs as well as different slides in PowerPoint.

▶ You can copy and paste multiple objects using the Office Clipboard.

▶ You can select multiple shapes for moving, copying, or deleting by holding down the SHIFT key as you click each one.

▶ Objects can be aligned on the same line at the top, middle, bottom, left, center, or right.

▶ The Format Painter feature allows you to copy the attributes of one object onto another object.

▶ You can add text to any AutoShape or drawing shape by clicking the shape and keying the text.

▶ You can add text to any part of a slide using the Text Box tool on the Drawing toolbar.

▶ You can arrange the order of objects, so that one object appears behind or in front of another.

▶ Grouping allows you to work with two or more objects as if they were one single object, to facilitate flipping, resizing, moving, and formatting.

Commands Review

Action	Menu Bar	Shortcut Menu	Toolbar	Task Pane	Keyboard
Display ruler	View, Ruler				ALT + V, R
Display grid	View, Grid and Guides		▦		ALT + V, I CTRL + G SHIFT + F9
Display guides	View, Grid and Guides		▦		ALT + V, I CTRL + G ALT + F9
Draw a rectangle			▢		
Draw a square			SHIFT + ▢		
Draw an oval			⬭		
Draw a circle			SHIFT + ⬭		
Draw a line			◺		
Draw a straight line			SHIFT + ◺		
Draw an arrow			↘		
Draw a straight arrow			SHIFT + ↘		
Resize shape		Double-click shape, click Size tab, change Height and Width	⤡		
Delete a selected shape					DELETE
Add AutoShapes	Insert, Picture, AutoShapes		AutoShapes ▾		ALT + I, P, A ALT + U
Display the Office Clipboard	Edit, Office Clipboard			▾ on task pane, then click Clipboard	ALT + E, B
Select all objects	Edit, Select All	SHIFT + Click each object, or draw a marquee box around all objects			ALT + E, L CTRL + A
Duplicate objects	Edit, Duplicate Edit, Copy, then Edit, Paste	Right-click object, Copy, then right-click, Paste; Right-drag, then Copy Here; CTRL + drag the left mouse		Click item on Clipboard task pane; or click list arrow on item and click Paste	ALT + E, I ALT + E, C, then ALT + E, P CTRL + D
Change fill and line colors	Format, AutoShape	Right-click object, Format AutoShape; Double-click object			ALT + O, O
Align selected objects	Draw, Align or Distribute				ALT + R, A
Distribute space between selected objects	Draw, Align or Distribute				ALT + R, A
Format Painter			🖌		

chapter four

Action	Menu Bar	Shortcut Menu	Toolbar	Task Pane	Keyboard
Add text to selected drawings and AutoShapes		Right-click shape, click Add Text			Key text in selected object
Change selected AutoShape	Draw, Change AutoShape				ALT D + C
Insert a text box	Insert, Text Box				ALT + I, X
Order selected objects	Draw, Order	Right-click, Order			ALT + R, R
Group selected objects	Draw, Group	Right-click, Grouping, Group			ALT + R, G
Ungroup object	Draw, Ungroup	Right-click, Grouping, Ungroup			ALT + R, U

Concepts Review   SCANS

Circle the correct answer.

1. Rulers, grids, and guides:
[a] help position objects on the slide.
[b] print on the slide.
[c] cannot be turned on or turned off.
[d] automatically appear when drawing shapes.

2. When you want to draw a perfectly shaped object, use the mouse and the:
[a] SHIFT key.
[b] CTRL key.
[c] ALT key.
[d] SPACEBAR.

3. If you release the mouse button before releasing the SHIFT key when you draw a square, the square will:
[a] be larger.
[b] be smaller.
[c] not be at the center of the slide.
[d] not be a perfect square.

4. The AutoShapes menu provides you with:
[a] clip art that is related to your presentation.
[b] any shape you want to add on a slide.
[c] commonly found shapes.
[d] fancy text to place on your slide.

5. Which option changes the fill color of an object back to the default color?
[a] fill colors
[b] patterns
[c] Automatic fill
[d] template

6. Special effects that can be applied to drawing shapes include all of the following *except*:
[a] 3-D shadows.
[b] rotating.
[c] gradient fills.
[d] copying.

7. When selecting multiple objects to format, you can select all objects at one time by pressing the:
[a] ALT + A keys.
[b] SHIFT + ENTER keys.
[c] CTRL + A keys.
[d] CTRL + SHIFT keys.

8. To place one object in front of another object, use the:
[a] Align and Distribute feature.
[b] Order feature.
[c] Duplicate feature.
[d] Rotate or Flip feature.

9. Which of the following is true of using the Text Box tool?

[a] You can create text anywhere on the slide.

[b] You can move the text box after you have keyed the text.

[c] You can format the text size and style easily.

[d] You can only have one text box on a slide.

10. To add text to a slide without using the standard placeholders, use the:

[a] AutoShapes tool.

[b] Drawing tool.

[c] Line tool.

[d] Text Box tool.

Circle **T** if the statement is true or **F** if the statement is false.

T   F   1. Grids and guides are nonprinting lines to help you place and position objects on a slide.

T   F   2. After drawing a perfect shape, you must release the mouse after releasing any other keys.

T   F   3. PowerPoint limits you to six colors for fill and line color changes.

T   F   4. Shadows and 3-D effects can be added to enhance the AutoShape object.

T   F   5. You can draw a marquee box around multiple objects to select them all at once.

T   F   6. You can duplicate an object by dragging the object to a new location on the slide.

T   F   7. You can copy objects by dragging them while holding down the CTRL key.

T   F   8. The Text Box tool enables you to type text anywhere on the slide area.

T   F   9. Gradients require the selection of two or more colors.

T   F   10. Grouping allows you to place certain shapes in categories that are easily accessed.

Skills Review

Exercise 1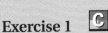

1. Open the *PowerPoint* presentation you modified in Chapter 3, and display the Slide Master view.

2. Add the 16-Point Star from the Stars and Banners AutoShapes category.

3. Resize the star AutoShape so it is approximately 0.5 inch high by 0.5 inch wide, and move it to the lower-right corner of the slide master.

4. Change the AutoShape fill to gradient fill using the gray color (Follow Accent and Followed Hyperlink Scheme Color) for the first color and the beige color (Follow Background Scheme Color) for the second color.

5. Use the From center shading style and the variant on the right.

6. Add the 3-D Style 5 to the AutoShape, and reposition the star, if necessary.

7. Add a blank slide at the end of the presentation.

8. Add the Bevel Shape from the Basic Shapes AutoShapes category (fourth row, third column). Draw or resize the bevel shape so that it is approximately 3.8 inches high by 6 inches wide.

9. Center the shape on the slide.

10. Key "PowerPoint will help sell your products and ideas" in the bevel shape. Change the font to Times New Roman, 44 point, bold, and italic.

chapter four

11. Format the bevel shape so that the text wraps within the shape.

12. Save the presentation, print only the slides with changes, and then close the presentation.

Exercise 2   C

1. Open the *Office* presentation you modified in Chapter 3, and add the Down Ribbon (third row, second column) from the Stars and Banners AutoShapes category to Slide 1.

2. Resize the Down Ribbon to approximately 1 inch high by 6 inches wide.

3. Add the following text to the AutoShape: "Software for the Future." (*Hint:* Press the ENTER key after the word "for" so the text wraps to the next line.) Change the fill color of the ribbon shape to match the color scheme of the slide, and change the font, font color, and font size as appropriate.

4. Select all three objects on the slide, and align them at their centers.

5. Add a blank slide at the end of the presentation.

6. Add two arrows from the Block Arrows AutoShapes category: a Curved Right Arrow, a Curved Left Arrow—each arrow should be 4 inches high by 1.5 inches wide—and a Curved Up Arrow, and a Curved Down Arrow—each arrow should be 1.5 inches high by 4 inches wide. Change the fill color of one of the arrows using a gradient or a texture fill effect. Then use the Format Painter to apply this fill coloring to the remaining three arrows.

7. Flip and position the arrows around the center section of the slide.

8. Add a text box with the following text: "All Roads Lead to Office XP"; use word wrap in the text box, and resize the text box until the text displays on three lines. Change the text size to 44 point, change the text color and font, and position the text box in the center of the slide.

9. Key "Excel" in the Curved Right Arrow, key "Word" in the Curved Left Arrow, key "PowerPoint" in the Curved Down Arrow, and key "Access" in the Curved Up Arrow.

10. Save the presentation, print only the slides with changes, and then close the presentation.

Exercise 3   C

1. Open the *Design* presentation you modified in Chapter 3, and add the Up Ribbon AutoShape from the Stars and Banners AutoShapes to Slide 1.

2. Align the ribbon shape on top of your name. Send the ribbon shape to the back so your name appears on top of the shape. Resize, move, and recolor the shape and text box as needed.

3. Add the 24-Point Star AutoShape from the Stars and Banners AutoShapes category to the slide with the WordArt object or any slide. Resize the star shape to approximately 5 inches high by 5.5 inches wide. Change the fill color to black (ScreenTip displays: Follow Accent Scheme Color).

4. Change the star shape to a 3-D effect. Drag the star shape and position it over the word "Design" of the WordArt object or any text object. Then send the star shape to the back. (*Hint:* Change the text color if you cannot read the text after the star shape is sent behind the text.)

5. Select and group the star shape with the WordArt object or the text object.

6. Add a blank slide at the end of the presentation. Omit the background graphics from this slide only.

7. Draw an oval approximately 2.5 inches high by 3.5 inches wide. Then key "Ovals and Circles Give a Feeling of Indecision" in the oval shape.

8. Format the shape to wrap the text.

9. Add the 3-D Style 2 to the oval. Change the fill color to black (ScreenTip displays: Follow Accent Scheme Color), and change the font of the text to Tahoma, 24 point, bold.

10. Draw a rectangle approximately 2.5 inches high by 3 inches wide, and key "Rectangles and Squares Relate to Rigidity" in this shape.

11. Add the Isosceles Triangle shape from the Basic Shapes AutoShapes category, resize it to approximately 4 inches high by 4 inches wide, and key "Triangles Allow All Ideas to be Considered" in it.

12. Use the Format Painter to copy the attributes of the oval shape to both the rectangle and the triangle shapes.

13. Position all three shapes attractively on the slide.

14. Save the presentation, print only the slides with changes, and close it.

Exercise 4

1. Open the *Precision Builders* presentation you modified in Chapter 3, and add the 5-Point Star from the Stars and Banners AutoShapes category to the slide with the WordArt object.

2. Resize the star shape to approximately 0.75-inch high by 0.75-inch wide.

3. Change the fill color of the star shape to the Parchment Texture in the Fill Effects dialog box.

4. Add a shadow effect to the star, and then recolor the shadow for greater visibility on the slide. (*Hint:* Use the Shadow Color button on the Shadow Settings toolbar.)

5. Position the star shape so that it is in the upper-left corner of the slide.

6. Make six copies of the star, and place them on the slide as you desire.

7. Add a blank slide at the end of the presentation, create a text box, and key the following: "Decisions Before Building a Home" in the text box.

8. Change the font to 36 point, and center the text within the text box.

9. Add the Flowchart Decision shape from the Flowchart AutoShapes.

10. Resize the shape to approximately 1.75 inches high and 3 inches wide, and add a shadow effect.

11. Change the font to Tahoma, 20 point, and word wrap the text.

12. Make three more copies of the decision shape.

13. Key the following text in the respective AutoShapes: "Location?"; "Split-level or Ranch?"; "Number of Bedrooms?"; and "Number of Bathrooms?"

14. Reposition, align, and distribute the space between the AutoShapes attractively on the page.

15. Save the presentation, print the slide with changes only, and then close the presentation.

Exercise 5

1. Open the *Nature Tours* presentation you modified in Chapter 3, and add a Title Only slide at the end of the presentation. The title should read "Special Tours."

2. Using the Basic Shapes AutoShapes category, add the Sun and the Moon shapes to the Title Only slide.

3. Using the Text Box tool, create two separate text boxes. Key "For the Early Risers" in one box and "For the Night Owls" in the other.

4. Rotate the text boxes and format the text in regard to font style, size, and color.

5. Format the shapes in regard to color, size, and placement on the slide.

6. Align the Sun and Moon images and their appropriate text boxes.

chapter four

7. Group the Sun and its appropriate text box. Repeat for the Moon and its text box.

8. Add an AutoShape from the More AutoShapes dialog box to any slide. Resize, recolor, and/or move the AutoShape.

9. Save the presentation, print only the slides with the changes, and then close the presentation.

Exercise 6   C

1. Open the *A Healthier You* presentation you modified in Chapter 3, and add the Heart AutoShape to the slide master.

2. Resize the Heart AutoShape, add a gradient fill effect to change the color of the heart, and use a 3-D effect.

3. Position the heart attractively on the slide master. If necessary, move the text placeholders on the slide master if the text overlaps with the heart shape.

4. Add a blank slide at the end of the presentation. Add an AutoShape of your choice, and key "Reduce Your Stress" in the AutoShape.

5. Add at least four copies of another AutoShape to this slide, and key "Relax" in each AutoShape.

6. Format the color and size of the AutoShapes. Use 3-D styles or shadows, if desired. Use the Format Painter.

7. Position the shapes attractively on the slide. Format the font, font size, and font color of the text.

8. Save the presentation, print only the slides with changes, and then close the presentation.

Exercise 7   C

1. Open the *Buying A Computer* presentation you modified in Chapter 3, and add a Title Only slide at the end of the presentation.

2. Key the title "Places to Buy a Computer" on the slide.

3. Add various computer and other AutoShapes to this slide indicating at least four types of places to purchase your computer (for example, retail store, Internet, computer catalog, computer outlet). Format the AutoShapes with regard to size, color, and 3-D effect.

4. Key each different place in an AutoShape. (*Hint:* Word wrap the text, if necessary.)

5. Use the Straight Arrow Connector from the Connectors AutoShapes category to connect the AutoShapes in the order that you would prefer to begin shopping for your computer. Change the arrow thickness and color, if appropriate.

6. Save the presentation, print only the slides with changes, and then close the presentation.

Exercise 8   C

1. Open the *Leisure Travel* presentation you modified in Chapter 3, and add a Title Only slide at the end of the presentation. The title should read "Your Season – Your Choice."

2. Add an appropriate AutoShape to the center of the slide. Change the color of the shape.

3. Key "Anywhere – Anytime" in the shape. Wrap the text and format the text as desired.

4. Add an appropriate Cloud AutoShape, and then make three copies of the cloud shape.

5. Key the name of one season (Summer, Fall, Winter, and Spring) into each of the cloud shapes.

6. Add appropriate fills to each of the cloud shapes to depict that season.

7. Format the font within the clouds as desired.

8. Save the presentation, print only the slides with changes, and then close the presentation.

Case Projects

Project 1

You are not quite sure you understand the difference between grouping and regrouping objects. You decide to access the online Help feature to determine the difference. Click Show All in the Help window, and then print the "Group, ungroup, or regroup objects" Help topic.

Project 2

Looking at the *Communicate* presentation, you decide that in addition to using clip images on some of the slides, you also could use AutoShapes that resemble the cartoon balloons or a phone or a sound file. Open the *Communicate* presentation you modified in Chapter 3, and add a blank slide using AutoShapes and text to encourage courteous telephone answering. Add AutoShapes to any slide where you feel the shape enhances the slide message. Change colors and size to fit the presentation. Save the presentation, and print only the slides with the AutoShapes.

Project 3

Open the *Souner* presentation you modified in Chapter 3, and view the presentation, looking for places where you may want to add an AutoShape. When finished, add AutoShapes to a slide or slides to help deliver the theme of the training organization. Add a blank slide at the end of the presentation incorporating AutoShape objects, lines or arrows, or text boxes. Make color, size, and font enhancements. If possible, duplicate an AutoShape object to add interest to your slide. Align shapes and order shapes as needed. Add 3-D or shadows to the shapes to enhance them. View the slide show. Save the presentation and print only the slides with the AutoShapes.

Project 4

You decide to view your *My Presentation* presentation to see where you can enhance it by adding AutoShapes. You want to add a text box inside an AutoShape to describe your company's service or product. Open the *My Presentation* presentation you modified in Chapter 3, and add a new blank slide or enhance an existing slide or slides. Be careful not to let the AutoShape become the dominant part of your presentation. If appropriate, consider adding an AutoShape or text box to the slide master. Rotate text boxes and shapes as needed to attract attention to that section of the slide. Save the presentation, and print only the slides with AutoShapes.

Project 5

You try to think of creative ways to show the paths to certain areas in the zoo. You decide that using the flowchart symbols and connecting lines would be a great way to help children find the zoo exhibits. Open the *Zoo* presentation you modified in Chapter 3, and add the appropriate AutoShapes to accomplish the task. Add 3-D and various fill effects to the AutoShapes to help enhance their interest to the children. Change the color and thickness of the arrows. Use the guides to place the shapes. Save the presentation, and print only the slide or slides with AutoShapes.

Project 6

You want to use clip art, WordArt, and AutoShapes to enhance slides, guide the eye through a slide, and bring attention to a concept on a slide. You also want to learn more about design tips that you can apply to your presentations. Connect to the Internet and search the Web for design tips. Be sure to check out the fonts available for specific moods or tones and additional clip art or images that can be downloaded for future use. Create a presentation consisting of a title slide, a text slide with several design tips, a slide illustrating several new fonts, and a slide with clip art or images accessed via the Internet. Include drawing shapes or AutoShapes in your presentation. Print the presentation.

chapter four

Project 7

You decide to incorporate some drawing shapes in the *Cars* presentation. You want to add shapes to display the different types of places that students can find information about new and used cars. Open the *Cars* presentation you modified in Chapter 3, and add text to some of the AutoShapes, as well as individual text boxes. To create interest on some of your existing slides, add shapes and send them behind some of the text already in your presentation. Resize, color, and align shapes as desired on each slide. If possible, add a shape to the slide master. Save the presentation, and print only the slides with the AutoShapes.

Project 8

In your *Internet* presentation, you and your partner discuss how to handle the lecture on search engines. Connect to the Internet to search the Web for information about the various search engines. Open the *Internet* presentation you modified in Chapter 3. Add AutoShapes to show why you would or should use a particular search engine on the Internet. You may need to create a new slide for each search engine you research. Format your AutoShapes and drawing shapes to fit the design and color scheme of your *Internet* presentation. Save the presentation, and print only the slides with the AutoShapes.

Working with Tables

Chapter Overview

When you need to present quantitative or relational information in a presentation, you may want to use a table. Tables display data in tabular format. In this chapter, you learn how to add, edit, and position a table on a slide. You also learn to format a table to make important information stand out.

LEARNING OBJECTIVES

- ► Create a table on a slide
- ► Add and delete rows and columns
- ► Format a table

Case profile

To alert employees to a host of upcoming Teddy Toys products, Ms. Hill asks you to include a slide containing several pieces of information. She wants the slide to display the names of new products in development, their team leaders, and the expected date they will be on the market. Because Teddy Toys is proud of their products and production teams, you want to display that information in a format that is compelling and easy to comprehend.

chapter five

C 5.a Creating a Table on a Slide

When creating a presentation it is important to anticipate your audience's needs and convey information so that they grasp it quickly and easily. Organizing information into a table enables them to see at a glance the information being conveyed.

The easiest way to create a table is to add a table slide to the presentation. A table slide contains a table placeholder that you complete by specifying the size of the table and then entering the information. You can insert an existing Word table or an Excel worksheet onto a PowerPoint slide. If you insert a table created in another software program, you must use that program to make editing and formatting changes to the table. To add a table slide at the end of the presentation:

Step 1	*Open*	the *Teddy Toys* presentation you modified in Chapter 4 and display the last slide
Step 2	*Click*	the New Slide button [New Slide] on the Formatting toolbar
Step 3	*Click*	the Title and Table layout in the Other Layouts area of the Slide Layout task pane

Your screen should look similar to Figure 5-1.

FIGURE 5-1
Slide with Table Placeholder

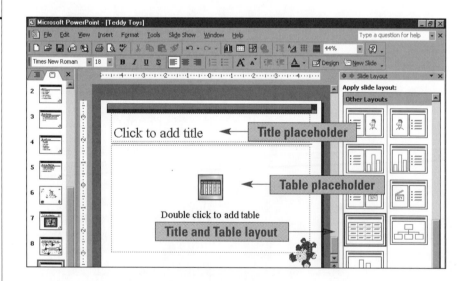

At the top of the new slide is a title placeholder, and at the center is a table placeholder. To add a title and insert the table:

| Step 1 | *Key* | New Product Production in the "Click to add title" placeholder |

Step 2	**Double-click**	the table placeholder

The Insert Table dialog box opens. Here you specify how many rows and columns you want in your table. You can key the desired numbers, or you can click the spin arrows until the boxes display the desired numbers.

Step 3	**Key**	3 in the Number of columns: text box
Step 4	**Key**	4 in the Number of rows: text box
Step 5	**Click**	OK

A table appears on your slide with three columns and four rows, forming twelve cells, as shown in Figure 5-2. The Tables and Borders toolbar may appear and obscure the table. If necessary, drag the toolbar out of the way.

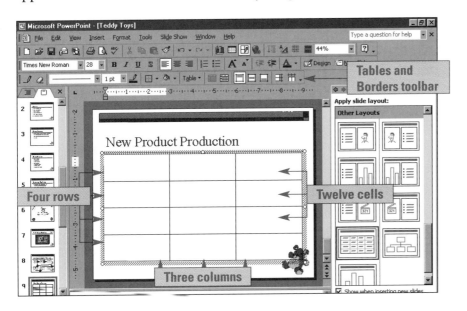

A **cell** is the intersection of a column and a row. Lines, called **borders**, separate the columns and rows. Above and to the left of the table, the ruler is displayed to help work in the table. Unless the data in your table is self-explanatory, you should begin a table by keying column headings in the first row. **Column headings** identify the contents of each column. PowerPoint automatically capitalizes the first word in a new cell. You can turn off automatic capitalization by clicking AutoCorrect Options on the Tools menu, and then removing the check mark in the Capitalize first letter of table cells check box.

The remaining rows contain information related to the column headings. To enter column headings:

Step 1	**Click**	in the first cell, if necessary

TASK PANE TIP

You can create a table by clicking any Content Layout or Text and Content Layout in the Slide Layout task pane and then clicking the Table icon on the placeholder.

FIGURE 5-2
Created Table

MOUSE TIP

The Tables and Borders toolbar displays when a table is selected. Or, you can right-click any toolbar, and then click Tables and Borders.

QUICK TIP

The maximum number of rows and columns you can specify in the Insert Table dialog box is 25. You add additional rows when working in the table by pressing the TAB key at the end of the last row.

chapter
five

Step 2	*Key*	New Product
Step 3	*Press*	the TAB key
Step 4	*Key*	Team Leader
Step 5	*Press*	the TAB key
Step 6	*Key*	Target Date
Step 7	*Press*	the TAB key

The headings are complete. By default, they are aligned at the left and at the top of the cells. To enter table data:

Step 1	*Key*	the following, pressing the TAB key after each entry except the last entry:
		Baby Teddy Leslie Skylar September 15
		Teddy Wagon Juan Ortiz October 31
		Rocking Horse Ran Un December 1
Step 2	*Save*	the *Teddy Toys* presentation

5.b Adding and Deleting Rows and Columns

Sometimes when you reach the end of a table, or after viewing a table slide, you want to add more information to the table. You can insert additional rows or columns anywhere in a table at any time. To add a row at the end of the table:

Step 1	*Move*	the insertion point to the last cell of the existing table, if necessary
Step 2	*Press*	the TAB key

A new row is created. The table is now too long for the slide; you fix this later in the chapter.

Step 3	*Key*	the following, pressing the TAB key after each entry, except the last entry:
		Toddler Bike Sara Jackson May 5

The new row and text have been added to the existing table. You also can add or delete rows and columns anywhere within a table, not just at an outer edge. First you select the row or column below or to the right of where you want to insert the new item. When you make the insertion, the item is inserted above or to the left of the row or column you selected. To add a column to a table:

Step 1	*Click*	outside the table object
Step 2	*Move*	the mouse pointer slightly above the Team Leader column until you see a solid black down arrow

Your screen should look similar to Figure 5-3.

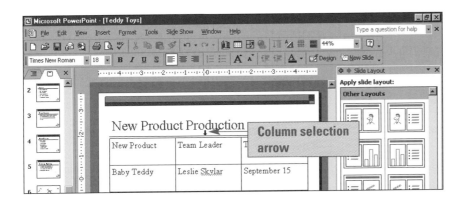

Step 3	*Right-click*	the top of the column to select the Team Leader column
Step 4	*Click*	Insert Columns

A new column is inserted to the left of the column you selected.
    You can delete rows and columns from a table when you no longer need the information. To delete a row or column, you must first select it. To delete a column:

Step 1	*Right-click*	the selected column
Step 2	*Click*	Delete Columns
Step 3	*Save*	the *Teddy Toys* presentation

FIGURE 5-3
Table with Column Selection Arrow

chapter
five

5.c Formatting a Table

After you complete a table, you can format it to change its appearance. Perhaps you want to make it larger or smaller. Perhaps the column headings do not stand out distinctly enough for quick reference and should be bolded, italicized, or shaded, or the column widths are too narrow or too wide for your purposes. Or, you may not want to see borders surrounding all cells, so you need to remove some or all of them. And, just like other text in PowerPoint, you can change font, font size, font style, and alignment to make the most of your information.

Resizing a Table

A table created in PowerPoint is an object. As such, it can be resized and moved using the same methods you use on other objects, such as clip art images and AutoShapes. When selected, a table displays eight sizing handles. To resize the table:

Step 1	Click	the table to display the sizing handles, if necessary
Step 2	Scroll	down to view the lower-right sizing handle of the table, if necessary
Step 3	Point to	the lower-right sizing handle until the mouse pointer changes to a double-tipped black arrow
Step 4	Drag	the sizing handle up and to the left until the vertical ruler guide reaches the 2.5-inch mark and the horizontal ruler guide reaches the 3-inch mark

Do not be concerned if the text wraps unattractively within the cell. You correct this later in the chapter.

Moving a Table

Often, you need to reposition a table on a slide to improve its appearance. Because the table is an object, you move the table object as you would any object—by selecting and dragging it to the desired location. To move the table:

Step 1	Select	the table object, if necessary
Step 2	Position	the mouse on the selection border on the left, right, top, or bottom of the table
Step 3	Verify	that the mouse pointer changes to a four-directional arrow

| Step 4 | *Drag* | to the right approximately 0.25 inch and down approximately 0.25 inch, being sure not to cover the teddy bear graphic |

The table is positioned more attractively on the slide. Your screen should look similar to Figure 5-4.

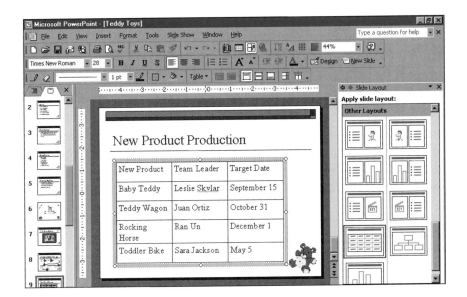

MOUSE TIP

To insert a row between two existing rows in a table, position the insertion point in the row below where you want the new row to appear, right-click the row, and then click Insert Rows.

| Step 5 | *Save* | the *Teddy Toys* presentation |

Changing Text and Cell Formatting

You can change formatting in any or all cells in a table to help guide the viewer's eye to important information. Because tables display information in a relational manner—the information in rows relates to the information in the column headings —you want to make sure the audience can quickly identify the column headings, especially in tables containing several rows. You can make text stand out by italicizing, bolding, shading, increasing font size, and/or changing text alignment. To format the cells containing the column headings:

Step 1	*Drag*	to select the column headings
Step 2	*Click*	the Italic button *I* on the Formatting toolbar
Step 3	*Click*	the Bold button **B** on the Formatting toolbar
Step 4	*Right-click*	the selected row

QUICK TIP

You can add a new cell, row, or column by splitting a cell, row, or column vertically or horizontally using the Draw Table button on the Tables and Borders toolbar.

You can merge any cell with the adjacent cell, if you want to join two or more cells to create one cell, by erasing the line between the cells. Click the Eraser button on the Tables and Borders toolbar, and then click the line to be erased.

Step 5	*Click*	Borders and Fill
Step 6	*Click*	the Fill tab in the Format Table dialog box
Step 7	*Click*	the Fill color: list arrow
Step 8	*Click*	the green color, sixth color from the left in the first row
Step 9	*Click*	the Semitransparent check box to add a check mark
Step 10	*Click*	OK
Step 11	*Click*	outside the column headings to deselect them

Notice how shading attracts the eye to the information within the shaded area. The current font of the title and table text is Times New Roman. **Font** refers to the design and appearance of printed characters. Each font has its own unique characteristics in terms of weight, height, and stroke. The font you choose helps set the mood or tone for your presentation. Times New Roman is a serif font. **Serifs** are fine cross strokes that appear at the bottom and the top of a letter. **Sans serif** means without serifs. Sans serif fonts have no cross strokes, are clean, modern looking, and very simple in appearance. Using an appropriate font also aids in the readability of text. Serif fonts are often used to guide the eye when reading large amounts of normal sized text. Sans serif fonts are often used when the text is going to be read at a distance or as headline text. To change the font style of selected table text:

Step 1	*Select*	the column headings
Step 2	*Change*	the font to Arial Narrow
Step 3	*Deselect*	the cells
Step 4	*Save*	the *Teddy Toys* presentation

Changing Indents and Setting Internal Margins

Each cell in a table has an indent marker. An **indent marker** enables you to change the position of the first line of text in a column, the second line (if there is any), or all the lines within a cell. Indent markers for the currently selected cell are displayed on the ruler that appears above the table. You can set a new indent for the current cell by moving the indent marker.

The indent markers on the Quadrant presentation template are at the extreme left edge of each column. You want to position the table text away from the left edge of the cell throughout your table. To achieve this, you could set new indents for each cell.

To move the existing indents:

| Step 1 | *Click* | in the New Product cell |

The horizontal ruler highlights the active column in white and displays indent markers for the columns. The first line indent marker (top triangle) shows the indent position of the first line of text in the cell. The bottom triangle shows the indent position of the second and any following lines of a paragraph in a cell. The left indent marker (rectangle box) shows the indent position of all lines of text in a cell.

| Step 2 | *Drag* | the left indent marker  to the 0.5 inch mark on the ruler |

If your goal is to position text in all columns in the same way, creating internal margins is quicker than setting new indents because you can set the internal margin of several cells at one time by selecting the cells first and then changing the internal margin—unlike an indent, which must be applied individually to cells.

Step 3	*Click*	the Undo button [icon] on the Standard toolbar
Step 4	*Right-click*	the table selection border
Step 5	*Click*	Borders and Fill
Step 6	*Click*	the Text Box tab

The Text Box tab in the Format Table dialog box has options for text alignment, internal margins, and rotating text. The dialog box on your screen should look similar to Figure 5-5.

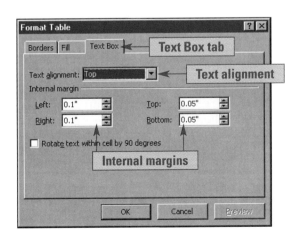

MOUSE TIP

You can change fills and borders by right-clicking the selected row, column, or table, and then clicking Borders and Fill.

MENU TIP

You can make changes to the font, font style, font size, font color, and font effects of slide text by clicking the Font command on the Format menu.

FIGURE 5-5
Format Table Dialog Box

chapter
five

Step 7	*Key*	0.2 in the Left: text box and the Right: text box under Internal margin
Step 8	*Click*	OK
Step 9	*Click*	outside the table object

Changing Text Alignment

Alignment refers to the position of text within a cell. **Horizontal alignment** refers to the horizontal position of text within a cell. **Vertical alignment** refers to the vertical position of text within a cell. To change horizontal alignment in a table:

Step 1	*Select*	the table object
Step 2	*Click*	the Center button ▦ on the Formatting toolbar

All of the table text is now center aligned. To change the horizontal alignment of a column and a cell:

Step 1	*Point*	slightly above the Target Date column until you see a solid black down arrow
Step 2	*Click*	the top of the column (the entire column should be selected)
Step 3	*Click*	the Align Right button ▦ on the Formatting toolbar
Step 4	*Click*	in the Target Date cell
Step 5	*Click*	the Center button ▦ on the Formatting toolbar
Step 6	*Drag*	to select the first column text, excluding the column heading
Step 7	*Click*	the Align Left button ▦ on the Formatting toolbar

The text below the column heading in the first column is aligned at the left, the Target Date column text is aligned at the right, and the New Product and Target Date column headings are centered.

Text can be vertically aligned within a cell in a table, at the top, center, or bottom of the cell. You want the text in the cells to be vertically centered so that there is equal space above and below the text within the cells.

CAUTION TIP

Be careful not to click in the white area of the ruler. If you do, you set a tab for that column. If you set a tab and no longer want it, simply drag it down off the ruler.

QUICK TIP

To center only the contents of one cell or a row, you can select the cell or row and click the desired alignment button.

Instead of changing the alignment of text or numbers in a table, you can set a tab by clicking the Tab button at the left of the horizontal ruler to display the type of tab you want, and then clicking the ruler where you want to set the tab. After the tab is set, hold down the CTRL key, press the TAB key to the desired tab, and key your data.

To change vertical alignment:

Step 1	*Click*	the Tables and Borders button 🗗 on the Standard toolbar to display the Tables and Borders toolbar, if necessary
Step 2	*Click*	the Table button ⬚Table▾ on the Table and Borders toolbar
Step 3	*Click*	Select Table
Step 4	*Click*	the Center Vertically button ▤ on the Tables and Borders toolbar
Step 5	*Click*	outside the table

The table text is vertically aligned within the cells. Your screen should look similar to Figure 5-6.

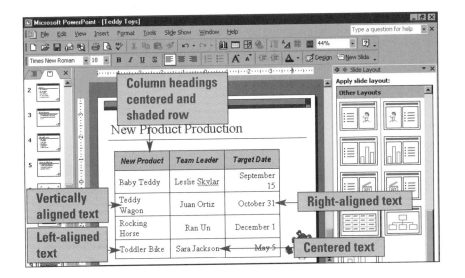

FIGURE 5-6
Table with Text Aligned Vertically and Horizontally

Adjusting Column Width and Row Height

After completing any table, you may need to adjust column width and/or row height to improve the table's appearance and readability. **Column width** refers to the horizontal size of a cell or column, and **row height** refers to the vertical size of a cell or row. You can drag row and column borders to quickly change column width and row height within a table. You can adjust the row height of one row, or the width of one column, and then use the Distribute Rows Evenly or Distribute Columns Evenly buttons on the Tables and Borders toolbar to automatically make the row heights even or the column widths even.

MOUSE TIP

You can change the horizontal and/or vertical alignment of several columns by dragging over the tops of the desired columns and then clicking the desired alignment button.

You can also select one or more columns or rows, click the Table button on the Tables and Borders toolbar, and then click the Select Column command to select the columns or the Select Row command to select the rows.

DESIGN TIP

For optimal readability, text in tables is usually left or center aligned, whereas numbers are right aligned.

The heights of the rows on the table you just created are equal, but you want the height of the first row to be larger so it stands out more than the rest of the rows. To change row height of the first row:

| Step 1 | *Position* | the mouse pointer on the horizontal border between the New Product and Baby Teddy rows until it changes to the row resizing arrow ÷ |
| Step 2 | *Drag* | the resizing arrow ÷ down approximately two marks on the vertical ruler |

Double-clicking the vertical border of a column automatically resizes that column to the longest item within the column.

Step 3	*Position*	the mouse pointer on the vertical border after the New Product column
Step 4	*Double-click*	the vertical border
Step 5	*Double-click*	the vertical border after the Team Leader and Target Date columns
Step 6	*Click*	outside the table

Your screen should look similar to Figure 5-7.

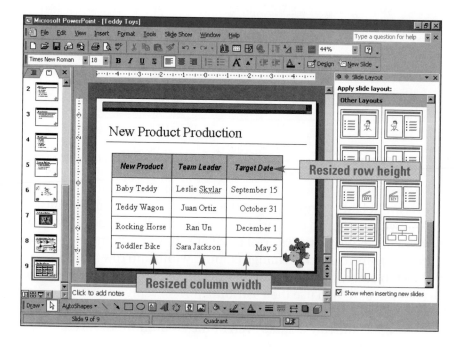

FIGURE 5-7
Table with Row Height and Column Width Changes

Each of the three column widths automatically adjusts to fit the longest item within the column.

Removing and Adding Borders

As you have learned, **borders** are lines that delineate or set off rows, columns, selected cells, or an entire table. PowerPoint provides the versatility to create any desired arrangement of borders or no borders at all. To change borders:

Step 1	*Select*	the table object
Step 2	*Click*	the Border button list arrow  on the Table and Borders toolbar
Step 3	*Click*	the No Border button in the first row, last column

The border button now displays nonprinting gridlines and no borders. If you position the mouse pointer over the button, the ScreenTip displays No Border. The Border button displays the last selected border style as its ScreenTip.

Step 4	*Click*	outside the table to view the table without the borders
Step 5	*Select*	the table object
Step 6	*Click*	the Border button list arrow on the Tables and Borders toolbar
Step 7	*Click*	the Outside Borders button in the first row, first column
Step 8	*Select*	the column headings
Step 9	*Click*	the Border button list arrow on the Tables and Borders toolbar
Step 10	*Click*	the Bottom Border button in the second row, second column
Step 11	*Click*	outside the table
Step 12	*Reposition*	the table so the right edge does not overlap the teddy bear image

chapter
five

Your screen should look similar to Figure 5-8.

FIGURE 5-8
Repositioned Table with
New Borders

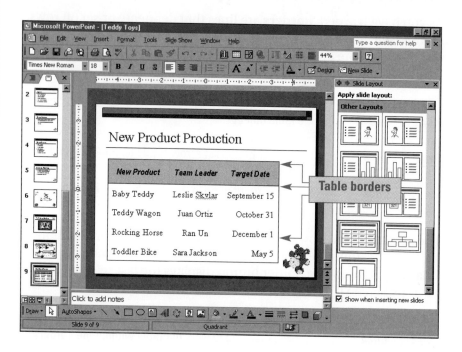

Q U I C K   T I P

You can select the table object by holding down the SHIFT key and clicking the table when no object is currently selected. You can also select the table by clicking the selection border.

Cell, column, and/or row text can be aligned vertically and horizontally by selecting the cell(s), column(s), or row(s), right-clicking the table, clicking Borders and Fill, clicking the Text Box tab, and then clicking the Top, Middle, Bottom, Top Centered, Middle Centered, or Bottom Centered option.

Step 13 | **Save** | the *Teddy Toys* presentation and close it

The table slide you added to the presentation makes it easy for the employees to determine what the new products are, who is responsible for the product, and when they will be ready for market.

Summary

▶ You can create a table on any slide in a PowerPoint presentation.

▶ The easiest way to create a table in PowerPoint is to add a new slide based on the table layout and then double-click the table placeholder on the new slide.

▶ You can insert an existing Word or Excel table in a PowerPoint slide.

▶ You can add or remove table borders to separate the columns and rows, one column or one row, or selected columns or rows.

▶ You can easily add a row or column at the end of a table or within the body of a table.

▶ You can easily delete columns or rows in a table.

▶ You can format all attributes of a table, including the font, font size, font style, alignment, borders, shading, column widths, and row heights.

▶ You can size table objects in PowerPoint by dragging the sizing handles with the mouse.

▶ You can easily adjust column widths or row heights by dragging the borders.

▶ The goal of column headings is to enable viewers to quickly identify the items in their respective columns.

▶ Cell, column, or row text can be horizontally and vertically aligned.

▶ Borders can be removed or added to cells, rows, or columns in a table, or to the entire table itself.

▶ Dragging the table object to a new position easily moves tables.

Commands Review

Action	Menu Bar	Shortcut Menu	Toolbar	Task Pane	Keyboard
Add a table	Insert, Table	Right-click, Slide Layout, click Title and Table layout Double-click table placeholder	Table ▼, Insert Table	Click Title and Table layout under Other Layouts on the Slide Layout task pane, or click any Content layout on the Slide Layout task pane, then click the Insert Table icon	ALT + I, B

chapter five

Action	Menu Bar	Shortcut Menu	Toolbar	Task Pane	Keyboard
Add a row to a table		Right-click a row, Insert Rows	Table ▾ , Insert Rows Above or Insert Rows Below		ALT + A, A or B
Delete a row in a table		Right-click the row beneath the desired rows, Delete Rows	Table ▾ , Delete Rows		ALT + A, W
Add a column to a table		Right-click a selected column, Insert Columns	Table ▾ , Insert Columns to the Left or Insert Columns to the Right		ALT + A, L or R
Delete a column from a table		Right-click a selected column, Delete Columns	Table ▾ , Delete Columns		ALT + A, C
Change table text font	Format, Font	Right-click selected text, Font	Comic Sans MS ▾		ALT + O, F
Select a row		Drag across the row to select it	Table ▾ , Select Row		ALT + A, T
Select a column		Drag down the column to select it, or click just above the column to select it	Table ▾ , Select Column		ALT + A, O
Select the entire table	Edit, Object	Right-click the table, Select Table, SHIFT + click table, or drag over entire table text	Table ▾ , Select Table		ALT + E, O ALT + A, S
Indent text within a column	Format, Table, Text Box tab	Drag indent marker on ruler in selected cell; Right-click cell, Borders and Fill, Text Box tab			ALT + O, T ALT + A, E
Change horizontal alignment of table text	Format, Table, Text Box tab	Right-click cell, row, column, or table, Borders and Fill, Text Box tab			ALT + O, T ALT + A, E
Change vertical alignment of table text	Format, Table, Text Box tab	Right-click cell, row, column, or table, Borders and Fill, Text Box tab			ALT + O, T ALT + A, E
Change column width		Drag border between columns, or double-click border between columns to AutoFit text to longest item			
Change row height		Drag border between rows			
Change table borders and fill	Format, Table, Borders or Fill tab	Right-click cell, row, column, or table, Borders and Fill, Borders or Fill tab	Table ▾ , Borders and Fill		ALT + O, T ALT + A, E
Move a table			Drag the selection border		

Concepts Review

Circle the correct answer.

1. Material consisting of relational information is best presented as a:
[a] title slide.
[b] text slide.
[c] table slide.
[d] drawing slide.

2. Which of the following statements is false?
[a] You can insert a Word table or an Excel worksheet on a PowerPoint slide.
[b] You can edit a table by double-clicking the table and using Microsoft Word's creating and editing capabilities.
[c] You can draw a table within PowerPoint.
[d] You can create a table by clicking any Content layout in the Slide Layout task pane.

3. A cell is defined as:
[a] a rectangular marker.
[b] a text box.
[c] the intersection of a column and a row.
[d] a border style.

4. To add a new row at the end of a table, you can position the insertion point in the last cell and:
[a] click the Insert Rows button on the Standard toolbar.
[b] press the ENTER key.
[c] press the TAB key.
[d] press the CTRL + ENTER keys.

5. To insert a row within a table, you position the insertion point:
[a] in the row above where you want to insert the new row, right-click the table, and click Insert Rows.
[b] in the row below where you want to insert the new row, right-click the table, and click Insert Rows Above.
[c] anywhere in the row where you want to insert the new row, right-click the table, and click Insert Rows.
[d] anywhere in the row where you want to insert the new row, click Format, Table, Row tab, and then click the Insert Row check box.

6. You format a simple table object by:
[a] right-clicking the table, and then clicking Edit Document Object.
[b] double-clicking the table.
[c] clicking the Edit subcommand of the Document Object command on the Edit menu.
[d] right-clicking the table, and then clicking the desired option.

7. The size of a table:
[a] is determined by the number of columns and rows.
[b] is determined by the presentation design and cannot be changed.
[c] is dependent on the intended look desired by the creator.
[d] cannot exceed 10 rows and 10 columns.

8. Which of the following enables viewers to quickly identify the items in the columns of a table?
[a] column names
[b] column headings
[c] row identifiers
[d] column markers

chapter five

9. To adjust the width of table columns, you:
[a] click the Column width command on the Format menu.
[b] drag the vertical line between two columns.
[c] right-click the table, and then click Column width.
[d] double-click the table and select the Column tab.

10. Which of the following statements concerning tables is not true?
[a] Individual cells can be aligned.
[b] Individual columns can be aligned.
[c] Individual rows can be aligned.
[d] Nonadjacent columns can be aligned at the same time.

Circle **T** if the statement is true or **F** if the statement is false.

T   F   1. A table slide displays data organized into columns and rows.

T   F   2. Tables can be created in Word and Excel and inserted in PowerPoint slides.

T   F   3. You can insert rows in a table only by clicking the Insert Rows command on the Table menu.

T   F   4. Pressing the ENTER key within a cell of a table adds another row.

T   F   5. Table border lines can be added or removed by right-clicking the table and clicking Borders and Fill.

T   F   6. You can automatically adjust the width of any column to its longest item by double-clicking the column's right border.

T   F   7. Shading in a table attracts the eye to the text or information within the shaded area.

T   F   8. You can change the vertical and horizontal alignment of cells, rows, and columns.

T   F   9. Column headings help viewers to quickly identify items within respective columns.

T   F   10. Once a table is created, it cannot be repositioned.

Skills Review

Exercise 1   C

1. Open the *PowerPoint* presentation you modified in Chapter 4, and add a table slide at the end of the presentation. The title should read "Slide Types."

2. Create a table consisting of two columns and four rows using the following information:

Slide Type	Function
Title	Introduce topic
Bullet	Summarize or prioritize
Table	Establish relationship between data

3. Add shading and bold the column headings. (Try to match one of the colors in the presentation design.)

4. Vertically center the text in the entire table, and change the font size to 24 point.

5. Increase the width of column 2 by decreasing the width of column 1.

6. Remove any indents in the column heading cells, and center the column headings horizontally.

7. Add an internal margin of 0.25 inches to all cells in the table.

8. Select the last three rows (do not include the column headings), and change the font to Times New Roman.

9. Reduce the height of rows 2, 3, and 4 by approximately 0.25 inch. (*Hint:* Change one row, then select the three rows, and then click the Distribute Rows Evenly button on the Tables and Borders toolbar.)

10. Resize and reposition the table to enhance the appearance of the slide.

11. Save the presentation, spell check it, resave if necessary, print the table slide, and close the presentation.

Exercise 2   C

1. Open the *Office* presentation you modified in Chapter 4, and add a table slide at the end of the presentation. The title should read "Microsoft Office XP."

2. Create a table using the Content layout consisting of two columns and six rows using the following information:

Software	*Application*
Word	*Word processing*
Excel	*Worksheets*
Access	*Databases*
PowerPoint	*Presentations*
FrontPage	*Web site creation and management tool*

3. Change the font size of the column headings to 28 point, Bold, Center Align.

4. Increase the row height of the column headings by approximately 0.25 inch, and vertically center the text.

5. Add an internal margin of 0.25 inch to the left and right margin for both columns.

6. Adjust the width of the columns, making column 1 narrower than column 2.

7. Italicize the names of the software in column 1, excluding the column heading.

8. Remove the existing table borders, add an outside border to the table, add a bottom border to the column headings, and add a right column border to column 1.

9. Resize and reposition the table attractively on the slide.

10. Save the presentation, spell check it, resave if necessary, print the table slide, and close the presentation.

Exercise 3   C

1. Open the *Design* presentation you modified in Chapter 4, and add a table slide at the end of the presentation. The title should read "Basic Color Tips."

2. Create a table consisting of two columns and six rows using the following information:

Color	*Message*
Blue	*Security, relaxation, conservatism*
Red	*Power, passion, competition*
Black	*Directness, force*
Green	*Intelligence, development*
Purple	*Entertainment, royalty*

3. Resize the columns to the longest item in each column.

4. Apply bold formatting to the column headings, and change the size to 26 point. (*Hint:* You can key 26 in the Font Size text box.)

5. Add the following row so that it appears above the "Purple" row:

Gray	*Neutral*

chapter five

6. Remove all the borders around the table.

7. Add an Inside Horizontal Border to the selected table.

8. Add a Bottom Border to the last row of the table.

9. Resize and reposition the table for readability and to insure that the entire table appears on the slide.

10. Vertically align the text to the bottom in the entire table.

11. Save the presentation, spell check it, resave if necessary, print the table slide, and close the presentation.

Exercise 4   C

1. Open the *Precision Builders* presentation you modified in Chapter 4, and add a table slide at the end of the presentation. The title should read "Quality Materials."

2. Create a table consisting of four columns and six rows using the following information:

Materials	Ranch	Two-story	Townhome
Brick	X	X	X
Hardwood floors	X	X	X
Ceramic baths	X	X	X
Two-story foyer		X	X
Thermal windows	X	X	X

3. Bold and italicize the column headings.

4. Adjust the width of the types of homes columns so that they are even.

5. Add shading (try to match one of the colors in the presentation design) to the column headings, and change the text color, if necessary.

6. Horizontally center columns 2, 3, and 4, and vertically center the column headings.

7. Vertically align all rows at the bottom, except the column headings.

8. Delete the row containing information about a Two-story foyer.

9. Resize and reposition the table, if necessary.

10. Save the presentation, spell check it, resave if necessary, print the table slide, and close the presentation.

Exercise 5   C

1. Open the *Nature Tours* presentation you modified in Chapter 4, and add a table slide at the end of the presentation. The title should read "Let Your Legs Do the Work."

2. Enter the following table text, pressing the ENTER key at the breaks shown:

Leg Tours	Locations
Hiking	Grand Canyon, Rocky Mountains, Glacier National Park, Lake Tahoe
Walking	Sonoran Desert, Maine Coast, Hawaiian Islands
Mountain climbing	Tetons, Seven Summits, High Sierras, Mount Olympus

3. Adjust column widths so that column 2 is wider than column 1.

4. Change the font, font size, style, and vertical and horizontal alignment of the column headings.

5. Align the text in the columns as necessary.

6. Resize the table, if necessary.

7. Save the presentation, spell check it, resave if necessary, print the table slide, and close the presentation.

Exercise 6   C

1. Open the *A Healthier You* presentation you modified in Chapter 4, and add a table slide at the end of the presentation. The title should read "Food Pyramid Guide."

2. Enter the following table text:

Food Group	Servings Per Day
Breads, Cereal, Rice, & Pasta	6 – 11
Vegetables	3 – 5
Fruits	2 – 3
Milk, Yogurt, & Cheese	2 – 3
Meat, Poultry, Fish, Dry Beans, Eggs, & Nuts	2 – 3
Fats, Oil, Sweets	use sparingly

3. Adjust column widths for ease of readability and appearance.

4. Add shading and determine where to place borders to enhance the table.

5. Change the border lines of the table to 2 ¼ point, and use an appropriate border color that matches the presentation.

6. Format the text within the table with regard to font style, font size, and alignment.

7. Adjust the row height of the column headings.

8. Change the vertical and horizontal alignment where necessary for readability.

9. Indent the text from the border for column 1.

10. Resize the table, if necessary.

11. Save the presentation, spell check it, resave if necessary, print the table slide, and close the presentation.

Exercise 7   C

1. Open the *Buying A Computer* presentation you modified in Chapter 4, and add a table slide at the end of the presentation. The title should read "Computer Essentials."

2. Enter the following table text:

What minimum options do I need?				
Processor	RAM	MHz	Hard Drive	Drives
Celeron	64MB	500	6.5GB	3 ½"
Pentium III	128MB	700	15GB	3 ½" (Press the ENTER key)
				250MB ZIP (Press the ENTER key)
				CD-ROM

3. Select the first row ("What minimum options do I need?") and merge the cells. (*Hint:* Use the Tables and Borders toolbar.)

4. Adjust the column widths for optimal readability.

5. Change the font, font size, style, and/or alignment of the first row.

6. Format the text within the table.

7. Add or remove borders and/or shading to improve the appearance of the table.

chapter five

8. Resize the table to fit attractively on the slide.

9. Save the presentation, spell check it, resave if necessary, print the table slide, and close the presentation.

Exercise 8

1. Open the *Leisure Travel* presentation you modified in Chapter 4, and add a table slide at the end of the presentation. The title should read "All-Inclusive Package Teasers."

2. Enter the following table text:

Pkg. #	Destination	# of Days	Approx. Cost*
1224	Aruba	7	$2,000
1335	Puerto Vallarta	6	$1,150
1129	St. Thomas	5	$1,500

3. Adjust column widths as necessary.

4. Horizontally and vertically align text as desired.

5. Add another row anywhere after the column headings row, and key the following:

1546	Cancun	5	$1,350

6. Resize and reposition the table.

7. Add a row at the bottom of the table, merge the cells, and key the following text: "*Average price quoted for the given number of days."

8. Reduce the font size and change the vertical alignment of the last row (the footnote) to center.

9. Remove the borders around the last row.

10. Save the presentation, spell check it, resave if necessary, print the table slide, and close the presentation.

Case Projects

Project 1

You decide that you want to learn more about the Draw Table button and the Eraser button on the Tables and Borders toolbar. You are particularly interested in how to use the buttons on an existing table, what type of tables you can draw with the Draw Table mouse pointer, and how to erase lines. Use the Ask A Question Box to find information on the Draw Table button and Eraser button. Using the information you find, create a presentation that consists of only a table slide using the Draw Table and Eraser buttons to draw rows and columns. Arrange the information you find from the online Help in a table format. Print the table slide.

Project 2

Your manager is concerned about the reaction of callers to the employees they deal with on the telephone. She believes that there is a correlation between the phone etiquette of employees and customers' needs, concerns, and expectations being satisfied. She asks you to create a checklist of basic phone etiquette employees should perform when talking to customers. Open the *Communicate* presentation you modified in Chapter 4, and add a table slide to your presentation that conveys at least three actions employees should do when receiving calls. Add shading and borders as you desire. Change alignment, fonts, font size, etc., as appropriate. After completing the table slide, you should make any adjustments necessary to aid readability. Spell check and save the presentation. Print the table slide.

Project 3

Because the owner of Souner & Associates believes that variety and a continuous offering of courses will satisfy most potential clients' needs, your manager wants you to add a table slide to the *Souner* presentation that indicates course offerings for the current month. Open the *Souner* presentation you modified in Chapter 4, and add a table that includes at least four classes that are being offered and indicate whether or not they are being offered each week. Change the borders within the table. After completing the table slide, make any adjustments necessary to aid readability. Spell check and save the presentation. Print the table slide.

Project 4

You have informed your employer that you think a table slide should be added to your presentation to best display additional information concerning your topic. Open the *My Presentation* presentation you modified in Chapter 4, and add a table slide. You want to display your data attractively in rows and columns for this presentation. After completing the table slide, make any adjustments necessary to aid readability. Be sure to spell check and save the *My Presentation* presentation. Print the table slide.

Project 5

The zoo has several special exhibits and showings scheduled for the current month. They are especially proud of the births of Chi Lo, the first panda ever born at the zoo, and Tweeky, the new son of Zelda, one of the female hippopotamuses, which occurred during the first week of the month. In addition, the newly renovated ape house and bird aviary are done and will open to the public the second and third week of the month. You need to add this information to your *Zoo* presentation. Open the *Zoo* presentation you modified in Chapter 4, and create a table slide that displays these special events and the dates of the events. Make any formatting decisions with regard to text alignment, borders and shading, and fonts. Save the presentation, and print the table slide.

Project 6

There are several very good integrated software suites on the market today. You are curious how they compare with each other. Connect to the Internet and search the Web for information that compares Microsoft Office with the latest Lotus SmartSuite and Corel WordPerfect Suite. Print the information you find. Create a new presentation consisting of a title and table slide that compares the three suites. View the slide show, save the presentation with an appropriate filename, and print the presentation.

Project 7

You have just read an article relating the survival rate of car drivers and passengers in car accidents. The article has indicated that the fate of drivers and passengers in some accidents is dependent on the safety features found in the cars on the highway today. You found the article to be extremely interesting and want to share this information with your fellow students. Connect to the Internet and search the Web for current information about your car's safety features. Open the *Cars* presentation you modified in Chapter 4, and add a table slide to your presentation that lists several of the safety features you found and their descriptions. Make any formatting decisions with regard to alignment of text, column widths, typeface, type size, and table size. Replace the presentation fonts for this presentation. Save the presentation and print the table slide.

Project 8

You and your partner decide that a table slide would be a good way to display several of the terms and their definitions that you found while searching the Internet. Open the *Internet* presentation you modified in Chapter 4, and add a table slide at the end that displays the top six terms you found vital to understanding the Internet. If necessary, connect to the Internet and search the Web for appropriate terms. Make any formatting changes to shading, typeface, font size, column widths, and table size to improve the readability and appearance of the table. Save the presentation, and print the table slide.

chapter five

Working with Charts

Chapter Overview

Charts are important tools in PowerPoint; they present complex data in a simple, graphical form that an audience can easily understand. You might use a chart to compare results such as monthly product sales or to identify trends such as weather patterns. Like a table, a chart organizes data, but it also interprets the data as a visual picture, so the audience gets the message without having to read every number. In this chapter, you learn how to create chart slides and how to work with different types of charts. You also learn how to edit and format a chart to convey your information most effectively.

LEARNING OBJECTIVES

- Add a chart to a slide
- Work with a datasheet
- Format a chart
- Add a pie chart to a slide
- Format a pie chart

Case profile

To present the current market status of Teddy Toys, Ms. Hill wants you to include two charts in the *Teddy Toys* presentation. First, she would like you to create a graph depicting sales within each of Teddy Toys' four product areas over the last two years. In addition, two of Teddy Toys' competitors hold a significant portion of the toy market, with Teddy Toys coming in as the leader. To highlight the need to maintain Teddy Toys' position in the marketplace, Ms. Hill wants you to create a slide that compares the market share among all three top toy manufacturers.

chapter six

6.a Adding a Chart to a Slide

To add a chart to a presentation, you can create a chart from scratch in PowerPoint or you can insert an existing chart that you created in another program, such as Word or Excel. You can create a chart in PowerPoint using **Microsoft Graph**, a charting program shared by the Office suite of products. In Microsoft Graph, you can quickly create almost any type of chart, including column, bar, line, pie, XY (scatter), area, doughnut, radar, surface, bubble, stock, cylinder, cone, and pyramid charts. Within each chart type available in Microsoft Graph, you can choose from at least two or three subtypes. If one of these standard chart types does not meet your needs, you can choose a custom chart type.

You can create a chart in any slide, or you can use one of the layouts in the New Slide task pane that contains a chart placeholder. To add a chart using a chart layout slide at the end of a presentation:

Step 1	*Open*	the *Teddy Toys* presentation you modified in Chapter 5 and display the last slide in the presentation
Step 2	*Click*	the New Slide button [New Slide] on the Formatting toolbar
Step 3	*Scroll*	to the Other Layouts area of the Slide Layout task pane
Step 4	*Click*	the Title and Chart layout in the Other Layouts area of the Slide Layout task pane

Your screen should look similar to Figure 6-1.

> ### TASK PANE TIP
>
> You can add a chart to a PowerPoint slide by clicking one of the Content layouts in the Slide Layout task pane and then clicking the Insert Chart icon.
>
> You can also create a chart by clicking any Content Layout or Title and Text and Content Layout in the Slide Layout task pane and then clicking the Insert Chart icon on the placeholder.

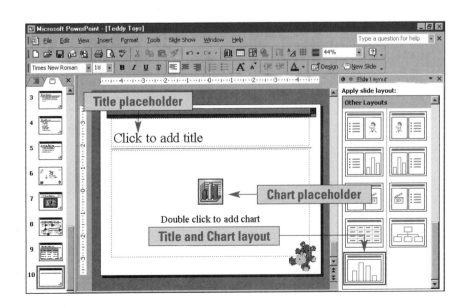

FIGURE 6-1
Slide with Chart Placeholder

chapter
six

MENU TIP

You can create a chart in any slide by clicking the Chart command on the Insert menu. You also can create a chart by clicking the Object command on the Insert menu, and then clicking Microsoft Graph Chart.

To add a title and create the chart:

Step 1	*Click*	the "Click to add title" placeholder
Step 2	*Key*	Market Status
Step 3	*Double-click*	the chart placeholder

Microsoft Graph opens and displays a default chart on the slide and a **datasheet**, a worksheet that is linked to your new chart. It contains default data that you replace with the your own data. Your screen should look similar to Figure 6-2.

FIGURE 6-2
Default Chart with Datasheet

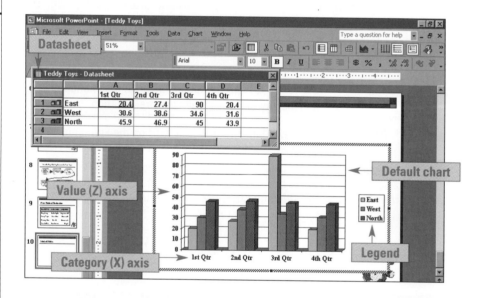

The data in the datasheet is depicted visually in the chart. When you create a new chart, Microsoft Graph displays the datasheet with **default data**, sample data that it uses to draw the sample chart. Once you enter or edit information in the datasheet, the chart changes accordingly. In the chart, each data series is represented by a different color. A **data series** represents one set of related data on the datasheet, such as 1st Qtr sales. The **Category (X) axis** (the horizontal axis), created from the first row in the datasheet, consists of categories, such as 1st Qtr. The **Value (Y) or (Z) axis** (the vertical axis), created from the actual data values keyed in the datasheet, consists of measurements of the categories listed on the Category (X) axis, such as sales. If the chart is a 3-D chart, you have a Value (Z) axis instead of a Value (Y) axis. A **legend**, displayed on the right, indicates the various series being used in the chart, such as East, West, North. The legend is created from the first column in the datasheet. The columns for one category represent a data series in a chart. Each series has a unique color, fill, or pattern and is represented in the chart legend. You can plot one or more data

MOUSE TIP

You can create a chart by clicking the Insert Chart button on the Standard toolbar.

series in a chart, with the exception of pie charts, which have only one data series. A **data point** represents one data series in a chart, such as one slice of a pie or one column in a series of columns.

6.b Working with a Datasheet

On the datasheet, columns are identified by letters, and rows are identified by numbers. In the first column and first row of the datasheet are sample labels for the data. When you replace the default labels with your own, you replace the sample column labels with text descriptions of the data categories in your chart and the sample row names with descriptions of the data values. You enter labels and data in cells, as you do in Microsoft Excel, though there are some important differences in the entry process.

Deleting Default Data

Before entering data in a datasheet, you delete the default data. You could delete this information one cell at a time, but doing so is time consuming and may leave you with undesired cells. Deleting individual cell contents clears only the data; the empty cell, row, or column still remains, which may cause the chart to produce gaps between the data series. To delete the data and the empty rows or columns, it's better to select all the data at once and then delete it. The datasheet contains a Select All button in the upper-left corner of the datasheet that you can click to select all the rows and columns in the datasheet. To delete all the default data from the datasheet:

Step 1	*Click*	the Select All button in the upper-left corner of the datasheet

The datasheet on your screen should look similar to Figure 6-3.

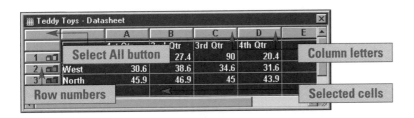

Step 2	*Press*	the DELETE key to delete the existing default data

CAUTION TIP

If you drag and select the text in a datasheet, or delete the text cell by cell, your chart may contain large blank areas without columns or bars. Click the Select All button to ensure that you delete all previous text.

FIGURE 6-3
Datasheet with Selected Cells

chapter
six

Keying Chart Data

You key data in a datasheet just as you key data into an Excel worksheet. After keying data in a cell, you complete your entry and move to a different cell by pressing the TAB key, the ENTER key, or any of the ARROW keys. If you wish to return to a previous cell, you can press the SHIFT + TAB keys, the LEFT ARROW key, the SHIFT + ENTER keys, or the UP ARROW key. As in an Excel worksheet, a cell is identified by a cell address, which represents the intersection of the lettered column and numbered row; cell A1, for example, is the cell located at the intersection of column A and row 1. The datasheet in Microsoft Graph also contains cells to the left of column A and above row 1 for text that identifies the data; these cells are not represented by a cell address. To key data into a datasheet:

Step 1	*Click*	the cell in the first row immediately below the column A indicator
Step 2	*Key*	Last Year
Step 3	*Press*	the TAB key
Step 4	*Key*	This Year
Step 5	*Click*	the cell immediately to the right of the row 1 indicator and to the left of cell A1
Step 6	*Key*	the following, pressing the ENTER key after each entry: Family Bears / Action Bears / Sports Clothes / Toys

Notice that the column labels, Last Year and This Year, are displayed on the Category (X) axis, and the row labels, Family Bears, Action Bears, Sports Clothes, and Toys, are displayed in the legend on the chart beneath the datasheet.

When entering a large section of data on the datasheet, you can preselect a range of cells. **Preselecting a range** temporarily changes the path of the active cell to make it easier to key quickly. After keying the first value in a preselected range and pressing the ENTER key, the active cell moves to the next cell in the range. This enables you to complete the data entry more efficiently. If the preselected range includes more than one column, the active cell moves down one column and then to the top of the next. To preselect a range, enter values in the range and then close the datasheet:

| Step 1 | *Drag* | from the center of cell A1 to cell B4 to select eight cells |

| Step 2 | Key | the following, pressing the ENTER key after each value:
25000
30000
15000
50000
28000
32000
12000
45000 |
| Step 3 | Observe | how the chart builds to reflect the data you are entering |

The columns on the chart represent the data series from the values in the datasheet.

| Step 4 | Click | the View Datasheet button 🖿 on the Standard toolbar to close the datasheet |

Notice that the Value (Z) axis displays a range of numbers based on the values in the datasheet. This represents the sales for each year. The Category (X) axis displays Last Year and This Year categories of comparison. The chart displays a different colored column or bar for each of the four major product areas. The legend displays a colored key box indicating each specific product. To close the Microsoft Graph application and view the chart slide:

| Step 1 | Click | outside the chart object |

Your screen should look similar to Figure 6-4.

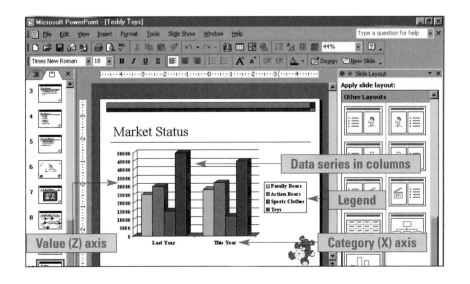

MOUSE TIP

You can adjust column width in a datasheet by dragging the border between the column letters to the desired width, or by double-clicking the border between the column letters.

MENU TIP

You can display or hide the datasheet at any time by clicking the Datasheet command on the View menu in Microsoft Graph.

FIGURE 6-4
Column Chart Slide

chapter
six

| Step 2 | *Save* | the *Teddy Toys* presentation |

6.c Formatting a Chart

A chart is an embedded object. An **embedded object** is an object that was created in a different program and must be opened in that program to make editing and formatting changes. Therefore, if you need to edit the information in a datasheet or format the chart on a slide, you must open Microsoft Graph. Microsoft Graph provides its own set of toolbars for editing and formatting charts. Some toolbar buttons are available when the chart is selected, and other buttons are available when the datasheet is displayed.

You can format a chart by changing the chart type, chart and series colors, number and text format, legend placement, axes titles, and data labels. A chart is actually made up of individual objects, such as columns or bars, gridlines, and a legend; to make formatting changes, you open Microsoft Graph, select the object you want to modify, and then make the necessary changes. To open Microsoft Graph:

| Step 1 | *Double-click* | the chart object |

Microsoft Graph opens, and the chart is ready to be edited or formatted. The selection border and eight sizing handles surrounding the chart indicate it is selected.

| Step 2 | *Close* | the datasheet, if necessary |

You must select a chart object to format it. You can select chart objects by clicking them or by selecting them from the Chart Objects list box on the Standard toolbar in Microsoft Graph. Immediately to the right of the Chart Objects list box is a Format Object button, which displays a ScreenTip indicating the selected object on the chart. ScreenTips identify each section of the chart when you point to it. You must pause for a moment to see the ScreenTip.

| Step 3 | *Point to* | the first column in the chart |

The ScreenTip displays: Series "Family Bears" Point "Last Year" Value: 25000.

| Step 4 | Point to | each chart object and observe its ScreenTip |

MENU TIP

You can edit the selected legend object by clicking the Selected Legend command on the Format menu.

Formatting a Chart Legend

The **legend** on a chart is an object that identifies the patterns, fills, or colors that are assigned to the categories or data series. The legend on the Teddy Toys slide contains the four products with their respective colored box indicating each series. Legends, like all objects, can be enhanced to improve readability and comprehension. To format and move the legend:

| Step 1 | Double-click | the Legend object |

The Format Legend dialog box opens, with options for changing fill and border colors, fonts, font styles, font sizes, font colors, and placement of the legend on the chart.

Step 2	Click	the Patterns tab, if necessary
Step 3	Click	the Shadow check box to insert a check mark
Step 4	Click	the pale orange color in the fifth row, second column under Area
Step 5	Click	the Font tab
Step 6	Click	Italic in the Font style: list box
Step 7	Click	16 in the Size: list box
Step 8	Click	the Placement tab
Step 9	Click	the Bottom option button
Step 10	Click	OK
Step 11	Save	the *Teddy Toys* presentation

MOUSE TIP

You can edit the legend object by right-clicking the Legend object and then clicking Format Legend. You also can edit a selected legend by clicking the Format Legend button on the Standard toolbar in Microsoft Graph.

You can move the legend by dragging it to a new location. (Be careful not to drag a sizing handle, or you will resize the legend.)

Changing the Chart Display

The chart display shows how your current chart plots the data from the datasheet. You can change the chart display to display by rows or by columns. You use the By Column display when you want the columns on the datasheet to represent the data series in the chart. You use the By Row display when you want the rows on the datasheet to represent the data

chapter
six

series in the chart. The chart compares each product's sales for last year and each product's sales for this year. To change the chart display:

| Step 1 | *Click* | the By Column button ⊞ on the Standard toolbar |

The legend and the Category (X) axis labels are reversed, and the chart now compares each product's last year's sales with this year's sales. Comparing all product sales for last year with all product sales for this year gives a better picture of how sales have changed in the marketplace, so you change the display back to By Row.

| Step 2 | *Click* | the By Row button ▤ on the Standard toolbar |

Changing the Chart Type

When you create a chart in Microsoft Graph, the default chart type, a column chart, is created. You can change to any chart type available in Microsoft Graph, including column, bar, line, pie, XY (scatter), area, doughnut, radar, surface, bubble, stock, cylinder, cone, and pyramid charts. Each type is best for presenting a particular type of information. Column and bar charts, for example, are most effective when the goal is to show changes in data over a period of time or comparisons among items. Line charts are most effective when the goal is to show trends over a period of time. Cone, pyramid, or cylinder charts create a dramatic 3-D effect when showing changes in data over a period or time or when comparing data. Stock charts are most effective when the goal is to display high-low-close ratings of stocks. To change the chart type:

| Step 1 | *Click* | the Chart Type button list arrow ◪▾ on the Standard toolbar |
| Step 2 | *Click* | various chart types to view your chart in different forms |

Generally, the choices on the left of the Chart Type list are 2-D examples, whereas the choices in the middle are 3-D choices. After viewing different chart types, you want to return to your original 3-D column chart. The 3-D column chart found in the Chart Type list displays 3-D columns, but it also displays 3-D walls and floors around the columns. You decide to return to your original column chart.

| Step 3 | *Click* | <u>C</u>hart |

Step 4	*Click*	Chart Type

Step 5	*Click*	the Standard Types tab, if necessary

The Chart Type dialog box opens with the Standard Types tab displaying the chart types in the column on the left and previews of various sub-types on the right. The dialog box on your screen should look similar to Figure 6-5.

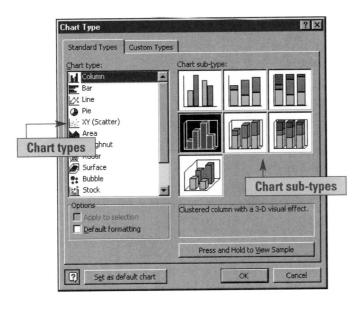

FIGURE 6-5
Chart Type Dialog Box

Step 6	*Click*	Column in the Chart type: list

Step 7	*Click*	the Clustered column with a 3-D visual effect in the second row, first column in the Chart sub-type: list

Step 8	*Click*	OK

Formatting a Data Series

A data series in a chart can be formatted by changing the border and fill styles and colors, the depth and width, the shape, and the data labels. You can add different types of fill effects to each different series. Gradients are shaded colors that are usually comprised of two colors blending from one color to the other. You can use various shading styles, patterns, or solid fill colors. Textures reflect fills that represent a realistic effect, such as bubbles or wood fills. When you change a series color and fill, the legend reflects that change in the legend key box. When you change the fill of a data series, you select the entire series. If you select only one of the columns in the series, the changes only affect that column.

chapter
six

To format a data series with a different fill color and gradient:

Step 1	*Double-click*	the Toys series column for either year
Step 2	*Click*	the Patterns tab in the Format Data Series dialog box, if necessary
Step 3	*Click*	Fill effects in the Format Data Series dialog box
Step 4	*Click*	the Gradient tab, if necessary
Step 5	*Click*	the Two colors option button under Colors
Step 6	*Click*	the Color 1: list arrow under Colors
Step 7	*Click*	the Dark Red color in the second row, first column
Step 8	*Click*	the From center option button under Shading styles
Step 9	*Click*	the preview on the right under Variants
Step 10	*Click*	OK twice
Step 11	*Press*	the ESC key to deselect the current chart objects

After previewing a gradient fill effect, you decide to add a texture fill effect and a pattern fill to the Sports Clothes and Action Bears data series to see which effect you want to use. To format a data series with texture and pattern fill effects:

Step 1	*Double-click*	the Sport Clothes series column for either year
Step 2	*Click*	Fill effects in the Format Data Series dialog box
Step 3	*Click*	the Texture tab
Step 4	*Click*	the Papyrus texture in the fourth row, first column
Step 5	*Click*	OK twice
Step 6	*Double-click*	the Action Bear series column for either year
Step 7	*Click*	Fill Effects
Step 8	*Click*	the Pattern tab
Step 9	*Click*	the Solid diamond pattern (last row, last column)

| Step 10 | *Click* | OK twice |
| Step 11 | *Press* | the ESC key |

All the columns display different fill effects, from solid, to pattern, to texture, to gradient. Your screen should look similar to Figure 6-6.

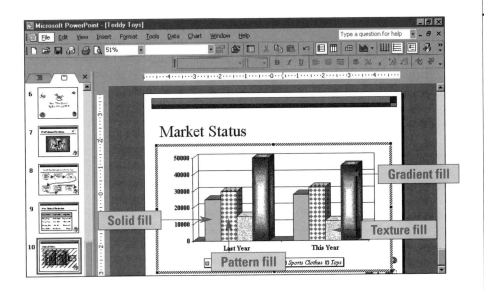

FIGURE 6-6
Columns with Different
Fill Effects

MOUSE TIP

You can change the chart type by right-clicking the series, plot area, or chart area in a chart and then clicking Chart Type.

From a design point of view, the columns in a chart should have a consistent look. For example, if you use a gradient fill effect, then all columns in the chart should use that same effect. To format a data series with a solid fill color:

Step 1	*Double-click*	the Toys series column for either year
Step 2	*Click*	the Patterns tab, if necessary
Step 3	*Click*	the medium brown color in the sixth row, third column under Area
Step 4	*Click*	OK
Step 5	*Double-click*	the Sports Clothes series column for either year
Step 6	*Change*	the series color to the pale orange color in the fifth row, second column under Area
Step 7	*Double-click*	the Action Bears series column for either year
Step 8	*Change*	the series color to the green color in the sixth row, second column under Area
Step 9	*Save*	the *Teddy Toys* presentation

CAUTION TIP

When accessing the Format Data Series dialog box, be sure to double-click—do not click twice. If you click twice, you may select only one of the columns. To be safe, be sure that all columns of a series are selected before making changes.

chapter
six

Formatting the Value Axis

The Value (Z) axis displays numbers corresponding to the values listed on the datasheet. You can format a Value (Z) axis to display currency to indicate that the numbers represent sales in terms of dollars or to add or remove decimals. In addition, you can also format a Value (Z) axis to change the scale minimum, maximum, or interval units. This affects how the data series is displayed according to the chart data. You have the option of changing the scale, font, font size, style and color, and the alignment of the Value (Z) axis.

To change the format of the numbers on the Value (Z) axis to include a $, a comma, and no decimal places:

Step 1	Double-click	any number on the Value (Z) axis to open the Format Axis dialog box
Step 2	Click	the Number tab
Step 3	Click	Currency in the Category: list box
Step 4	Key	0 in the Decimal places: text box
Step 5	Verify	that a $ symbol appears in the Symbol: list box
Step 6	Click	OK

Adding titles to the axes in a chart helps the audience to clearly understand the categories and measurements being displayed. You want to add a title to the Value (Z) axis to indicate that the dollar amounts are in thousands. The Value (Z) axis title appears on the slide in a horizontal format. The more you add to a chart, the smaller the columns become. You can rotate the Value (Z) axis title to increase the size of your columns. There is no need to add a Category (X) axis title at this time because the labels, Last Year and This Year are self-explanatory. To add a title to the Value (Z) axis and rotate it:

Step 1	Click	Chart
Step 2	Click	Chart Options
Step 3	Click	the Titles tab, if necessary

Your screen should look similar to Figure 6-7.

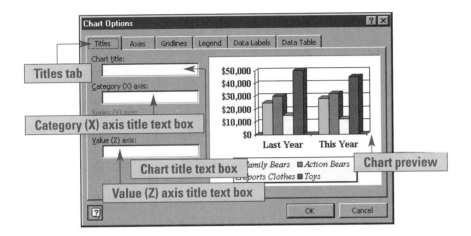

FIGURE 6-7
Chart Options Dialog Box

QUICK TIP

You can change the orientation of the Value axis title by clicking anywhere on the Orientation dial or by dragging the red orientation diamond or the Text arm in the Chart Options dialog box.

Step 4	*Click*	in the Value (Z) axis: text box
Step 5	*Key*	Total Sales
Step 6	*Click*	OK
Step 7	*Right-click*	the Value Axis Title (Total Sales)
Step 8	*Click*	Format Axis Title
Step 9	*Click*	the Alignment tab
Step 10	*Key*	90 in the Degrees: text box
Step 11	*Click*	OK
Step 12	*Click*	outside the chart object
Step 13	*Save*	the *Teddy Toys* presentation

Your screen should look similar to Figure 6-8.

MOUSE TIP

You can display labels and values by right-clicking the series, clicking Format Data Series, and then clicking the Data Labels tab.

chapter
six

FIGURE 6-8
Formatted Column
Chart Slide

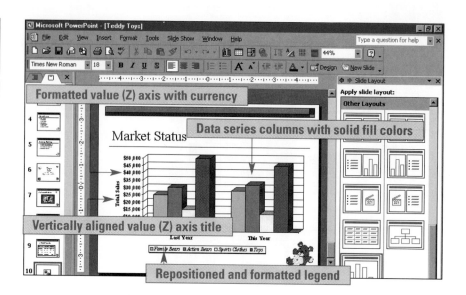

6.d Adding a Pie Chart to a Slide

Column and bar graphs are most effective for showing the relationship among groups of data, trends, or time changes. When you want to show the relationship of parts the whole, pie charts are the best choice. In addition, a pie chart is useful when you want to emphasize a major component of a series; say, for example, you want to show the sales for only one quarter or one area. To add a pie chart to a slide at the end of a presentation:

Step 1	*Display*	the column chart slide, if necessary
Step 2	*Add*	a new slide based on the Title and Chart layout
Step 3	*Key*	Market Share in the title placeholder
Step 4	*Double-click*	the chart placeholder

The default column chart with default data appears every time you add a chart to a slide. You need to delete the default data and key in your own data for a pie chart. To delete the sample data from the datasheet and enter new data:

Step 1	*Click*	the Select All button in the upper-left corner of the datasheet to select the contents of the datasheet

QUICK TIP

When you key data for a pie chart, you can key the pie slice data in the first column, column 0. The values are keyed directly to the right of each slice label. When completed, click the By Column button on the Standard toolbar.

Step 2	Press	the DELETE key
Step 3	Click	the cell immediately below the column A indicator
Step 4	Key	Andy's Amusements and press the TAB key
Step 5	Key	Gary's Games in cell B0 and press the TAB key
Step 6	Key	Teddy Toys in cell C0
Step 7	Click	cell A1
Step 8	Key	the following values, pressing the TAB key after each value: 75000 90000 120000
Step 9	Close	the datasheet

The data you just keyed in the datasheet reflects total sales from last year for each of three toy manufacturers. When you create a chart in Microsoft Graph, it is automatically displayed as a column chart. To display the data in a different chart type, you must change the chart type. Because you keyed data for only one data series, you decide to change the column chart to a pie chart. To change the default chart to a pie chart:

| Step 1 | Click | the Chart Type button list arrow on the Standard toolbar |
| Step 2 | Click | the 3-D Pie Chart button in the fifth row, second column |

6.e Formatting a Pie Chart

After you create a pie chart, you have many options for enhancing its appearance. You can display names of series, categories, values, and percentages instead of using a legend for clarity. The pie may be rotated, tilted, resized, and moved to make it easier for the audience to interpret the data. Individual pie slices (as well as the entire pie) can be pulled out for emphasis and the border and fill colors can be changed to match the presentation design. Two-dimensional and three-dimensional pies create different effects.

DESIGN TIP

Data labels can be displayed on a column or bar chart, but they sometimes are too large and difficult to read. A legend displays better on a column chart, whereas data labels display better on a pie chart.
As a general design rule, a pie chart should contain no more than seven slices. Too many slices cause a pie chart to lose its effectiveness. If you find that your series of information consists of more than seven values, consider using a different type of chart to display your data.

MENU TIP

You can access the 3-D View dialog box by clicking the 3-D View command on the Chart menu in Microsoft Graph.

chapter six

Hiding a Legend and Displaying Data Labels

Instead of displaying a legend with a pie chart, it is usually more effective to use data labels and values. Legends tend to take up a lot of room on a pie chart, and the eye has to travel off the pie to see the label for the slices. **Data labels** can be set to display series names, category names, values, percentages, or any combination.

The pie chart displays three colored slices representing the three toy manufacturers. You can display data labels and percentages for each, so that the audience readily identifies each competitor and its market share. To hide the legend and display labels and percentages:

Step 1	*Click*	the Legend button 📇 on the Microsoft Graph Standard toolbar to hide the legend
Step 2	*Click*	Chart
Step 3	*Click*	Chart Options
Step 4	*Click*	the Data Labels tab
Step 5	*Click*	the Category name and Percentage check boxes
Step 6	*Click*	OK
Step 7	*Click*	outside the chart area

Your screen should look similar to Figure 6-9.

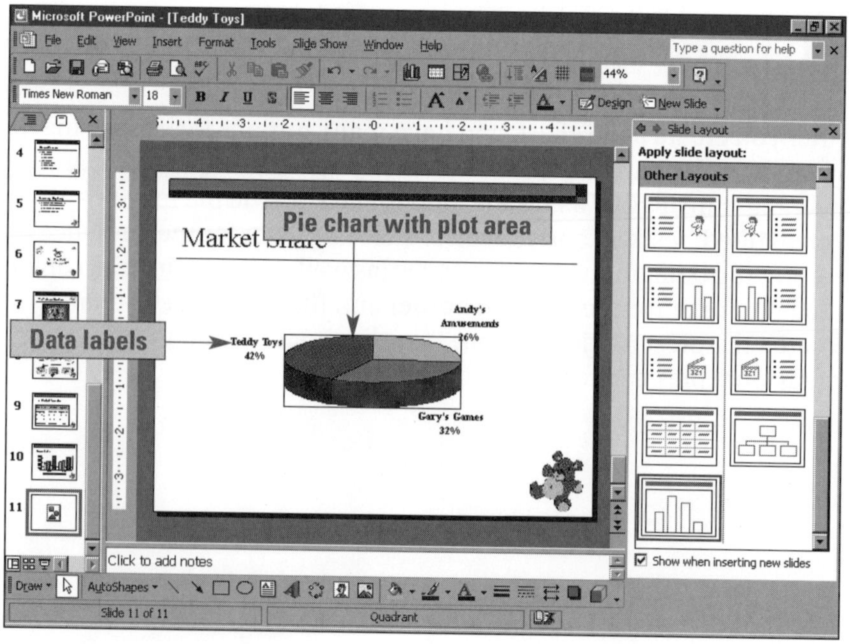

FIGURE 6-9
Pie Chart with Data Labels

> **QUICK TIP**
>
> You can redisplay the legend by clicking the Show legend box on the Legend tab after clicking the Chart Options command on the Chart menu.
>
> You can hide a legend by selecting the legend and pressing the DELETE key. The legend is not deleted, just hidden.
>
> You can hide or show a legend by clicking the Legend button on the Standard toolbar in Microsoft Graph.

Rotating and Tilting a Pie Chart

After creating a pie chart, the slices and labels can be rotated so they fit better in the chart slide area. You can tilt and change the height of the pie to create a different 3-D visual effect. You decide to change the tilt and rotation of the Teddy Toys pie slice to emphasize that Teddy Toys holds a large slice of the current market. To change the 3-D view options:

Step 1	*Double-click*	the pie chart object
Step 2	*Close*	the datasheet, if necessary
Step 3	*Right-click*	the chart area (ScreenTip displays: Chart Area)
Step 4	*Click*	3-D View

The 3-D View dialog box on your screen should look similar to Figure 6-10. This dialog box contains options for rotating, tilting, and changing the base height.

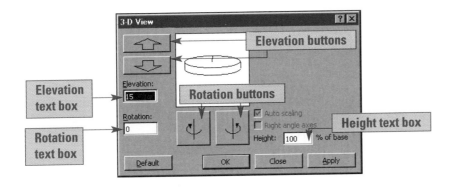

FIGURE 6-10
3-D View Dialog Box

Step 5	*Drag*	the 3-D View dialog box so that you can see the pie chart
Step 6	*Click*	the Up arrow button to change the elevation (tilt) of the pie to 35
Step 7	*Click*	Apply and observe the change
Step 8	*Click*	the Left rotate button until the Rotation: text box displays 150
Step 9	*Click*	Apply and observe the change
Step 10	*Click*	OK
Step 11	*Save*	the *Teddy Toys* presentation

chapter
six

Pulling Out a Pie Slice

You can pull out an individual slice to emphasize the importance of that particular slice, or data point. To select one slice of a pie chart object, you click once to select the data series (entire pie), and then again to select just that data point (one slice). If you select the pie instead of one slice, you pull out all the slices of the pie. As you pull out a slice, or all the slices, you might need to adjust the labels and percentages so that you can read them. The size of the labels and percentages may change depending on how you pull out the slices. To pull out a slice:

| Step 1 | Click | the Teddy Toys slice twice to select it; do not double-click the slice |
| Step 2 | Drag | the Teddy Toys slice to the right approximately 0.5 inch |

Formatting the Plot Area of a Pie Chart

The plot area of a chart is the area of a chart that graphically displays statistical data being plotted. The plot area border line can be formatted with a different style, color, and weight, while the plot border area can be formatted with different fill colors and fill effects. You resize the plot area by dragging one of the corner handles. You move the plot area by dragging the selection border. Although resizing and moving the plot area is very helpful, you still have the option of moving and resizing the entire chart object on the PowerPoint slide. When you resize the pie object, the data labels size may change. To change the size of the pie in the plot area, remove the plot area border, and make any final plot area adjustments:

Step 1	Click	the plot area border line (ScreenTip displays: Plot Area)
Step 2	Drag	any corner handle to increase the size of the pie chart so that it fits better in the chart area
Step 3	Resize	the plot area as necessary to make sure all labels and percentages fit in the chart area
Step 4	Drag	the plot area border to center the pie object in the chart area
Step 5	Select	the plot area border, if necessary
Step 6	Press	the DELETE key to delete the Plot Area border
Step 7	Click	any data label to select all of the labels
Step 8	Change	the font size to 20 point

Step 9	*Click*	outside the chart area

The pie chart on your slide should look similar to Figure 6-11.

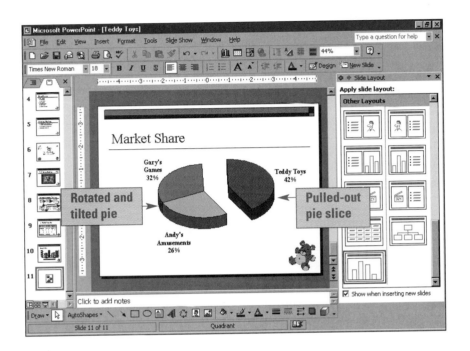

FIGURE 6-11
Completed Market Share Pie Chart

Step 10	*Save*	the *Teddy Toys* presentation and close it

The pie chart clearly shows the Teddy Toys' market share.

chapter
six

Summary

▶ You can add a chart slide to a presentation to illustrate statistical and quantitative information in a graphical representation so that the audience can quickly interpret your message.

▶ You create a chart in PowerPoint using Microsoft Graph, a program that comes with PowerPoint.

▶ You can insert an existing chart that you created in another program, such as Word or Excel, in a PowerPoint slide.

▶ Because a chart in a PowerPoint slide is an embedded object, you edit and format it using the program in which it was created.

▶ A data series represents one set of related data on the datasheet, such as one set of columns on a chart.

▶ A data point represents only one item in a data series, such as one column in a series of columns or one slice in a pie chart.

▶ The datasheet is used to key values in the form of rows and columns, similar to a Microsoft Excel worksheet, to create a chart that reflects those values.

▶ When keying data in the datasheet, preselecting a range temporarily changes the path of the active cell, to make it easier to key quickly.

▶ The Select All button on the datasheet is used to select all the default data before deleting it.

▶ The category (X) axis on a chart displays the categories being measured.

▶ The value (Y) or (Z) axis displays a scale based on the values that are entered on the datasheet.

▶ When working on three-dimensional charts, the value (Y) axis displays as value (Z).

▶ A chart legend is a chart object that identifies the patterns, fills, or colors that are assigned to the categories or data series on a chart.

▶ Depending on the chart type, rows and columns can be switched to display data differently.

▶ Depending on the type of data you want to project, you can choose many different types of charts including column, bar, line, pie, XY, area, doughnut, radar, surface, bubble, stock, cylinder, cone, or pyramid.

▶ Column and bar charts show changes in data over a period a time or show comparisons among individual items.

▶ Line charts show trends over a period of time.

▶ Pie charts are best for displaying the relationship of parts to the whole.

▶ Cone, pyramid, or cylinder charts add a dramatic 3-D effect when showing changes in data over time or when comparing data values.

▶ Stock charts are most effective for showing the high-low-close ratings of stocks.

▶ You can format the Value (Y) or Value (Z) axis to display currency, to represent dollar amounts, change the axis scale, change the text alignment, and change the font.

▶ Titles can be added to a chart and rotated on the axes for clarity.

▶ Labels and values or percentages should be used instead of a legend to identify the series on a pie chart.

▶ You can rotate and tilt the pie chart to create a different visual effect.

▶ You can cut a slice of the pie or explode the entire pie for emphasis.

▶ The colors of individual slices of a pie can be changed.

▶ The plot area displays the actual chart series such as columns, bars, lines, and pie slices.

▶ The plot area can be used to resize the chart within the chart area, and the plot area border can be deleted.

Commands Review

Action	Menu Bar	Shortcut Menu	Toolbar	Task Pane	Keyboard
Add a chart	Insert, Chart Insert, Object, Microsoft Graph Chart	Double-click chart placeholder	📊	Click Title and Chart layout on the Slide Layout task pane under Other Layouts, or click any Content layout on the Slide Layout task pane and then click the Insert 📊 Chart icon	ALT + I, H ALT + I, O
Edit the selected legend	Format, Selected Legend	Right-click legend, Format Legend Double-click legend			ALT + O, E CTRL + 1
Change the chart display	Data, Series in Rows or Series in Columns		📊 📊		ALT + D, R ALT + D, C
Change the chart type	Chart, Chart Type	Right-click series, plot area, or chart area, then Chart Type	📈▾		ALT + C, Y
Format the selected data series	Format, Selected Data Series	Right-click series, Format Data Series Double-click the series object	📝		ALT + O, E CTRL + 1
Format the selected axis	Format, Selected Axis	Right-click axis, Format Axis Double-click the axis	📝		ALT + O, E CTRL + 1
Add axis titles	Chart, Chart Options	Right-click plot area or chart area, Chart Options			ALT + C, I
Display labels and percentages	Chart, Chart Options, Data Labels	Right-click plot area or chart area, Chart Options, Data Labels Double-click the pie object, Data Labels			ALT + C, I
Format the selected data labels	Format, Selected Data Labels	Right-click the data labels, Format Data Labels Double-click any data label	📝		ALT + O, E CTRL + 1
Rotate, tilt, and change the pie height	Chart, 3-D View	Right-click the plot area or chart area, 3-D View			ALT + C, V
Cut a pie slice		Drag the selected pie slice			
Format a selected slice	Format, Selected Data Point	Right-click selected slice, Format Data Point Double-click selected slice	📝		ALT + O, E CTRL + 1
Format selected plot area	Format, Selected Plot Area	Right-click the plot area, Format Plot Area Double-click plot area	📝		ALT + O, E CTRL + 1

chapter six

Concepts Review

SCANS

Circle the correct answer.

1. A chart slide is created by using Microsoft:
[a] Word.
[b] Excel.
[c] Table.
[d] Graph.

2. The name of the form used to input chart values is:
[a] AutoForm.
[b] Microsoft Graph Chart.
[c] Microsoft Excel.
[d] Datasheet.

3. The values entered in a datasheet are displayed on the:
[a] (X) axis.
[b] (Y) or (Z) axis.
[c] legend.
[d] title area.

4. Which of the following formatting options allows you to display dollar signs on the Value axis?
[a] Number
[b] Date and Time
[c] Currency
[d] Percentage

5. Titles can be added to all of the following except the:
[a] (Y) or (Z) axis.
[b] (X) axis.
[c] chart.
[d] gridlines.

6. Charts should be used to display statistical data on a slide to show all of the following *except*:
[a] comparisons.
[b] parts of a whole.
[c] trends.
[d] a bulleted list.

7. A pie chart best displays statistical data using which of the following?
[a] trends over time
[b] comparisons of ten products
[c] comparisons of parts to the whole
[d] comparisons of many different categories of data

8. All of the following may appear near each slice of the pie *except*:
[a] titles.
[b] percentages.
[c] values.
[d] category names.

9. To pull out a slice of a pie:
[a] right-click the selected slice.
[b] drag the selected slice.
[c] double-click the selected slice.
[d] press the CTRL + X keys.

10. The part of a chart slide that holds the actual series objects (columns, bars, pie slices, and so on) created from the datasheet, is the:
[a] plot area.
[b] chart area.
[c] category axis.
[d] legend.

Circle **T** if the statement is true or **F** if the statement is false.

T   F   1. In a chart, a series represents one set of related data.

T   F   2. Double-clicking a chart in PowerPoint enables you to make formatting changes to the chart.

T   F   3. A legend displays the series color and the series name.

T   F   4. All column charts display a Value (Z) axis.

T   F   5. The (X) axis displays the values that were keyed on the datasheet.

T   F   6. A legend should always be used in a pie chart.

T   F   7. You should have as many slices on a pie chart as you desire.

T   F   8. You can display values, percentages, series name, or category name, but not all at one time on a pie chart.

T   F   9. The reason you pull out a slice is usually to emphasize that particular slice of the pie chart.

T   F   10. The plot area of a pie chart is the only element of the chart that cannot be changed.

Skills Review

Exercise 1 C

1. Open the *PowerPoint* presentation you modified in Chapter 5, and add a chart slide at the end of the presentation with the title "Comparing Slide Types."

2. Clear the datasheet of sample data, and complete the chart using the information below:

	Accounting	Marketing
Title	15	30
Bullet	35	50
Table	25	15
Chart	60	40

3. Change the chart to display By Column.

4. Change the location of the legend to the top.

5. Change the color of the Accounting column to display a texture that complements the presentation design and the color of the Marketing column to display a texture that complements the presentation design.

6. Add the following title to the Value axis: "number of slides".

7. Rotate the Value axis title to 90 degrees.

8. Save the presentation, print the chart slide, and then close the presentation.

Exercise 2 C

1. Open the *Office* presentation you modified in Chapter 5, and add a chart slide at the end of the presentation with the title "Daily Office Use."

2. Clear the datasheet of sample data, and complete the chart using the information below:

Word	Excel	PowerPoint	Access	Outlook
80	65	50	40	35

3. Change the chart to a 3-D pie.

4. Hide the legend, and display data labels with category names and percentages.

5. Rotate the pie to 130 degrees.

6. Tilt or elevate the pie to 40 degrees.

7. Remove the plot area border.

8. Pull out the PowerPoint slice.

chapter six

9. Resize the pie chart within the chart area so you can read all the data labels.

10. Save the presentation, print the chart slide, and then close the presentation.

Exercise 3   ©

1. Open the *Design* presentation you modified in Chapter 5, and add a chart slide at the end of the presentation with the title "Design Element Frequency."

2. Clear the datasheet of sample data, and complete the chart using the information below:

Clip Art	*100*
AutoShapes	*75*
Music	*50*
Videos	*25*

3. Change the chart to a 3-D horizontal bar chart.

4. Change the chart to display By Column.

5. Hide the legend.

6. Change the bar fill to either a gradient fill or a texture fill to match the presentation design.

7. Change the wall colors to enhance the bars, and then change the gridline color, if necessary.

8. Add the following title to the Value (Z) axis: "Percentage Used in Presentations."

9. Resize and reposition the chart as needed.

10. Save the presentation, print the chart slide, and then close the presentation.

Exercise 4   ©

1. Open the *Precision Builders* presentation you modified in Chapter 5, and add a chart slide at the end of the presentation with the title "New Homes Built This Year."

2. Clear the datasheet of sample data, and complete the chart using the information below:

Ranch Homes	*Townhomes*	*Two-story Homes*
8	*5*	*10*

3. Change the chart to a 3-D pie chart.

4. Tilt or elevate the pie to 35 degrees.

5. Rotate the pie to 260 degrees.

6. Pull out the Ranch Homes slice of the pie.

7. Hide the legend, and display data labels with category names and percentages.

8. Change the color of all the slices to match the presentation design.

9. Remove the plot area border.

10. Resize and reposition the chart as needed.

11. Resize the labels for readability.

12. Save the presentation, print the chart slide, and then close the presentation.

Exercise 5 [C]

1. Open the *Nature Tours* presentation you modified in Chapter 5, and add a chart slide at the end of the presentation with the title "National Park Visitors."

2. Complete the chart using the information below:

	1998	1999	2000
Glacier	150000	175000	160000
Yellowstone	200200	195000	175000
Rocky Mountain	95000	105000	100000
Teton	75000	80000	85000

3. Select a column chart using cylinders, cones, pyramids, or any other chart type.

4. Add commas (thousands' separators), 0 decimals to the Value axis.

5. Add an appropriate title to the Value axis.

6. Change the font, font style, font color, and font size for the axes labels.

7. Format the legend, and change the position of the legend on the chart.

8. Resize and reposition the chart as needed.

9. Save the presentation, print the chart slide, and then close the presentation.

Exercise 6 [C]

1. Open the *A Healthier You* presentation you modified in Chapter 5, and add a chart slide at the end of the presentation with the title "Books on Nutrition."

2. Complete the chart using the information below:

Diets and You	15000
Today's Foods	35000
Eating Wisely	30000

3. Decide on the type of chart you want to use to show the relationship between the different books on nutrition.

4. Make changes regarding size, position, font, and so forth to the chart.

5. Add the following chart title: "Copies Sold."

6. Save the presentation, print the chart slide, and then close the presentation.

Exercise 7 [C]

1. Open the *Buying A Computer* presentation you modified in Chapter 5, and add a chart slide at the end of the presentation with the title "Home Computer Prices."

2. Complete the chart using the information below:

	1997	1998	1999	2000	2001
Home PCs	3000	2400	1800	1550	1200

3. Use a line chart to show the trend over the past five years.

4. Change the line color and weight.

5. Change the line marker—style, color, shape, and size.

6. Display the legend and format it in regard to location, size, color, and so forth.

chapter six

7. Display currency on the Value axis.

8. Resize and reposition the chart as needed.

9. Save the presentation, print the chart slide, and then close the presentation.

Exercise 8 C

1. Open the *Leisure Travel* presentation you modified in Chapter 5, and add a chart slide at the end of the presentation with the title "Future Cruises."

2. Complete the chart using the information below:

	2001	2002	2003
Aruba	45	50	30
Cancun	50	52	48
Puerto Vallarta	40	30	25
St. Thomas	30	40	30

3. Select an appropriate chart to show future bookings for cruises.

4. Decide whether to compare the years or the locations.

5. Display the legend and format it in regard to location, size, color, and so forth.

6. Add a title on the Value axis.

7. Make any other formatting changes to the chart.

8. Resize and reposition the chart as needed.

9. Save the presentation, print the chart slide, and then close the presentation.

Case Projects

Project 1 C

You want to import a Microsoft Excel chart into a PowerPoint slide. Access the Microsoft Graph online Help, and find information on importing a Microsoft Excel chart. In addition, you want to find out what other file formats Microsoft Graph can import. Print all information, as well as any linked information.

Project 2 C

Communicate Corporation wants employees to know the typical types of customer calls that are handled daily so they can anticipate what to expect when the phone rings. Your manager wants you to create a chart slide for the *Communicate* presentation you modified in Chapter 5 that compares the types of telephone calls received on a daily basis. You decide which chart type best fits your data. Make any formatting changes in regard to size, color, shape, font, and so forth. Save the presentation, print the chart slide, and close the presentation.

Project 3 C

Souner & Associates has been very successful during the past few years. However, the owners want to see how their training company compares with the competition. They ask you to create a chart slide for the *Souner* presentation you modified in Chapter 5 that compares the number of training classes held by Souner & Associates with three competitors for the past year. It is your decision to select an appropriate chart type that reflects your company's position and share in the market. Enhance the chart by formatting and customizing various parts of the chart. Remember that your chart should match your presentation design. Save the presentation, print the chart slide, and close the presentation.

Project 4

As you continue working on your own presentation, you find that a chart slide helps to display and present your data. Create a chart slide for the *My Presentation* you modified in Chapter 5 that provides additional information concerning your topic. Think about comparing, showing trends, or displaying parts of a whole when you create the chart slide. You can select any chart type you desire to present your data. Make any formatting changes you feel necessary. Save the presentation, print the chart slide, and close the presentation.

Project 5

As the season progresses, you want to compare the attendance figures for various exhibits at the zoo. This will help determine staffing needs for next year. Add a chart to the *Zoo* presentation you modified in Chapter 5 listing at least four exhibits and comparing the visitors' attendance. Make the chart as attractive as possible; however, the data must be clearly expressed. Save the presentation, print the chart slide, and close the presentation.

Project 6

You have been using PowerPoint for a few weeks, and you want to find out more information regarding Microsoft Graph Chart. Connect to the Internet and search the Web for new features about Microsoft

Graph Chart. Print the information you find. Create a presentation consisting of a title slide and one or two charts displaying the information you discovered. Save, print, and close the presentation.

Project 7

In the *Cars* presentation that you modified in Chapter 5, you want to compare the sales of the most popular cars on the market today. Connect to the Internet and search the Web for the most popularly sold cars and their current selling prices. You decide on the type of chart slide to add to your presentation. Make any formatting changes and enhancements to help display your message. Save the presentation, print the chart slide, and close the presentation.

Project 8

As an example of how people use various sites on the Internet, you and your partner want to add a chart slide comparing the number of hits (visits) per site in a given period of time. You each choose three Internet sites, and track the number of hits for a two-week period. After that time, you compile your data and show each Internet site and its number of hits. Enhance the chart slide as needed to present your findings in the *Internet* presentation you modified in Chapter 5. Save the presentation, print the chart slide, and close the presentation.

chapter six

Preparing and Running a Slide Show

Chapter Overview

A slide show is a PowerPoint slide presentation that can be viewed on a computer screen or projected onto a large screen by a specially designed projection device connected to the computer. Although you can output PowerPoint slides for use in a slide projector or an overhead projector, running a slide show in PowerPoint lets you control the transition of slides and even add special effects. In this chapter, you learn to run a slide show in PowerPoint, add transitions and animation schemes to slides, enhance transitions with special effects, and set timings to run the slide show automatically.

Case profile

During a meeting with your boss, Ms. Hill, you review the various media options available for the presentation you have been working on for her. Ms. Hill tells you that there will be less than twenty people at the initial presentation. She has learned that the room is equipped with an overhead projection system. Because Ms. Hill has a laptop computer she can use with the overhead projection system, you suggest that she run the presentation as a slide show in PowerPoint.

chapter seven

7.a | Running a Slide Show

You decide to run the slide show of the *Teddy Toys* presentation as it is so you can determine what transitions to add to the slides as they appear on the screen. To run a slide show:

Step 1	*Open*	the *Teddy Toys* presentation you modified in Chapter 6 and display Slide 1
Step 2	*Click*	the Slide Show (from current slide) button

After the "Starting slide show" message appears briefly, the current slide fills the screen. Your screen should look similar to Figure 7-1.

Step 3	*Click*	anywhere on the slide

The second slide appears. Each time you click or press certain keys, the next slide appears. As you progress through the slide show, pay careful attention to how each slide comes on to the screen.

Step 4	*Press*	the PAGE DOWN key to display the next slide
Step 5	*Press*	the RIGHT ARROW key to display the next slide
Step 6	*Press*	the DOWN ARROW key to progress to the next slide
Step 7	*Key*	N to progress to the next slide
Step 8	*Press*	the SPACEBAR to progress to the next slide

FIGURE 7-1
Title Slide in Slide Show

chapter
seven

QUICK TIP

If you move the mouse slightly while in Slide Show, the shortcut icon appears.

You also can press one of several keys to move to previous slides in a presentation. To move to a previous slide in Slide Show:

Step 1	*Press*	the PAGE UP key to move to the previous slide
Step 2	*Press*	the LEFT ARROW key
Step 3	*Press*	the UP ARROW key
Step 4	*Key*	P
Step 5	*Press*	the BACKSPACE key
Step 6	*Press*	the END key to move to the last slide
Step 7	*Press & hold*	both mouse buttons for two seconds to move to the first slide
Step 8	*Press*	the ESCAPE key to end the slide show

Working with Slide Show Options

As you view a slide show, you can click an onscreen icon to open a shortcut menu displaying controls, commands, and options for use during the slide show. To display this shortcut icon initially during a slide show, you simply move the mouse slightly on the screen; the icon then remains on the screen until the slide show ends. This shortcut menu also appears when you right-click anywhere on the screen during a slide show. To display the shortcut icon in Slide Show:

MENU TIP

You can turn off the black slide option by clicking Options on the Tools menu, clicking the View tab, and clicking the End with black slide check box to remove the check mark.

Step 1	*Start*	the slide show from the beginning
Step 2	*Point*	anywhere on the screen
Step 3	*Click*	the shortcut icon at the lower-left corner of the screen

The shortcut menu on your screen should look similar to Figure 7-2.

FIGURE 7-2
Shortcut Menu in
Slide Show

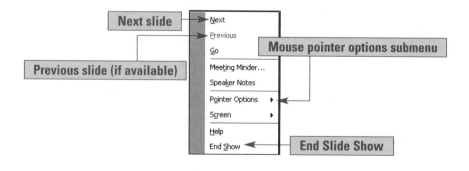

You can move from slide to slide during a presentation by clicking the Next, Previous, and Go commands on this shortcut menu. You also can navigate through a slide show to any desired slide according to its title by clicking the By Title command on the Go submenu.

By default, the mouse pointer in Slide Show appears as an arrow. You can, however, hide the mouse pointer or change the mouse pointer shape to a pen you can use to temporarily write or draw on the slide as it is being viewed in a slide show. To use the pen pointer during a presentation:

Step 1	*Point to*	Pointer Options
Step 2	*Click*	Pen
Step 3	*Press & hold*	the SHIFT key
Step 4	*Draw*	a line under the title text

Pressing the SHIFT key constrains the line you draw to a straight line. Any marks you draw while in slide show appear only in slide show and only while the current slide is displayed. The marks you make are removed as soon as you move to a different slide or end the slide show. You also can remove pen marks on the current slide by pressing the E key. In addition, you can change the color of the pen. To draw circles with a different pen color:

Step 1	*Click*	the shortcut icon
Step 2	*Point to*	Pointer Options
Step 3	*Point to*	Pen Color
Step 4	*Click*	Red
Step 5	*Draw*	a circle around the word "Focusing" and the word "Products"

Your screen should look similar to Figure 7-3.

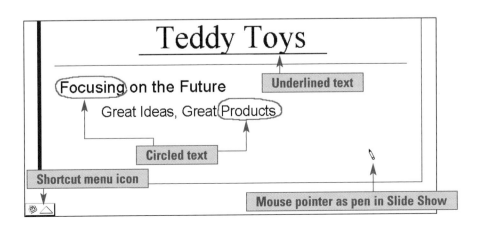

FIGURE 7-3
Pen Options in Slide Show

chapter
seven

To use keyboard shortcuts to remove the line and circles and change the mouse pointer back to the arrow shape:

Step 1	*Press*	the E key to remove all the pen marks
Step 2	*Press*	CTRL + A to change the mouse pointer from a pen to an arrow
Step 3	*Press*	the ESCAPE key to return to Normal view

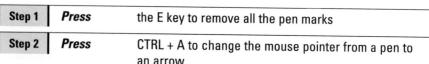

7.b Applying Transition Effects and Animation Schemes

A slide show visually reinforces the ideas, comments, solutions, or suggestions you are presenting. By using creative techniques to move from slide to slide, such as transition effects and animation schemes, you also are conveying to the audience that you and your company use the most creative and innovative methods to achieve your goals.

Applying Transitions

When you run a slide show, each slide replaces the previous slide whenever you click the mouse button or press a key to change slides. You may, however, want to add special effects when moving from one slide to the next in the slide show. **Transitions** are special display effects used to introduce a slide during the slide show. Transitions determine how the display changes as the user progresses from one slide to another. Examples of transitional effects include a slide that wipes down across the screen, a slide that is formed out of a set of blinds closing, and a slide that appears as a spoke turns clockwise, exposing more and more of the slide as the spoke turns.

You can add slide transitions and animation schemes to slides in any of the PowerPoint views except Slide Show. To add transitions and times to slides, you can use the Slide pane, the Slides tab, or Slide Sorter view. You can add transitions to each slide individually, you can add the same transition to multiple slides by preselecting them in the Slides tab, or you can add the same transition to all slides by clicking the Apply to All Slides button in the Slide Transition task pane. To apply transition effects:

Step 1	*Switch to*	Normal view, if necessary
Step 2	*Click*	Slide Show

Step 3	*Click*	Slide Transition
Step 4	*Verify*	that the AutoPreview check box at the bottom of the Slide Transition task pane contains a check mark
Step 5	*Click*	the first effect (Blinds Horizontal) in the Apply to selected slides: list box in the Slide Transition task pane

Your screen should look similar to Figure 7-4.

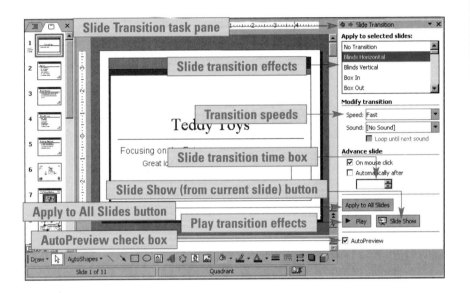

FIGURE 7-4
Slide Transition Task Pane

The slide in Normal view illustrates the effect. To view the effect again, click the transition effect in the Apply to selected slides: list box or click the Play button at the bottom of the Slide Transition task pane. You can try other effects from the Slide Transition effects list in the same way.

Step 6	*Click*	Blinds Vertical
Step 7	*Continue*	to view the remaining transitions, scrolling when necessary
Step 8	*Click*	Newsflash

In addition to changing the transition effect, you can change the speed of the transition effect in the Speed: list box under Modify transition in the Slide Transition task pane. To apply a transition speed to all the slides:

| Step 1 | *Click* | Slow in the Speed: list |

chapter
seven

You like this speed. To apply this transition effect to all slides in the presentation:

Step 2	Click	the Apply to All Slides button in the Slide Transition task pane
Step 3	Display	Slide 1, if necessary
Step 4	Click	the Slide Show button [Slide Show] in the Slide Transition task pane
Step 5	View	each slide in the presentation until you reach the end of the slide show
Step 6	Save	the *Teddy Toys* presentation

Adding Animation Schemes to Slides

Another useful presentation technique is animation. **Animation** is special visual effects that you can add to parts of a slide. Animation effects enable the presenter to direct focus to important points as they are being presented, to control the flow of information to the audience, or to capture the audience's attention. To apply an animation scheme to a text slide:

Step 1	Display	Slide 2
Step 2	Click	Slide Show
Step 3	Click	Animation Schemes

The Slide Design-Animation Schemes task pane opens. Your screen should look similar to Figure 7-5.

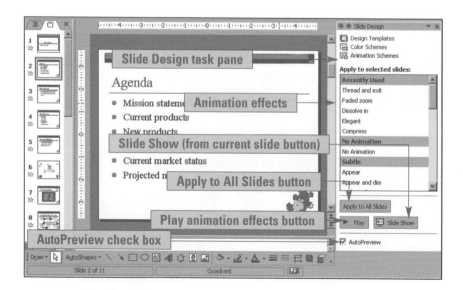

FIGURE 7-5
Animation Schemes in
Slide Design Task Pane

The task pane displays a list box of animation schemes that can be applied to the current slide or to all slides in the presentation. The animation schemes in the Apply to selected slides: list box enable you to pick schemes from the following categories: Recently Used, No animation, Subtle animation, Moderate animation, and Exciting animation.

Step 4	*Click*	Elegant in the Moderate category

A ScreenTip displays when you point to an animation effect indicating the exact Slide Transition, Title, and/or Body effects. If an animation scheme also changes the slide transition, that transition replaces any previously applied transition. You can see the slide transition and animation scheme by clicking the Play button at the bottom of the Slide Design task pane or by clicking the effect in the animation schemes list again.

Step 5	*Click*	several effects in each category and observe the different animation schemes
Step 6	*Click*	the Slide Show button in the Slide Design task pane, and view the animation effects for the current slide
Step 7	*Click*	to view each bullet item

Because the default for progressing through slides is manual progression, you have to click the mouse or press the SPACEBAR, the ENTER key, the PAGE DOWN key, or an ARROW key to see each effect.

Step 8	*Press*	the ESCAPE key after viewing the bullets on the slide to end the slide show
Step 9	*Click*	Elegant in the Moderate category
Step 10	*Click*	the Apply to All Slides button in the Slide Design task pane
Step 11	*Run*	the slide show from the beginning, clicking to progress through each slide and then return to Normal view
Step 12	*Save*	the *Teddy Toys* presentation

7.c Rehearsing Presentations

There are four steps involved in creating presentations: plan, prepare, practice, and present. **Planning** involves establishing the goal of the presentation and researching information to find the essential

DESIGN TIP

All the slides in a presentation should have a similar look and function as a unit. Using the same transition effect on all the slides in a presentation aids in accomplishing this design principle; using a wide assortment of transition effects defeats it. Of course, there are always exceptions to this general rule. The key is to remember your message and your audience and adjust transition effects to them.

Setting timings enables a presenter to appear more natural, polished, and professional, but you must set timings that are appropriate to the time needed for each slide. Therefore, establishing appropriate timings for slides involves plenty of practice.

chapter
seven

facts or concepts to support or establish that goal. **Preparing** involves using presentation graphics software to provide the medium to display that goal. **Practicing** involves learning the material, equipment, and software to present the information. **Presenting** involves the actual conveying of information in an effective and effective manner. PowerPoint provides you with the tools necessary to prepare and practice presentations.

A PowerPoint feature that aids in rehearsing and presenting is the ability to set timings for your slides. When you set **timings** for slides, the slides in the presentation progress from one to the other automatically when running a slide show. You do not have to click the mouse, press the SPACEBAR, or otherwise manually advance the slides. This way, the presenter is not tied to a computer console and can walk around the room while the slides progress when new topics, points, or ideas are being discussed. You can manually set what you consider appropriate timings for the slides and then rehearse the presentation, or you can work with PowerPoint to set timings while you rehearse.

Setting Slide Times Manually

Setting times manually is advisable when you know you have only so many minutes available in which to give a presentation. In this way, when you practice your presentation, you work within the allotted time frame established for each slide.

To manually set slide times in a slide show, you can be in either Normal or Slide Sorter view. In Normal view, you select the slide or slides in the Slides tab. In Slide Sorter view, you can see all the slides of the presentation and then "guesstimate" how long it will take to go over the information on each slide. The time for each slide can be set independently of the others or all slides can be set for the same time.

 notes For purposes of practice, you set minimal times in this chapter. This enables you to view the effects quickly.

To manually set times for individual slides and view the slide show:

Step 1	*Click*	the Other Task Panes list arrow in the Slide Design task pane
Step 2	*Click*	Slide Transition
Step 3	*Display*	Slide 1
Step 4	*Key*	2 in the Automatically after text box
Step 5	*Click*	anywhere on the slide in Normal view

Notice that the time "00:02" appears in the Automatically after text box in the Advance Slide area.

Step 6	*Select*	every even-numbered slide (press and hold the CTRL key as you click each even-numbered slide) in the Slides tab
Step 7	*Key*	4 in the Automatically after text box
Step 8	*Click*	anywhere on the slide in Normal view
Step 9	*Select*	the remaining odd-numbered slides
Step 10	*Key*	2 in the Automatically after text box
Step 11	*Click*	anywhere on the slide in the Normal view
Step 12	*Press*	the F5 key to start the slide show from the beginning

You can now view the slide show from the beginning without clicking the mouse. If you were planning to make this presentation, you could rehearse your comments and see whether you needed to lengthen or shorten any timings.

| Step 13 | *Click* | to end the slide show, if necessary |

Setting Slide Times During Rehearsal Mode

You can also set timings while you rehearse a presentation. It is important to practice timings with the material so that your words match the flow of the presentation. This can be very difficult if you plan to orally present the material with the slide show running with preset times. You need to be extremely familiar with the material and practice it many times to successfully match your words, ideas, and timing with that of the preset times. You can use rehearsal mode to accurately determine the length of a presentation. To set timings while rehearsing:

| Step 1 | *Click* | Slide Show |
| Step 2 | *Click* | Rehearse Timings |

The first slide and the Rehearsal toolbar appear. Your screen should look similar to Figure 7-6. The Rehearsal toolbar includes a Next button for progressing to the next slide, a Pause button to stop the clock, the time spent on each slide, a Repeat button to rehearse a slide again, and the time spent on the total presentation.

DESIGN TIP

Animation schemes work well with title and text slides because each part of the slide can be introduced by itself.

CAUTION TIP

Setting times to a slide show should only be done after much practice by a presenter who is sure of the time required for each slide. Inexperienced presenters often have more success by manually progressing through a presentation.
Do not click the Apply to All Slides button in the Slide Transition task pane unless you want the same time applied to all the slides.

MOUSE TIP

You can start rehearsing timings in Slide Sorter view by clicking the Rehearse Timings button on the Slide Sorter toolbar.

chapter seven

FIGURE 7-6
Rehearsal Toolbar in
Slide Show

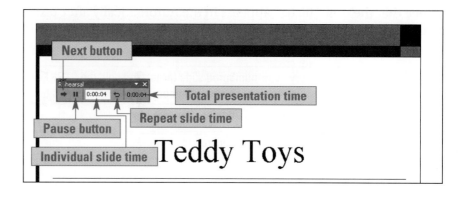

Step 3	*Click*	the Next button on the Rehearsal toolbar after the time clock displays 2 to 4 seconds for each bullet and/or slide
Step 4	*Click*	Yes in the dialog box displaying the total time for the presentation

After you accept the new slide show timings, PowerPoint displays
the slides in Slide Sorter view.

The times displayed below the slides in Slide Sorter view for your
presentation are the times you set during your rehearsal. Your screen
should look similar to Figure 7-7, though your times may vary. You can
rehearse the material again at any time and set new times.

FIGURE 7-7
Slide Sorter View with
Rehearsal Times

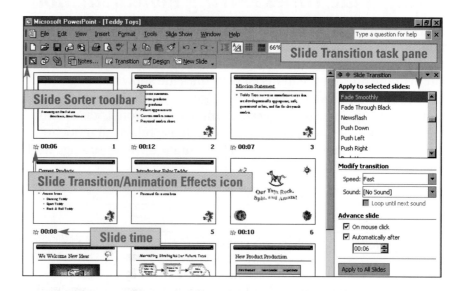

To cycle through all the slides quickly, you decide to change the times
for all the slides to 4 seconds. To apply the same time to all the slides:

Step 1	*Key*	4 in the Automatically after text box

Step 2	*Click*	the Apply to All Slides button in the Slide Transition task pane
Step 3	*Run*	the slide show
Step 4	*Save*	the *Teddy Toys* presentation

7.d Preparing Slide Shows for Delivery

Slide Sorter view is a good view for adding transitions, animation schemes, and times. In addition, this view is ideal for rearranging and managing the slides in your presentation. Because your presentations may consist of many slides, it is easier to move, copy, hide, and delete the slides when they are displayed in Slide Sorter view than when in Normal view.

Changing the Order of Slides

Moving a slide from one location to another within a presentation, or from one presentation to another, is a common task when managing presentations. After practicing a presentation or giving a presentation for the first time, you may need to rearrange slides to match your flow of thought or maintain a logical progression. In Slide Sorter view, you can move the slide miniatures as you would any object to rearrange them. To change the order of slides in Slide Sorter view:

Step 1	*Select*	any slide in the presentation
Step 2	*Drag*	the selected slide to the right of the next slide
Step 3	*Drag*	the last slide to the left of the first slide of the presentation
Step 4	*Click*	the Undo button ↺ on the Standard toolbar twice

As you drag the slide, a vertical line and the Move arrow ⬚ are displayed to the right of the slide to indicate where the slide will be repositioned. When you release the mouse button, the move is complete.

QUICK TIP

You can undo an action by pressing the CTRL + Z keys. You can redo an action by pressing the CTRL +Y keys.

QUICK TIP

You can select multiple slides in Slide Sorter view by holding down the SHIFT or CTRL key and clicking each slide. The SHIFT key enables you to select slides in a continuous order, whereas the CTRL key enables you to select slides individually, in no particular order.

You can select all slides in Slide Sorter view by pressing the CTRL + A keys.

chapter
seven

Copying Slides in Slide Sorter View

Copying slides in Slide Sorter view involves the same techniques as copying any object. You can use the menu, toolbar, and mouse methods to copy slides within a presentation. To copy a slide in Slide Sorter view:

Step 1	*Right-click*	any slide in the presentation
Step 2	*Click*	Copy
Step 3	*Right-click*	to the right of the last slide in the presentation
Step 4	*Click*	Paste

You have created a copy of the slide. The copied slide has the same transition and time as the original slide.

Deleting Slides

When viewing a presentation in Slide Sorter view, you may decide that a slide or slides do not work well within the presentation or are no longer necessary to the goal of the presentation. When that happens, you need to delete slides. Again, because the miniature slides are objects, you delete them just as you would delete any object. To delete slides in the Slide Sorter view:

Step 1	*Select*	the copied slide and the Our Toys Rock, Spin, and Amaze! slide
Step 2	*Press*	the DELETE key

Hiding Slides

Sometimes you may need to give a presentation to two different groups. Because the groups are different, you may not want to show all the slides in each presentation. When this happens, it is not necessary to delete the slide or slides for the next group. Instead, you can **hide** a slide or slides for a particular presentation. Then, if you wish to use the entire presentation again, you simply show or **unhide** the slide or slides.

To hide slides in Slide Sorter view:

| Step 1 | *Select* | the New Product Production and the Introducing Baby Teddy slides |
| Step 2 | *Click* | the Hide Slide button 🔲 on the Slide Sorter toolbar |

An icon displays under the lower-right corner of each slide with a diagonal line covering the slide number, indicating that the slide is hidden.

| Step 3 | *Run* | the slide show from the beginning and observe that the hidden slides do not appear |

To show or unhide slides in Slide Sorter view:

Step 1	*Select*	the hidden slides, if necessary
Step 2	*Click*	the Hide Slide button 🔲 on the Slide Sorter toolbar
Step 3	*Save*	the *Teddy Toys* presentation

Removing Transitions, Animation Effects, and Timings

Transitions, animations, and timings can be removed while in Slide Sorter or Normal view using the Slide Design and Slide Transition task panes. To remove transitions, animations, and timings:

Step 1	*Click*	the Slide Transition button 🔳 Transition on the Slide Sorter toolbar
Step 2	*Click*	No Transition in the Apply to selected slides: list box in the Slide Transition task pane
Step 3	*Click*	the Automatically after check box to remove the check mark
Step 4	*Click*	the Apply to All Slides button in the Slide Transition task pane
Step 5	*Click*	the Other Task Panes list arrow in the Slide Transition task pane
Step 6	*Click*	Slide Design - Animation Schemes
Step 7	*Click*	No Animation in the No Animation section in the Apply to selected slides: list box
Step 8	*Click*	the Apply to All Slides button in the Slide Design task pane
Step 9	*Save*	the *Teddy Toys* presentation

chapter
seven

C   7.e   Creating a New Blank Presentation from Existing Slides

You can create a new presentation by moving or copying existing slides from another presentation and then saving the new presentation. Any slide copied or moved from one presentation to another is formatted based on the design template of the destination presentation. To create a new presentation from existing slides:

Step 1	*Verify*	that the presentation is in Slide Sorter view
Step 2	*Click*	the New button on the Standard toolbar to create a new, blank presentation
Step 3	*Key*	Teddy Toys Products in the title placeholder
Step 4	*Key*	Striving for Customer Satisfaction in the subtitle placeholder
Step 5	*Click*	the Slide Design button Design on the Formatting toolbar
Step 6	*Click*	the Crayons design template
Step 7	*Click*	the Slide Sorter View button
Step 8	*Click*	Window
Step 9	*Click*	Arrange All

The presentations are arranged side by side. This makes it easier to copy slides. Your screen should look similar to Figure 7-8.

FIGURE 7-8
Side-by-Side Presentations in Slide Sorter View

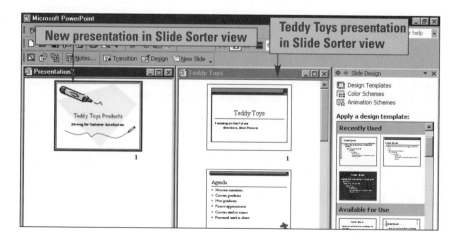

Step 10	**Click**	in the Teddy Toys window to activate the Teddy Toys presentation
Step 11	**Select**	the following Mission Statement, Current Products, Introducing Baby Teddy, and We Welcome New Ideas slides
Step 12	**Drag**	the selected slides to the new presentation window (see Figure 7-9 for placement)

When you drag to copy, the mouse pointer displays a rectangle at the lower-right corner of the mouse and a + sign at the upper-right corner of the mouse. This indicates that you are copying, not moving the slides. A vertical guide indicates the position of the moved or copied slide or slides. Your screen should look similar to Figure 7-9.

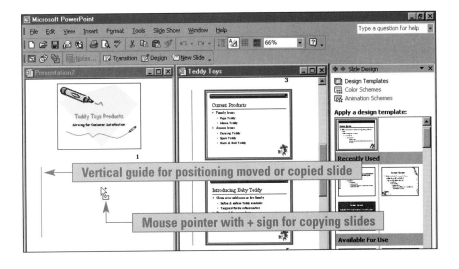

FIGURE 7-9
Mouse Pointer for Copying Slides

| Step 13 | **Release** | the mouse button when a vertical guide appears in the new presentation window under the title slide |

Because your newly created presentation used the Crayons design template, the copied slides no longer retain the formatting of the Quadrant design template. A Smart Tag, the Paste Options button, appears in the newly created presentation that enables you to Keep Source Formatting (the Quadrant design template formatting) or Use Design Template Formatting (the Crayons design template formatting).

| Step 14 | **Save** | the new presentation as *Teddy Toys Products* |
| Step 15 | **Close** | both presentations |

Copying slides from an existing presentation is a quick way to create a new presentation.

MOUSE TIP

You can copy or move a slide or slides from one presentation to another in Slide Sorter view by selecting the slide or slides you want to copy or move and then right-clicking the selected slide or slides and then clicking Copy or Cut. To paste the copied or cut slide or slides in a different presentation, right-click in front of the slide where you want to place the moved or copied slide or slides, and then click Paste.

Summary

▶ A slide show is a computer-based slide presentation that can be viewed on a computer monitor or projected onto a large screen.

▶ Transitions are special effects that introduce slides in Slide Show.

▶ PowerPoint offers a variety of effects for transitions.

▶ You can change the speed at which a transition appears from slow to medium or fast.

▶ Animations are special visual effects that can be added to parts of the slides.

▶ Animation schemes allow the presenter to focus on important points, control the flow of information, and capture the audience's attention.

▶ Setting times to the slides in a presentation can be done before rehearsing the presentation or as you rehearse the presentation.

▶ Setting times to the slides in a presentation allows the presentation to run in Slide Show without clicking the mouse.

▶ You can create a new presentation using slides in an existing presentation.

▶ You can move, copy, hide, and delete slides in Slide Sorter view.

▶ You can move and copy slides from one presentation to another.

Commands Review

Action	Menu Bar	Shortcut Menu	Toolbar	Task Pane	Keyboard
View slide show from the beginning	Slide Show, View Show; View, Slide Show				ALT + D, V ALT + V, W F5
View slide show from current slide			🖵	▣ Slide Show on Slide Design-Animation Schemes or Slide Transition task pane	
Move to the next slide in the slide show		Right-click slide, Next	📇 △ , Next		PAGE DOWN, RIGHT or DOWN ARROW, N, SPACEBAR, ENTER
Move to the previous slide in the slide show		Right-click slide, Previous	📇 △ , Previous		PAGE UP, LEFT or UP ARROW, P, BACKSPACE
End a slide show		Right-click slide, End Show	📇 △ , End Show		ESCAPE, HYPHEN

Action	Menu Bar	Shortcut Menu	Toolbar	Task Pane	Keyboard
Display the Slide Transition task pane	Slide Show, Slide Transition	Right-click empty area on slide, Slide Transition		▼, Slide Transition	ALT + D, T
Set transitions	Slide Show, Slide Transition	Right-click slide in Slide Sorter view, Slide Transition	🔁 Transition on Slide Sorter toolbar	ALT + D, T	
Display the Slide Design-Animation Schemes task pane	Slide Show, Animation Schemes	Right-click empty area on slide, Slide Design, then click Animation Schemes on the Slide Design task pane; Right-click slide in Slide Sorter view; Animation Schemes		▼, Slide Design - Animation Schemes	ALT + D, C
Add animation schemes	Slide Show, Animation Schemes				ALT + D, C
Set times to slides rehearsing	Slide Show, Rehearse Timings		⚙ on Slide Sorter toolbar		ALT + D, R
Set times to slides before rehearsal	Slide Show, Slide Transition	Right-click slide in Slide Sorter view, Slide Transition			ALT + D, T
Move slides in Slide Sorter view	Edit, Cut; position cursor; Edit, Paste	Right-click slide, Cut; right-click, Paste; Right-drag slide, Move	✂ 📋		ALT + E, T; then ALT + E, P CTRL + X; then CTRL + V
Copy slides in Slide Sorter view	Edit, Copy; position cursor; Edit, Paste	Right-click slide, Copy, right-click, Paste; Right-drag slide, Copy	📋 📋		ALT + E, C; then ALT + E, P CTRL + C; then CTRL + V
Hide and unhide slides in Slide Sorter view	Slide Show, Hide Slide	Right-click slide, Hide Slide	🔲		ALT + D, H
Delete selected slides in Slide Sorter view	Edit, Delete Slide	Right-click slide, Delete Slide			ALT + E, D DELETE
Delete selected slide in Normal view	Edit, Delete Slide				ALT + E, D DELETE

Concepts Review

Circle the correct answer.

1. **You cannot advance slides in Slide Show with:**
   [a] the mouse button.
   [b] the ENTER key.
   [c] the SPACEBAR.
   [d] the ESCAPE key.

2. **Slide show options available to the presenter include all of the following except:**
   [a] navigation commands.
   [b] Pointer Options.
   [c] End Show.
   [d] Transitions command.

3. **You can show the shortcut menu during the slide show by:**
   [a] clicking the title area of the current slide.
   [b] right-clicking the current slide.

   [c] clicking the Shortcut button on the Formatting toolbar.
   [d] clicking the Shortcut icon at the bottom right of the slide.

4. **Special effects that are applied to a slide to introduce the slides in a presentation are called:**
   [a] animation schemes.
   [b] transitions.
   [c] special effects.
   [d] predesigned effects.

chapter seven

5. The best view for setting transition effects for all slides in a presentation is:
[a] Outline view.
[b] Transition view.
[c] Notes Pages view.
[d] Normal view.

6. You would use animation schemes to:
[a] show bullet items as they are discussed.
[b] add times to selected slides.
[c] add clip art images to your slides.
[d] customize animation effects.

7. Which of the following is not a transition effect?
[a] Blinds Vertical
[b] Fade Through Black
[c] Dissolve
[d] Blinds Diagonal

8. Which of the following features allows you to view slides in a slide show without manually advancing each slide?
[a] adding transitions
[b] setting slide times
[c] adding build effects
[d] setting animation schemes

9. To select several nonadjacent slides in Slide Sorter view or in the Slides tab:
[a] CTRL + Click each slide.
[b] SHIFT + Click each slide.
[c] CTRL + SHIFT click each slide.
[d] ALT + Click each slide.

10. Which of the following does *not* allow you to add times to the slides in a presentation?
[a] Slide Transition button
[b] Rehearse Timings button
[c] Slide Show menu
[d] Animation Schemes list box

Circle **T** if the statement is true or **F** if the statement is false.

T   F   1. The shortcut icon in Slide Show is located at the lower-right corner of the screen.

T   F   2. Slide shows should be center stage in your presentation.

T   F   3. Using a variety of transition effects on each slide of the presentation contributes to the cohesiveness of your presentation.

T   F   4. Transition effects control the flow of information in a presentation.

T   F   5. Slide shows are a visual medium; therefore, sound is never used.

T   F   6. You must apply transition effects, slide times, and animation schemes to only one slide at a time.

T   F   7. The speed of transition effects can be adjusted from slow, to medium, and fast.

T   F   8. There are only a few animation schemes that can be applied to your slides.

T   F   9. After rehearsing timings, you are given an option of accepting or rejecting the rehearsed times.

T   F   10. Hidden slides are hidden in both Slide Show and Slide Sorter view.

Skills Review

Exercise 1

1. Open the *PowerPoint* presentation you modified in Chapter 6.

2. Using the Slide Transition task pane, apply a transition effect to all the slides.

3. Add an animation scheme to any title and text slides by accessing the Slide Design–Animation Schemes task pane and selecting an animation scheme.

4. Set times to the slides in the presentation using the Rehearse Timings button in Slide Sorter view.

5. Run the slide show. Save and close the presentation.

Exercise 2 [C]

1. Open the *Office* presentation you modified in Chapter 6.
2. Use the Slide Transition task pane to select the Wipe Right effect, and apply that effect to all the slides in the presentation.
3. Use the Animation Schemes list box to apply the Wipe animation effect to the title and text slides in your presentation.
4. Add different slide times to slides in the presentation.
5. Run the slide show. Save and close the presentation.

Exercise 3 [C]

1. Open the *Design* presentation you modified in Chapter 6.
2. Use the Slide Transition task pane to apply the Wheel Clockwise, 1 Spoke effect, using medium speed, to all the slides in the presentation.
3. Use the Animation Scheme list box to apply the Spin animation effect to the title and text slides in your presentation, and then observe the change in the slide transitions.
4. Add the same slide times to all slides in the presentation by selecting all slides and using the slide time text box.
5. Move the Basic Color Tips slide to the fourth position (before the WordArt slide).
6. Run the slide show. Save and close the presentation.

Exercise 4 [C]

1. Open the *Precision Builders* presentation you modified in Chapter 6.
2. Add the Box Out effect for the transition to each of the slides in the presentation.
3. Add the Zoom animation scheme to the title and the two title and text slides in the presentation.
4. Add different slide times to slides in the presentation.
5. Hide the WordArt slide.
6. Run the slide show.
7. Show the WordArt slide.
8. Save the presentation. With the *Precision Builders* presentation still open, create a new presentation.
9. Apply the Balance design template to the new presentation.
10. Add the title "Builders of Distinction." Add the subtitle: "Your Name, President."
11. Using Slide Sorter view, arrange the windows to view both presentations, and copy the three slides with clip art and AutoShapes from the *Precision Builders* presentation to the new presentation, keeping the Balance design template.
12. Add transitions to the slides in the new presentation. Run the slide show.
13. Save the new presentation as *Distinctive Designs*. Close both presentations.

Exercise 5 [C]

1. Open the *Nature Tours* presentation you modified in Chapter 6, and display the slides in Slide Sorter view.
2. Add a transition effect to all of the slides in the presentation.
3. Move the WordArt slide to the right of the title slide.
4. Add an animation scheme to one or more title and text slides.
5. Add times to the slides in the presentation using the Rehearse Timings button.
6. Hide the AutoShapes slide.
7. Run the slide show.
8. Change the pen color in Slide Show, and use the pen on various slides in the slide show.
9. Unhide the hidden slide.
10. Run the slide show. Save and close the presentation.

chapter seven

Exercise 6

1. Open the *A Healthier You* presentation you modified in Chapter 6, and display the slides in Slide Sorter view.
2. Add transitions to all the slides and an animation scheme to the title and text slides in the presentation.
3. Add different slide times to slides in the presentation using the Slide Transition task pane.
4. Make two copies of any slide in the presentation, and place one copy at the beginning of the presentation and one copy at the end of the presentation.
5. Run the slide show.
6. Delete the copied slides.
7. Move the WordArt slide to the right of the title slide.
8. Run the slide show. Save and close the presentation.

Exercise 7

1. Open the *Buying A Computer* presentation you modified in Chapter 6.
2. Add transitions to all the slides in the presentation.
3. Add an animation scheme to the title and text slides.
4. Add the same slide times to slides in the presentation.
5. Rearrange the slides in a different but logical sequence.
6. Run the slide show. Save and close the presentation.

Exercise 8

1. Open the *Leisure Travel* presentation you modified in Chapter 6, and display the slides in Slide Sorter view.
2. Add a slow transition to all the slides.
3. Add times to slides in the presentation using the Rehearse Timings button.
4. Rearrange the slides in a different but logical sequence.
5. Run the slide show.
6. Save the *Leisure Travel* presentation, and keep it open.
7. Create a new presentation, and save it as *Travel Ideas*.
8. Add the title "Travel Ideas" and the subtitle "By (press ENTER) Leisure Travel."
9. Copy the two slides with WordArt and AutoShapes from the *Leisure Travel* presentation to the *Travel Ideas* presentation.
10. Apply a presentation design template to the *Travel Ideas* presentation.
11. Add a transition to all the slides in the *Travel Ideas* presentation, and run the slide show.
12. Save the *Travel Ideas* presentation, and close both presentations.

Case Projects

Project 1

Your immediate supervisor has asked you about the Custom Shows command on the Slide Show menu. Using online Help, search for information about Custom Shows. Print the information you find, including all the linked information.

Project 2

The Director of Human Relations has asked to see the *Communicate* presentation you modified in Chapter 6 displayed as a slide show. You decide to add transition and animation effects to the presentation. Experiment with different effects to find the one that best fits the presentation. After completing the effects, practice setting times to the slides using the presentation-rehearsal method so that you can show her how to set times for the slides and make a decision as to whether or not she would prefer the slide show to run automatically or manually. Save the presentation.

Project 3

Your employer informs asks you to add different transitions to the *Souner* presentation you modified in Chapter 6 and she wants those transitions to be obvious to the audience. Your employer understands that you can assign times to the slides so that they automatically progress as she presents the material. She asks you not to add times. Because she is not that comfortable with the process, she wants to manually progress through the slide show. She also wants to use more than one method for progressing through the slides. Review the various methods of viewing the next and previous slides. When you are done reviewing, add transition to all the slides and an animation scheme to the text slides. Save the presentation.

Project 4

You just learned about transitions, animation schemes, and times for slide shows, and you want to practice what you learned on your *My Presentation* presentation you modified in Chapter 6. As you practice, review the various transition and animation schemes. Remember to use the same effect on all slides for consistency. Rearrange the slides in a different but logical sequence. Hide a slide of your choice. Practice giving the presentation using the Rehearsal Mode feature. Save the presentation.

Project 5

Children's Day is rapidly approaching. Your employer wants to welcome the children by presenting the information in the *Zoo* presentation you modified in Chapter 6. There will be a projection system hooked up to a computer in the room where children will view the presentation. You want to add some special effects to the presentation. Add transitions, an animation scheme, and times to the *Zoo* presentation. If necessary, rearrange the order of the slides. Save the presentation.

Project 6

You are excited about what you have learned so far about slide shows, and you want to know more. Connect to the Internet and search the Web for the words "slide show" to find more information about this medium for presentation. View a slide show of your choice, and print at least one or two slides of the selected presentation.

Project 7

As an instructor, you realize that it is very important to keep the students' attention as you present information. After learning about slide transitions, you find it extremely important to add slide transitions so the students keep their attention focused on the *Cars* presentation you modified in Chapter 6. You decide to add transitions to all the slides in the presentation as well as an animation scheme to many of the slides. Connect to the Internet and search the Web for slide shows of other presentations to determine how to make your presentation stand out. Save the presentation.

Project 8

Your professor asks to see the *Internet* presentation you modified in Chapter 6. You and your partner think that adding transitions and an animation scheme to the title and text slides will further impress the professor with what you have done thus far. Both you and your partner are comfortable with transitions and animation, but you want to find more information about slide shows. You connect to the Internet and search the Web for additional research. Make sure that the transitions and animations you select fit the goal of the presentation. The professor wants the presentation to be interesting, but the transition effects should not overpower the topic presented. This presentation will be used for two different level classes. Your professor wants you to create a new presentation from the existing slides and save it as *Internet Level II*. Apply a different presentation design and hide at least two slides in the *Internet Level II* presentation. Save the presentation.

chapter seven

Preparing, Previewing, and Printing Presentation Documents

Chapter Overview

▶ **Prepare speaker notes**
▶ **Prepare audience handouts**
▶ **Preview a presentation**
▶ **Print presentation documents**

There are many ways to ensure the success of your PowerPoint presentations with helpful support materials. In this chapter, you learn how to create and customize speaker notes for presenters and handouts for audience members. You also learn to preview all types of presentation materials, such as individual slides, outlines, notes pages, and audience handouts, to ensure they look the way you want when printed. Finally, you learn about the different options you have for printing these materials.

Case profile

Ms. Hill gives you some individual notes for certain slides in the *Teddy Toys* presentation. She wants you to create notes pages to accompany her presentation. In addition, she wants you to distribute handouts that display the slides, the name of the presentation, and her name so that members of the meeting have a hard copy of the presentation to which they can refer during the presentation.

**chapter
eight**

8.a Preparing Speaker Notes

Speaker notes consist of information the presenter needs to remember during a presentation. **Notes pages** are printouts that contain a picture of a slide along with the speaker notes for that slide, so a presenter can quickly refer to them during a presentation as each slide appears in the slide show. The audience sees the slides in the presentation, while the presenter glances at the printed notes page. In PowerPoint, a notes pane automatically accompanies each slide in Normal view, allowing you to key notes for each slide. You can key speaker notes either in Notes Page view, which displays a small miniature of the slide in the top section and a large notes pane, or in the notes pane located below the slide pane in Normal view. You edit and format the notes in a notes page in the same way that you work with any other text box or placeholder on a slide. To change to Notes Page view and create speaker notes for a slide:

Step 1	*Open*	the *Teddy Toys* presentation you modified in Chapter 7 and display Slide 1 in Normal view
Step 2	*Click*	View
Step 3	*Click*	Notes Page

Notes Page view displays a reduced view of the slide at the top of the page with a notes pane below it for any notes regarding this slide. The **notes pane** is a text box where you key the lecture or speaker notes for the first slide. Your screen should look similar to Figure 8-1.

FIGURE 8-1
Notes Page View

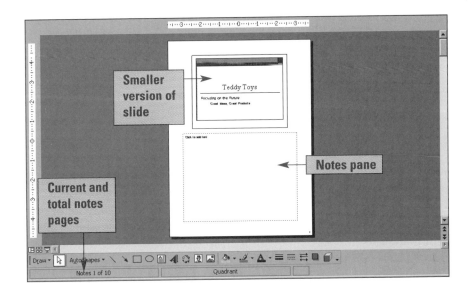

MENU TIP

You can access Notes Page view by clicking the Notes Page command on the View menu.

You can open the Notes Layout dialog box in Notes Page view by clicking the Notes Layout command on the Format menu.

You can open the Zoom dialog box by clicking the Zoom command on the View menu.

It is advisable to zoom in so that you can see the text as you key.

Step 4	*Click*	the Zoom button list arrow on the Standard toolbar
Step 5	*Click*	75%
Step 6	*Click*	the "Click to add text" placeholder
Step 7	*Key*	Thank all participants for attending the meeting.
Step 8	*Press*	the ENTER key twice
Step 9	*Key*	Be sure to show the new Baby Teddy and distribute one to each of the participants. Indicate that they will be able to pick up additional bears for their sales reps when they leave the meeting.
Step 10	*Click*	the Next Slide button on the vertical scroll bar
Step 11	*Click*	the "Click to add text" placeholder for Slide 2
Step 12	*Key*	Briefly highlight what will be covered in today's meeting. Remind participants that old, current, and new products are what determine market share.
Step 13	*Continue*	to key the following notes text in the notes pages: Notes page 3 (Mission Statement): Reiterate that the mission statement guides everything done at Teddy Toys. Teddy Toys wants parents to believe, and rightfully so, that any toy manufactured by Teddy Toys can be trusted to be appropriate for the intended ages, that no harm will come to their children when playing with the toys, that the toys will last, and that the fun will continue from their first child to their last child. Notes page 8 (New Product Production): Discuss the new schedule for producing the four new products. Introduce the team leaders and emphasize the importance of meeting the deadlines.
Step 14	*Spell check*	the notes pages
Step 15	*Save*	the *Teddy Toys* presentation

Working with the Notes Master

Just as the slide master controls the formatting, color, and graphic elements for the slides in a presentation, the notes master serves as a template for notes pages. The **notes master** determines the layout of the placeholders, typeface, font, and style of text on the page, as well as any additional items the presenter wants printed on every page. Additional items you can add are clip art images, text, headers and footers, and page numbers. If you add an item to a notes page, it appears only on that particular notes page in Notes Page view and on the printed page.

INTERNET TIP

Speaker notes can be used for a different purpose for presentations that you broadcast over the Internet. When you save a presentation as a Web page, you can display speaker notes on the screen below each slide; the effect is similar to viewing a presentation in Normal view. These notes can give your viewing audience the background and details that they would receive during a live presentation.

However, if you add an item to the notes master, it appears on every notes page in Notes Page view and on every printed page.

To add text and an image on the notes master:

Step 1	*Click*	View
Step 2	*Point to*	Master
Step 3	*Click*	Notes Master
Step 4	*Scroll*	to the top of the notes master

Your screen should look similar to Figure 8-2. The Notes Master View toolbar appears. You can click the Notes Master Layout button to open the Notes Master Layout dialog box. Here you can redisplay any deleted placeholders. Clicking the Close Master View button closes Notes Master view and returns you to Notes Page view.

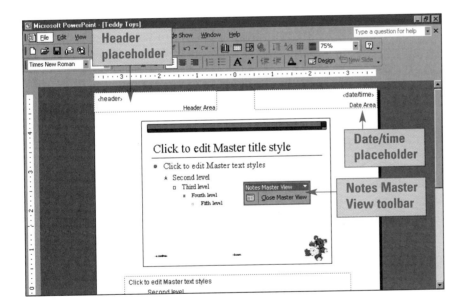

Step 5	*Click*	the <header> text placeholder in the Header Area text box
Step 6	*Key*	Teddy Toys
Step 7	*Scroll*	to the bottom of the notes master
Step 8	*Click*	the <footer> text placeholder in the Footer Area text box
Step 9	*Key*	Sandra Hill
Step 10	*Click*	the Insert Picture button 🖼 on the Drawing toolbar

FIGURE 8-2
Notes Master View with Notes Master View Toolbar

chapter
eight

Step 11	*Switch to*	the Data Disk
Step 12	*Double-click*	the *teddybear.wmf* graphics file
Step 13	*Drag*	the teddy bear image to the upper-right corner of the notes master
Step 14	*Flip*	the teddy bear image horizontally so it faces the miniature slide
Step 15	*Click*	the Close Master View button Close Master View on the Notes Master View toolbar
Step 16	*Save*	the *Teddy Toys* presentation

C 8.b Preparing Audience Handouts

PowerPoint provides the option of printing **handouts**, pages that contain a selected number of miniature slides of your presentation. Handouts provide your audience with reference materials during and after your presentation. They make it easier for your audience to concentrate on watching and listening to your presentation and provide them with a convenient place for taking any additional notes.

Working with the Handout Master

Just as notes pages have a master to control the formatting, color, and graphic elements for the notes pages, so do handouts. The **handout master** serves as a template for the placeholders, typeface, font, and style of text on handout pages, as well as on printed outline pages. You can add clip art images, text, headers and footers, page numbers, and other items to a handout master. These items print on each handout, but do not print on each slide. To add text to a handout master:

Step 1	*Point to*	the Slide Sorter View button ⊞
Step 2	*Press & hold*	the SHIFT key until the ScreenTip displays Handout Master View
Step 3	*Click*	the Handout Master View button ⊞
Step 4	*Click*	the Show positioning of 6-per-page handouts button ⊞ on the Handout Master View toolbar, if necessary

The handout master displays with a Handout Master View toolbar. Your screen should look similar to Figure 8-3. The toolbar contains buttons for printing two, three, four, six, or nine slides per page, as well as an outline layout. The outline layout displays only the text of a presentation in an outline format, excluding any design templates or graphic images. It provides a quick reference to the title and bullet text items displayed on slides in a presentation. The handout master contains placeholders for a header, footer, date, and page number.

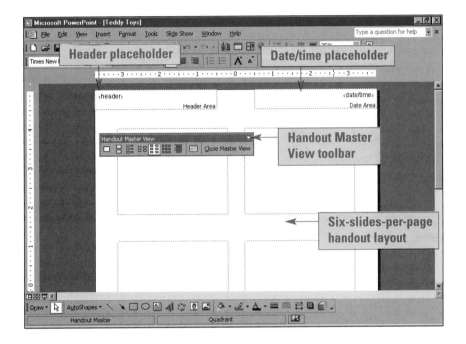

FIGURE 8-3
Handout Master with Handout Master View Toolbar

To add text to all pages of the handout:

Step 1	*Click*	the \<header\> text placeholder in the Header Area text box
Step 2	*Key*	Teddy Toys
Step 3	*Click*	the \<date/time\> text placeholder in the Date Area text box
Step 4	*Click*	Insert
Step 5	*Click*	Date and Time
Step 6	*Click*	the Update automatically check box so that the presentation displays the current date each time it is opened and printed
Step 7	*Double-click*	the fourth date format
Step 8	*Click*	the Close Master View button Close Master View on the Handout Master View toolbar
Step 9	*Save*	the *Teddy Toys* presentation

chapter eight

MOUSE TIP

You can click the Normal View or Slide Sorter View buttons to close the handout master or the notes master and return to the desired view.

CAUTION TIP

You can restore placeholders that were deleted on the handout master by right-clicking anywhere in Handout Master view, clicking the Handout Master Layout command on the shortcut menu, and then clicking the appropriate placeholder check box. You can restore placeholders that were deleted on the notes master by right-clicking anywhere in Notes Master view, clicking the Notes Master Layout command on the shortcut menu, and then clicking the appropriate placeholder check box.

8.c Previewing a Presentation

Most PowerPoint presentations are designed to display in color in Normal view. However, when you print handouts and/or slides to a black and white printer, PowerPoint prints in grayscale. PowerPoint provides the option of viewing slides in grayscale or pure black and white, instead of color, while working on slides in Normal view. The Color/Grayscale button on the Standard toolbar displays options for viewing a presentation in grayscale or black and white when the design template may appear too dark while keying or formatting. To view a presentation in grayscale or black and white, you can be in any view except Slide Show. When viewing slides in Slide Show, slides are always displayed in color. To view a presentation in black and white in Normal view:

Step 1	*Display*	Slide 1 in Normal view
Step 2	*Click*	the Color/Grayscale button 🔲 on the Standard toolbar
Step 3	*Click*	Grayscale
Step 4	*Click*	the Next Slide button ⬇ on the vertical scroll bar to view each of the slides
Step 5	*Run*	the slide show to view the slides in color
Step 6	*Click*	the Close Grayscale View button [Close Grayscale View] on the Grayscale View toolbar

Working in Print Preview

Before sending any PowerPoint presentation to the printer, you can **preview** it to see how the presentation will look in printed form. When you preview a presentation, you have many different options for viewing and printing presentation materials, such as slides, handouts, notes pages, and an outline.

You can make a few global changes to a presentation in Print Preview, such as adding a header or footer and changing the scale of a presentation to fit on the paper, but you cannot edit other presentation elements in the Print Preview window. This view is most useful for viewing different output formats and making sure your printed presentation looks the way you want. If your computer is connected to a color printer, your presentation appears in color; you can change options in print preview to color, grayscale, or pure black and white. If your computer is connected to a black and white printer, your preview appears in grayscale or pure black and white. The Color (On Black and White Printer) option in Print Preview displays the presentation in black and white. You want to preview the slides before printing. To preview a presentation as slides:

Step 1	*Display*	Slide 1, if necessary
Step 2	*Click*	the Print Preview button 🔲 on the Standard toolbar

The Print Preview window opens and displays the title slide. You can navigate in Print Preview by clicking the Previous Page and Next Page buttons on the Print Preview toolbar. You can print slides, handouts, notes pages, and an outline view directly from this window. You can add a Header or Footer, Scale to Fit Paper, Frame Slides, Print Hidden Slides, Include Comment Pages, and change the Printing Order in the Options list box in the Print Preview window. When previewing handouts, notes pages, or an outline view of your presentation, you can change the page orientation from portrait to landscape.

Your screen should look similar to Figure 8-4.

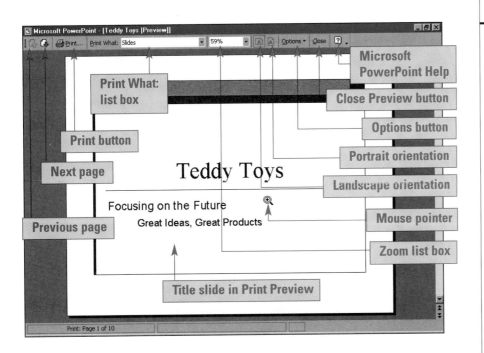

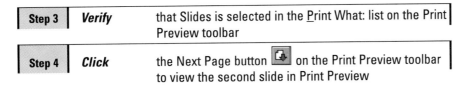

Step 3	*Verify*	that Slides is selected in the Print What: list on the Print Preview toolbar
Step 4	*Click*	the Next Page button 🔲 on the Print Preview toolbar to view the second slide in Print Preview

FIGURE 8-4
Teddy Toys Title Slide in Print Preview

You decide to preview notes pages, handouts, and an outline view of the *Teddy Toys* presentation to see how the final printed copies will look. To preview notes pages, handouts, and an outline view:

| Step 1 | *Click* | Notes Pages in the <u>P</u>rint What: list on the Print Preview toolbar |

Your screen should look similar to Figure 8-5.

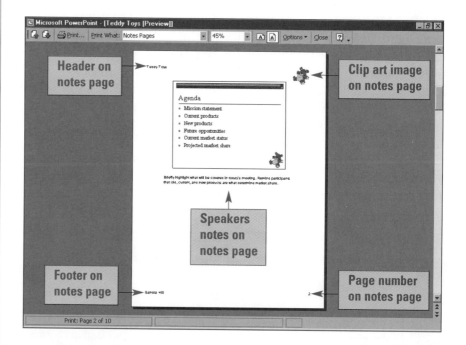

FIGURE 8-5
Notes Page in Print Preview

| Step 2 | *Navigate* | through all the notes pages in the preview window, viewing the header, footer, page number, and graphic on each notes page |

The text Teddy Toys appears on each notes page in the upper-left corner, the teddy bear image appears in the upper-right corner, and the name Sandra Hill and the page number appear at the bottom of the page. Page numbers appear by default on the notes pages. This text prints on each notes page, but not on the individual slides.

| Step 3 | *Click* | Handouts (6 slides per page) in the <u>P</u>rint What: list |

Your screen should look similar to Figure 8-6. Slides display two across and three down.

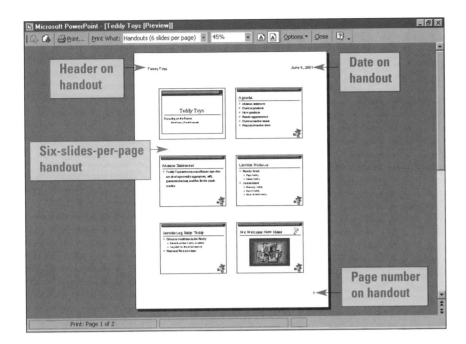

FIGURE 8-6
Handouts Page in Print Preview

Step 4	*Click*	the Options button Options ▾ on the Print Preview toolbar
Step 5	*Click*	Frame Slides if it is not checked to display a thin border around each miniature slide
Step 6	*Navigate*	through the two pages of the handout

The text Teddy Toys appears on each handouts page in the upper-left corner, the date appears in the upper-right corner, and the page number appear at the bottom of the page. Page numbers appear by default on the handouts pages. This text prints on each handouts page, but not on the individual slides.

Step 7	*Click*	Outline View in the Print What: list on the Print Preview toolbar

Your screen should look similar to Figure 8-7. Outline View displays the same settings as the handouts page. The handout master determines the text and objects placed on both the handout pages and the outline view pages.

chapter
eight

FIGURE 8-7
Outline View in Print
Preview

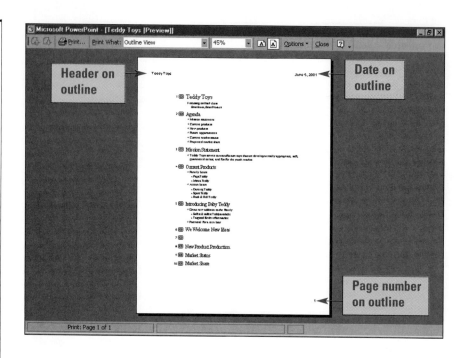

| Step 8 | *Click* | the Close Preview button `Close` on the Print Preview toolbar |

Changing Page Orientation

Page orientation refers to the vertical or horizontal position of the printed page. In **portrait orientation**, the page is printed across the short edge, or top, of the page; this is the common orientation for documents that are narrower than they are wide. In **landscape orientation**, the page is printed across the long edge, or the side. Landscape is the default orientation for slides because you can fit more text across a landscape page than a portrait page. However, you can change the presentation from landscape to portrait orientation. When you do, your slides may need to be readjusted so that all items fit appropriately on the slides. To change the orientation of a presentation:

Step 1	*Click*	File
Step 2	*Click*	Page Setup
Step 3	*Click*	the Portrait option button in the Slides section under Orientation
Step 4	*Click*	OK
Step 5	*Run*	the slide show and notice the placement and distortion of objects on each slide

You decide to return the presentation to landscape orientation.

Step 6	*Open*	the Page Setup dialog box
Step 7	*Click*	the Landscape option button in the Slides section under Orientation
Step 8	*Click*	OK

Print Preview allows you to change the orientation of notes pages, handouts, and outline view to provide another format for your presentation output. To change the orientation in Print Preview:

Step 1	*Click*	the Print Preview button on the Standard toolbar
Step 2	*Click*	Outline View in the Print What: list on the Print Preview toolbar, if necessary
Step 3	*Click*	the Landscape button 🅰 on the Print Preview toolbar and observe the change
Step 4	*Close*	the Print Preview window

8.d Printing Presentation Documents

The Print dialog box provides options for printing your presentation in different forms. You can print in grayscale or pure black and white, include animations, scale to fit the paper, frame the slides, print hidden slides, and include comment pages. You can print all slides, the current slide, a selection, a custom show, a range of slides, audience handouts, notes pages, and an outline. PowerPoint provides options for printing more than one copy and for collating. In addition, the Print dialog box provides a Preview button that opens Print Preview.

Printing Selected Slides

In some situations, you may want to print only selected slides of your presentation. You can print the current slide, a specific slide, or a range of slides. The default orientation for slides is landscape. To print selected slides:

Step 1	*Click*	File
Step 2	*Click*	Print

chapter
eight

The Print dialog box on your screen should look similar to Figure 8-8.

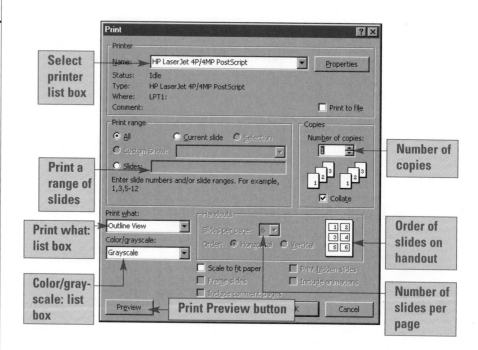

CAUTION TIP

If you click the Print button on the Standard toolbar, you bypass the Print dialog box and print based on the current print defaults, so you don't have the option of making specific changes in regard to printing.

QUICK TIP

You can open the Print dialog box by pressing the CTRL + P keys.

Step 3	*Click*	the Slides: option button in the Print range box
Step 4	*Key*	4,8 in the text box
Step 5	*Verify*	that Slides appears in the Print what: list box
Step 6	*Click*	Preview to view the slides
Step 7	*Click*	the Print button  on the Print Preview toolbar
Step 8	*Click*	OK

Slides 4 and 8 print one slide per page.

Printing an Outline View

For situations when you want to print primarily the slide text of a presentation, PowerPoint includes a feature for printing an Outline View. An **Outline View** lists all slides in the presentation without displaying backgrounds, colors, or clip art images. The default orientation for outlines is portrait. To print an outline:

| Step 1 | *Click* | the Print button  on the Print Preview toolbar |

Step 2	*Click*	the <u>A</u>ll option button in the Print range box, if necessary
Step 3	*Click*	Outline View in the Print <u>w</u>hat: list box
Step 4	*Click*	Pr<u>e</u>view
Step 5	*Change*	the orientation to Portrait
Step 6	*Click*	the <u>P</u>rint button 🖨 <u>P</u>rint... on the Print Preview toolbar
Step 7	*Click*	OK

An outline prints, displaying all slides in the presentation. Notice that Teddy Toys, the current date, and the page number are printed on each page of the outline. Any edits to a handouts master also appear on the printed outline for the same presentation.

Printing Notes Pages

Each notes page prints with a small slide at the top and your lecture or speaker notes at the bottom. The default orientation for notes pages is portrait. To print notes pages:

Step 1	*Click*	the <u>P</u>rint button 🖨 <u>P</u>rint... on the Print Preview toolbar
Step 2	*Click*	the Sl<u>i</u>des: option button in the Print range box
Step 3	*Key*	1-3, 8 to print notes pages for Slides 1 through 3, and 8
Step 4	*Click*	Notes Pages in the Print <u>w</u>hat: list box
Step 5	*Click*	Pr<u>e</u>view
Step 6	*Verify*	that the orientation is Portrait
Step 7	*Click*	the <u>P</u>rint button 🖨 <u>P</u>rint... on the Print Preview toolbar
Step 8	*Click*	OK

Any text keyed in the header and/or footer areas of the notes master, along with any images, print on the notes pages. The page number appears at the lower-right corner by default.

Printing an Audience Handout

Handouts can be printed in layouts of two, three, four, six, or nine slides per page. When you decide to print handouts, you have the option of printing the slides in order horizontally or vertically. Two slides per page print one above the other in portrait orientation or side by side in landscape orientation. Three slides per page print down the left side of the

page with horizontal lines to the right for taking notes in portrait orientation and three slides across the page with horizontal lines below. Four slides print two slides side by side in two columns. Six slides print two slides side by side in three rows in portrait orientation, and three slides side by side in two rows in landscape orientation. Nine slides print three slides across and three slides down. The default orientation for handouts is portrait. To print an audience handout:

Step 1	*Click*	the Print button ⧉ Print... on the Print Preview toolbar
Step 2	*Click*	the All option button in the Print range box
Step 3	*Click*	Handouts in the Print what: list box

When you want to print four, six, or nine slides per page, you have the option of changing the order of the slides. You can print the slides on a handout in order horizontally across the page or vertically down the page.

Step 4	*Click*	the Slides per page: list arrow in the Handouts box
Step 5	*Click*	6 as the number of slides per page, if necessary
Step 6	*Click*	Horizontal for the Order so the handout slides print in order across the page, if necessary
Step 7	*Click*	the Frame slides check box to insert a check mark, if necessary, to put a frame around each slide on the handout
Step 8	*Click*	Preview and verify that the orientation is Portrait
Step 9	*Click*	the Print button ⧉ Print... on the Print Preview toolbar
Step 10	*Click*	OK
Step 11	*Close*	the Print Preview window

Two pages print with six slides on the first page and four slides on the second page. The slides are in order from left to right across the page. Each handout displays Teddy Toys, the current date, and automatic page numbers.

Step 12	*Save*	the *Teddy Toys* presentation and close it

Ms. Hill will distribute the handout you created to the meeting attendees.

Summary

► Speaker notes contain information that a presenter can refer to during a presentation.

► Speaker notes can be keyed in Notes Page view or in the notes pane below the slide in Normal view.

► A notes master allows you to add text or clip art images that print on each notes page.

► Audience handouts display miniature slides printed on paper in two, three, four, six, or nine slides per page.

► The Handout Master Layout dialog box displays placeholders for the date, page number, header, or footer that appears on printed handouts.

► You can access the handout master to add text or clip art images that print on each audience handout.

► Print Preview allows you to preview how a presentation will actually look when it is printed. You can preview slides, handouts, outlines, and notes pages.

► A presentation can be viewed in color, grayscale, or black and white.

► You can change orientation of slides, handouts, outlines, and notes pages in the Page Setup dialog box.

► You can navigate in Notes Page view using the previous and next slide buttons on the scroll bar.

► Portrait orientation refers to the paper being printed across the short edge, or top, of the page.

► Landscape orientation refers to the paper being printed along the long edge, or side, of the page.

► By default, slides in a presentation print in landscape orientation.

► By default, notes pages, handouts, and outlines print in portrait orientation.

► You can change the page orientation of notes pages, handouts, and outlines in the Print Preview window.

► The Print dialog box provides several options for printing, including printing selected slides, outlines, notes pages, and handouts.

► You can print an entire presentation based on the current print defaults by clicking the Print button on the Standard toolbar.

chapter eight

Commands Review

Action	Menu Bar	Shortcut Menu	Toolbar	Task Pane	Keyboard
Add a notes page	View, Notes Page				ALT + V, P
Change the Zoom control	View, Zoom		50%		ALT + V, Z
Display the notes master	View, Master, Notes Master				ALT + V, M, N
Display the handout master	View, Master, Handout Master		SHIFT + [icon]		ALT + V, M, D
Preview a presentation	File, Print Preview		[icon]		ALT F, V CTRL + P, ALT + E
Preview a slide in grayscale or black and white	View, Color/Grayscale, Grayscale or Pure Black and White		[icon]		ALT + V, C, G ALT + V, C, U
Change page orientation	File, Page Setup				ALT + F, U
Change page orientation in Print Preview window for notes pages, handouts, outlines			[icon] [icon]		
Print selected slides	File, Print, Slides				ALT + F, P, ALT + I
Print an outline	File, Print, Print what: Outline View				ALT + F, P, ALT + W
Print notes pages	File, Print, Print what: Notes Pages				ALT + F, P, ALT + W
Print handouts	File, Print, Print what: Handouts				ALT + F, P, ALT + W

Concepts Review

Circle the correct answer.

1. **Which of the following provides a way to print out speaker notes with a miniature slide on a printed page?**
   [a] audience handout
   [b] notes page
   [c] Outline view
   [d] slides with animation

2. **Which of the following provides a printed copy of your presentation with horizontal lines for taking notes?**
   [a] audience handout
   [b] notes page
   [c] Outline view
   [d] slides with animation

3. **The handout master contains placeholders for all of the following *except* the:**
   [a] header.
   [b] footer.
   [c] title.
   [d] page number.

4. **Which of the following provides a printed copy of your presentation without the slide or clip art images?**
   [a] audience handouts
   [b] notes pages
   [c] outlines
   [d] slides

5. **When printing handouts, you cannot print:**
   [a] two slides per page.
   [b] three slides per page.
   [c] six slides per page.
   [d] ten slides per page.

6. **Previewing a presentation before printing provides a(n):**
   [a] audience handout.
   [b] printed copy of all the slides.
   [c] actual representation of how slides will appear when printed.
   [d] color notes page.

7. **In the Print Preview window, you cannot change the page orientation of:**
   [a] slides.
   [b] handouts.
   [c] notes pages.
   [d] outlines.

8. **The default page setup orientation for slides in PowerPoint is:**
   [a] portrait.
   [b] landscape.

   [c] vertical.
   [d] sideways.

9. **To print only Slides 5 and 12 in a presentation, click the:**
   [a] All option button in the Print dialog box.
   [b] Current slide option button in the Print dialog box.
   [c] Custom Show option button in the Print dialog box.
   [d] Slides option button in the Print dialog box.

10. **To bypass the Print dialog box when printing individual slides or an entire presentation, use:**
   [a] the CTRL + P keys.
   [b] File, Print.
   [c] the Print button.
   [d] File, Print Preview.

Circle **T** if the statement is true or **F** if the statement is false.

T   F   1. Notes page text can be only one sentence long per slide.

T   F   2. The purpose of the notes page is to aid the presenter when delivering the presentation.

T   F   3. Audience handouts can only be printed for an even number of slides.

T   F   4. Placeholders cannot be restored on a master once they have been deleted.

T   F   5. You can preview a presentation only to see how the slides look in color.

T   F   6. When printing an outline, clip art images do not print for each slide.

T   F   7. When printing a presentation, printing audience handouts and outlines can use less paper than printing the entire presentation as slides.

T   F   8. Audience handouts can be printed either across or down the page when printing more than three slides per page.

T   F   9. You can add the current date, page number, header, or footer to the audience handouts.

T   F   10. You cannot change the default orientation for printing notes pages, handouts, and outlines.

chapter eight

Skills Review

Exercise 1

1. Open the *PowerPoint* presentation you modified in Chapter 7.

2. Create the following notes page for the title slide: "Welcome everyone. Inform them that your goal today is to get them to appreciate PowerPoint, the popular presentation graphics software program."

3. Print the notes page for the title slide.

4. Prepare an audience handout using the six-slides-per-page option.

5. Add your name in the header area.

6. Add the name of the presentation in the footer area.

7. Preview the handout for the presentation, and then print the audience handout for the *PowerPoint* presentation using the six-slides-per-page option. Save and close the presentation.

Exercise 2

1. Open the *Office* presentation you modified in Chapter 7.

2. Add your name to the footer area and the current date on the handout master.

3. Add an appropriate clip art image to the handout master.

4. Preview and print the outline for the *Office* presentation.

5. Print an audience handout using the two-slides-per-page option. Save and close the presentation.

Exercise 3

1. Open the *Design* presentation you modified in Chapter 7.

2. Create the following notes page for the title slide: "Creating a presentation takes careful planning. Remember to keep the interest of the audience and the objective of the presentation in mind while you create each slide."

3. Create the following notes page for the WordArt slide: "Design is an important factor in every presentation. However, there are three main focus points of every presentation—the Audience, the Audience, the Audience."

4. Select the text box on the notes master, and change the font to Times New Roman 16 point.

5. Add an appropriate AutoShape to the notes master.

6. Preview and print the notes pages for Slides 1 and 5. Save and close the presentation.

Exercise 4

1. Open the *Precision Builders* presentation you modified in Chapter 7.

2. Add your name to the footer area on the handout master.

3. Add the name of the presentation to the header area on the handout master.

4. Select the four-slides-per-page layout.

5. Add an appropriate AutoShape to the top right of the handout master.

6. Preview and print the audience handout using the four-slides-per-page layout with the vertical option. Save and close the presentation.

Exercise 5 C

1. Open the *Nature Tours* presentation you modified in Chapter 7.

2. Preview the presentation in grayscale and then close the Grayscale view.

3. Create a notes page that contains relevant text for each of the even-numbered slides in the presentation.

4. Add an appropriate clip art image to the notes master. Add your name to the footer area on the notes master.

5. Change the page orientation of the notes pages to Landscape.

6. Preview and print only the even-numbered notes pages. Save and close the presentation.

Exercise 6 C

1. Open the *A Healthier You* presentation you modified in Chapter 7.

2. Prepare an audience handout to print three slides per page.

3. Add the title of the presentation in the header area. Add your name in the footer area.

4. Add an AutoShape to the handout master.

5. Verify that the page orientation of the handouts is Portrait.

6. Preview and print the handout with frames. Save and close the presentation.

Exercise 7 C

1. Open the *Buying A Computer* presentation you modified in Chapter 7.

2. Add the name of the presentation and the current date to the top of the handout master and your name to the footer area.

3. Select the nine-slides-per-page layout.

4. Add a computer clip art image to the handout master.

5. Preview and print the outline and the handout for the presentation. Save and close the presentation.

Exercise 8 C

1. Open the *Leisure Travel* presentation you modified in Chapter 7.

2. Preview the presentation in grayscale, pure black and white, and then in color.

3. Add the name of the presentation and the current date to the top of the handout master and your name to the footer area.

4. Change the page orientation for notes, handouts, and outline to Landscape.

5. Add an appropriate clip art image to the handout master.

6. Preview and print the audience handout using the four-slides-per-page option. Save and close the presentation.

Case Projects
SCANS

Project 1

One of your coworkers is having problems using the notes and handout masters. You remember how to create notes pages, but you need to use the Ask A Question Box and online Help to search for information on using the notes and handout master. Print a copy of help topics including any additional links for notes and handout masters.

chapter eight

Project 2

Your employer is new to presenting to a large audience. She asks you to provide notes pages for every even-numbered slide in the *Communicate* presentation you modified in Chapter 7. Create notes pages for each slide with information relevant to that slide. Add the title of the presentation in the header and your name in the footer area on the notes master. Preview and print the notes pages for all the even-numbered slides. Save the presentation and close it.

Project 3

The owners of Souner & Associates are masters when it comes to presenting slide show presentations. They want to make it easy for the audience to take notes during their upcoming slide show presentation. They ask you to create a handout that prints three slides per page so audience members can take notes next to each slide during the presentation. Prepare the handouts for the *Souner* presentation you modified in Chapter 7, including a clip art image and/or text on the handout master. Change the page orientation to landscape for the handout. Preview and print the handouts horizontally in the three-slides-per-page layout. Save the presentation and close it.

Project 4

While working on your own presentation, you decide that it might be beneficial to create a few notes pages for slides that need some clarification or reminders for the speaker. You also want to print an outline displaying a brief overview of the slides in the presentation. Create notes pages, an audience handout, and an outline for *My Presentation* you modified in Chapter 7. Add text and/or clip art images to your master. Preview and print the notes pages, handouts, and the outline. Save the presentation and close it.

Project 5

You work on the *Zoo* presentation you modified in Chapter 7 with enthusiasm, and you want to show your employer a quick overview of the slides. Instead of printing each slide of the presentation on a full sheet of paper, you decide to print a handout

displaying the best layout for the number of slides in your presentation. Add text and/or clip art images to the handout master. Preview and print the audience handout in both portrait and landscape orientation. Save the presentation and close it.

Project 6

You are interested in finding out new information about PowerPoint. Connect to the Internet and search the Web for current articles on PowerPoint 2002. Create a presentation consisting of at least three slides detailing the new features you found. Print the presentation as an outline and as an audience handout with three slides per page. Add text and clip art images as needed to the handout master. Save and close the presentation.

Project 7

You are getting close to finishing the details of your *Cars* presentation you modified in Chapter 7. You know that it would be helpful for your students to have a printed copy of the presentation you plan to give. You decide to add appropriate clip art images to the handout master to add some interest for the students. You also want to print one of the most interesting slides on a full page for the students. Preview and print the audience handout and any slide of interest. Save the presentation and close it.

Project 8

Your professor wants to distribute the entire *Internet* presentation you modified in Chapter 7 to his class. Because he expects the class to take notes on the handout of the presentation, he asks you to find a layout that accommodates lines next to the slides so that students have room to write notes. He also wants the current semester, year, course name, and his own name to appear on the handout. The pages should be numbered as well. In addition, the professor wants an outline of the presentation for his files. It is up to you and your partner to add clip art images to the masters and print the requested handouts. Save the presentation and close it.

Working with Windows 2000

Appendix Overview

The Windows 2000 operating system creates a workspace on your computer screen, called the desktop. The desktop is a graphical environment that contains icons you click with the mouse pointer to access your computer system resources or to perform a task such as opening a software application. This appendix introduces you to the Windows 2000 desktop by describing the default desktop icons and showing how to access your computer resources, use menu commands and toolbar buttons to perform a task, and review and select dialog box options.

LEARNING OBJECTIVES

- ▶ Review the Windows 2000 desktop
- ▶ Access your computer system resources
- ▶ Use menu commands and toolbar buttons
- ▶ Use the Start menu
- ▶ Review dialog box options
- ▶ Use Windows 2000 shortcuts
- ▶ Understand the Recycle Bin
- ▶ Shut down Windows 2000

appendix

A.a Reviewing the Windows 2000 Desktop

Whenever you start your computer, the Windows 2000 operating system automatically starts. You are prompted to log on with your user name and password, which identify your account. Then the Windows 2000 desktop appears on your screen. To view the Windows 2000 desktop:

| Step 1 | *Turn on* | your computer and monitor |

The Log On to Windows dialog box opens, as shown in Figure A-1.

FIGURE A-1
Log On to Windows
Dialog Box

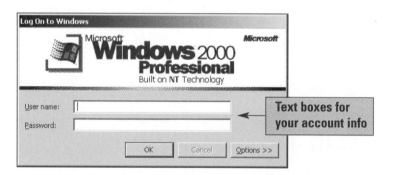

Step 2	*Key*	your user name in the <u>U</u>ser name: text box
Step 3	*Key*	your password in the <u>P</u>assword: text box
Step 4	*Click*	OK
Step 5	*Click*	the Exit button in the Getting Started with Windows 2000 dialog box, if necessary
Step 6	*Observe*	the Windows 2000 desktop work area, as shown in Figure A-2

The Windows 2000 desktop contains three elements: icons, background, and taskbar. The icons represent Windows objects and shortcuts to opening software applications or performing tasks. Table A-1 describes some of the default icons. The taskbar, at the bottom of the window, contains the Start button and the Quick Launch toolbar, and tray. The icon types and arrangement, desktop background, or Quick Launch toolbar on your screen might be different.

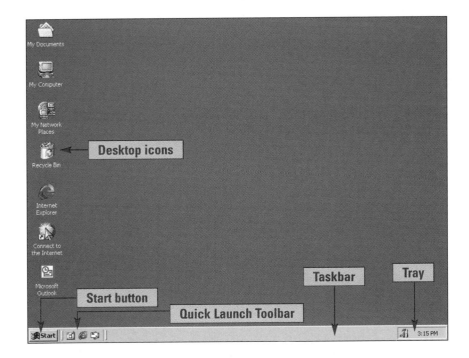

FIGURE A-2
Windows 2000 Desktop

Icon	Name	Description
	My Computer	Provides access to computer system resources
	My Documents	Stores Office documents (by default)
	Internet Explorer	Opens Internet Explorer Web browser
	Microsoft Outlook	Opens Outlook 2002 information manager software
	Recycle Bin	Temporarily stores folders and files deleted from the hard drive
	My Network Places	Provides access to computers and printers net worked in your workgroup

TABLE A-1
Common Desktop Icons

The Start button on the taskbar displays the Start menu, which you can use to perform tasks. By default, the taskbar also contains the **Quick Launch toolbar**, which has shortcuts to open the Internet Explorer Web browser and Outlook Express e-mail software, and to switch between the desktop and open application windows. You can customize the Quick Launch toolbar to include other shortcuts.

appendix
A

A.b Accessing Your Computer System Resources

The My Computer window provides access to your computer system resources. Double-click the My Computer desktop icon to open the window. To open the My Computer window:

Step 1	*Point to*	the My Computer icon on the desktop
Step 2	*Observe*	a brief description of the icon in the box, called a ScreenTip
Step 3	*Double-click*	the My Computer icon to open the My Computer window shown in Figure A-3

FIGURE A-3
My Computer window

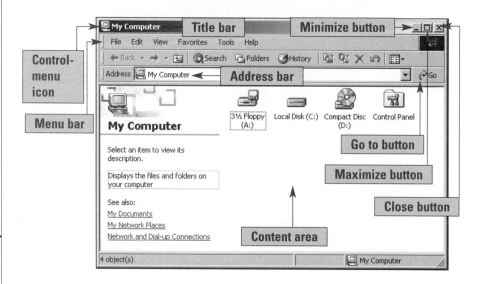

A window is a rectangular area on your screen in which you view operating system options or a software application, such as Internet Explorer. Windows 2000 has some common window elements. The **title bar**, at the top of the window, includes the window's Control-menu icon, the window name, and the Minimize, Restore (or Maximize), and Close buttons. The **Control-menu icon**, in the upper-left corner of the window, accesses the Control menu that contains commands for restoring, moving sizing, minimizing, maximizing, and closing the window. The **Minimize** button, near the upper-right corner of the window, reduces the window to a taskbar button. The **Maximize** button, to the right of the Minimize button, enlarges the window to fill the entire screen viewing area above the taskbar. If the window is already maximized, the Restore button appears in its place. The **Restore** button reduces the window size. The **Close** button, in the upper-right corner, closes the window. To maximize the My Computer window:

| Step 1 | *Click* | the Maximize button ▣ on the My Computer window title bar |
| Step 2 | *Observe* | that the My Computer window completely covers the desktop |

When you want to leave a window open, but do not want to see it on the desktop, you can minimize it. To minimize the My Computer window:

| Step 1 | *Click* | the Minimize button ▬ on the My Computer window title bar |
| Step 2 | *Observe* | that the My Computer button remains on the taskbar |

The minimized window is still open but not occupying space on the desktop. To view the My Computer window and then restore it to a smaller size:

Step 1	*Click*	the My Computer button on the taskbar to view the window
Step 2	*Click*	the Restore button 🗗 on the My Computer title bar
Step 3	*Observe*	that the My Computer window is reduced to a smaller window on the desktop

You can move and size a window with the mouse pointer. To move the My Computer window:

Step 1	*Position*	the mouse pointer on the My Computer title bar
Step 2	*Drag*	the window down and to the right approximately ½ inch
Step 3	*Drag*	the window back to the center of the screen

Several Windows 2000 windows—My Computer, My Documents, and Windows Explorer—have the same menu bar and toolbar features. When you size a window too small to view all its icons, a vertical or horizontal scroll bar may appear. A scroll bar includes scroll arrows and a scroll box for viewing different parts of the window contents.

appendix
A

MOUSE TIP

You can display four taskbar toolbars: Address, Links, Desktop, and Quick Launch. The Quick Launch toolbar appears on the taskbar by default. You can also create additional toolbars from other folders or subfolders and you can add folder or file shortcuts to an existing taskbar toolbar. To view other taskbar toolbars, right-click the taskbar, point to Toolbars, and then click the desired toolbar name.

To size the My Computer window:

Step 1	*Position*	the mouse pointer on the lower-right corner of the window
Step 2	*Observe*	that the mouse pointer becomes a black, double-headed sizing pointer
Step 3	*Drag*	the lower-right corner boundary diagonally up until the horizontal scroll bar appears and release the mouse button
Step 4	*Click*	the right scroll arrow on the horizontal scroll bar to view hidden icons
Step 5	*Size*	the window to a larger size to remove the horizontal scroll bar

You can open the window associated with any My Computer icon by double-clicking it. The windows open in the same window, not separate windows. To open the Control Panel Explorer-style window:

| Step 1 | *Double-click* | the Control Panel icon |
| Step 2 | *Observe* | that the Address bar displays the Control Panel icon and name, and the content area displays the Control Panel icons for accessing computer system resources |

A.c Using Menu Commands and Toolbar Buttons

You can click a menu command or toolbar button to perform specific tasks in a window. The **menu bar** is a special toolbar located below the window title bar that contains the File, Edit, View, Favorites, Tools, and Help menus. The **Standard Buttons toolbar**, located below the menu bar, contains shortcut "buttons" you click with the mouse pointer to execute a variety of commands. You can use the Back and Forward buttons on the Standard Buttons toolbar to switch between My Computer and the Control Panel. To view My Computer:

Step 1	*Click*	the Back button 🔙 on the Standard Buttons toolbar to view My Computer
Step 2	*Click*	the Forward button 🔜 on the Standard Buttons toolbar to view the Control Panel
Step 3	*Click*	View on the menu bar
Step 4	*Point to*	Go To
Step 5	*Click*	the My Computer command to view My Computer

| Step 6 | *Click* | the Close button ⊠ on the My Computer window title bar |

A.d Using the Start Menu

The **Start button** on the taskbar opens the Start menu. You use this menu to access several Windows 2000 features and to open software applications, such as Word or Excel. To open the Start menu:

| Step 1 | *Click* | the Start button 🔳Start on the taskbar to open the Start menu, as shown in Figure A-4 |

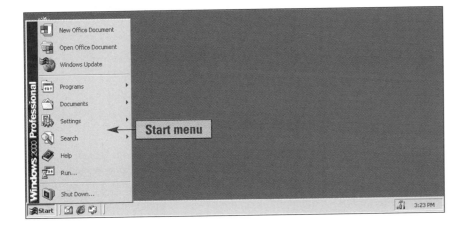

FIGURE A-4
Start Menu

| Step 2 | *Point to* | Programs to view the software applications installed on your computer |
| Step 3 | *Click* | the desktop outside the Start menu and Programs menu to close them |

A.e Reviewing Dialog Box Options

A **dialog box** is a window that contains options you can select, turn on, or turn off to perform a task. To view a dialog box:

| Step 1 | *Right-click* | the desktop |
| Step 2 | *Point to* | Active Desktop |

appendix
A

Step 3	*Click*	Customize My Desktop to open the Display Properties dialog box
Step 4	*Click*	the Effects tab (see Figure A-5)

QUICK TIP

Many dialog boxes contain sets of options on different pages organized on **tabs** you click. Options include drop-down lists you view by clicking an arrow, text boxes in which you key information, check boxes and option buttons you click to turn on or off an option, and buttons that access additional options.

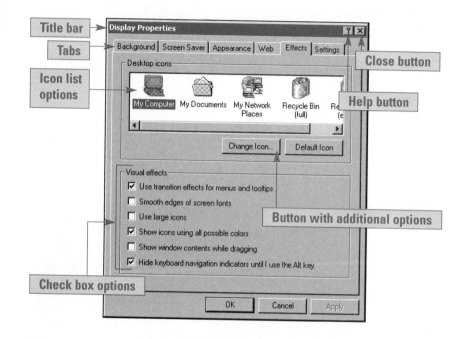

FIGURE A-5
Effects Tab in the Display Properties Dialog Box

MOUSE TIP

One way to speed up tasks is to single-click (rather than double-click) a desktop icon just like you single-click a Web page hyperlink. You can create a Web-style, single-click environment by opening the Folder Options dialog box from the Tools menu in any Windows 2000 window or the Control Panel from the Settings command on the Start menu. The Single-click to open an item (point to select) and Underline icon titles consistent with my browser options add an underline to icon titles, similar to a hyperlink.

Step 5	*Click*	each tab and observe the different options available *(do not change any options unless directed by your instructor)*
Step 6	*Right-click*	each option on each tab and then click What's This? to view its ScreenTip
Step 7	*Click*	Cancel to close the dialog box without changing any options

A.f Using Windows 2000 Shortcuts

You can use the drag-and-drop method to reposition or remove Start menu commands. You can also right-drag a Start menu command to the desktop to create a desktop shortcut. To reposition the Windows Update item on the Start menu:

Step 1	*Click*	the Start button 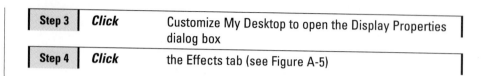 on the taskbar
Step 2	*Point to*	the Windows Update item
Step 3	*Drag*	the Windows Update item to the top of the Start menu

To remove the Windows Update shortcut from the Start menu and create a desktop shortcut:

Step 1	*Drag*	the Windows Update item to the desktop
Step 2	*Observe*	that the desktop shortcut appears after a few seconds
Step 3	*Verify*	that the Windows Update item no longer appears on the Start menu

To add a Windows Update shortcut back to the Start menu and delete the desktop shortcut:

Step 1	*Drag*	the Windows Update shortcut to the Start button [Start] on the taskbar and then back to its original position when the Start menu appears
Step 2	*Close*	the Start menu
Step 3	*Drag*	the Windows Update shortcut on the desktop to the Recycle Bin

You can close multiple application windows at one time from the taskbar using the CTRL key and a shortcut menu. To open two applications and then use the taskbar to close them:

Step 1	*Open*	the Word and Excel applications (in this order) from the Programs menu on the Start menu
Step 2	*Observe*	the Word and Excel buttons on the taskbar (Excel is the selected, active button)
Step 3	*Press & hold*	the CTRL key
Step 4	*Click*	the Word application taskbar button (the Excel application taskbar button is already selected)
Step 5	*Release*	the CTRL key
Step 6	*Right-click*	the Word or Excel taskbar button
Step 7	*Click*	Close to close both applications

You can use the drag-and-drop method to add a shortcut to the Quick Launch toolbar for folders and documents you have created. To create a new subfolder in the My Documents folder:

| Step 1 | *Double-click* | the My Documents icon on the desktop to open the window |
| Step 2 | *Right-click* | the contents area (but not a file or folder) |

appendix
A

Step 3	*Point to*	New
Step 4	*Click*	Folder
Step 5	*Key*	Example
Step 6	*Press*	the ENTER key to name the folder
Step 7	*Drag*	the Example folder to the end of the Quick Launch toolbar (a black vertical line indicates the drop position)
Step 8	*Observe*	the new icon on the toolbar
Step 9	*Close*	the My Documents window
Step 10	*Position*	the mouse pointer on the Example folder shortcut on the Quick Launch toolbar and observe the ScreenTip

You remove a shortcut from the Quick Launch toolbar by dragging it to the desktop and deleting it, or dragging it directly to the Recycle Bin. To remove the Example folder shortcut and then delete the folder:

Step 1	*Drag*	the Example folder icon to the Recycle Bin
Step 2	*Open*	the My Documents window
Step 3	*Delete*	the Example folder icon using the shortcut menu
Step 4	*Click*	Yes
Step 5	*Close*	the My Documents window

A.g Understanding the Recycle Bin

The **Recycle Bin** is an object that temporarily stores folders, files, and shortcuts you delete from your hard drive. If you accidentally delete an item, you can restore it to its original location on your hard drive if it is still in the Recycle Bin. Because the Recycle Bin takes up disk space you should review and empty it regularly. When you empty the Recycle Bin, its contents are removed from your hard drive and can no longer be restored.

MENU TIP

You can open the Recycle Bin by right-clicking the Recycle Bin icon on the desktop and clicking Open. To restore an item to your hard drive after opening the Recycle Bin, click the item to select it and then click the Restore command on the File menu. You can also restore an item by opening the Recycle Bin, right-clicking an item, and clicking Restore.

To empty the Recycle Bin, right-click the Recycle Bin icon and then click Empty Recycle Bin.

A.h Shutting Down Windows 2000

It is very important that you follow the proper procedures for shutting down the Windows 2000 operating system when you are finished, to allow the operating system to complete its internal "housekeeping" properly. To shut down Windows 2000 correctly:

| Step 1 | *Click* | the Start button **Start** on the taskbar |
| Step 2 | *Click* | Shut Down to open the Shut Down Windows dialog box shown in Figure A-6 |

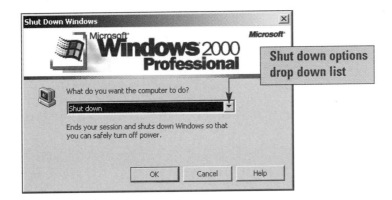

FIGURE A-6
Shut Down Windows
Dialog Box

You can log off, shut down, and restart from this dialog box. You want to shut down completely.

| Step 3 | *Click* | the Shut down option from the drop-down list, if necessary |
| Step 4 | *Click* | OK |

appendix
A

Formatting Tips for Business Documents

Appendix Overview

M ost organizations follow specific formatting guidelines when preparing letters, envelopes, memorandums, and other documents to ensure the documents present a professional appearance. In this appendix you learn how to format different size letters, interoffice memos, envelopes, and formal outlines. You also review a list of style guides and learn how to use proofreader's marks.

LEARNING OBJECTIVES

▶ Format letters
▶ Insert mailing notations
▶ Format envelopes
▶ Format interoffice memorandums
▶ Format formal outlines
▶ Use style guides
▶ Use proofreader's marks

appendix

B.a Formatting Letters

Most companies use special letter paper with the company name and address (and sometimes a company logo or picture) preprinted on the paper. The preprinted portion is called a **letterhead** and the paper is called **letterhead paper**. When you create a letter, the margins vary depending on the style of your letterhead and the length of your letter. Most letterheads use between 1 inch and 2 inches of the page from the top of the sheet. There are two basic business correspondence formats: block format and modified block format. When you create a letter in **block format**, all the text is placed flush against the left margin. This includes the date, the letter address information, the salutation, the body, the complimentary closing, and the signature information. The body of the letter is single spaced with a blank line between paragraphs.[1] Figure B-1 shows a short letter in the block format with standard punctuation.

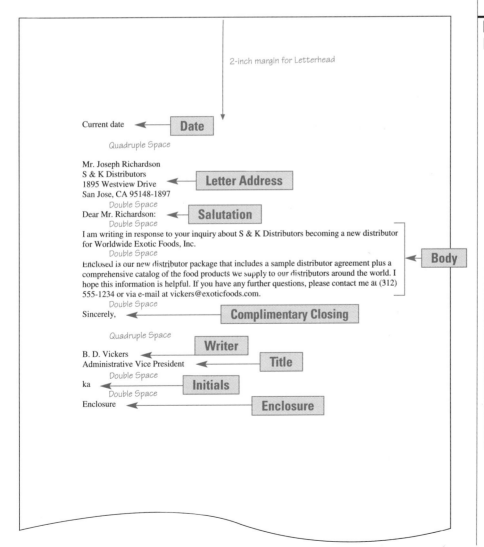

FIGURE B-1
Block Format Letter

appendix
B

In the **modified block format**, the date begins near the center of the page or near the right margin. The closing starts near the center or right margin. Paragraphs can be either flush against the left margin or indented. Figure B-2 shows a short letter in the modified block format with standard punctuation.

FIGURE B-2
Modified Block
Format Letter

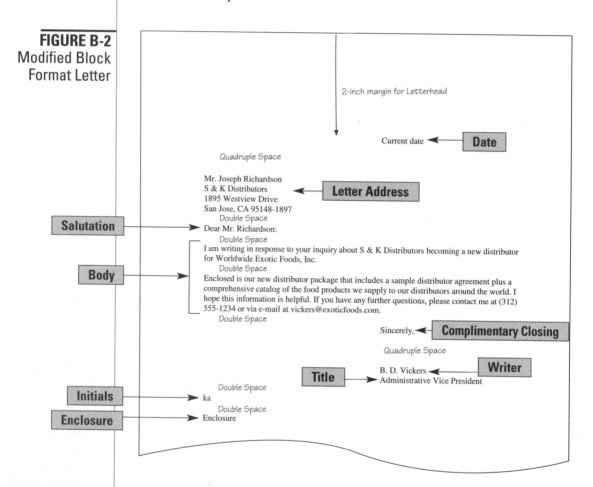

Both the block and modified block styles use the same spacing for the non-body portions. Three blank lines separate the date from the addressee information, one blank line separates the addressee information from the salutation, one blank line separates the salutation from the body of the letter, and one blank line separates the body of the letter from the complimentary closing. There are three blank lines between the complimentary closing and the writer's name. If a typist's initials appear below the name, a blank line separates the writer's name from the initials. If an enclosure is noted, the word "Enclosure" appears below the typist's initials with a blank line separating them. Finally, when keying the return address or addressee information, one space separates the state and the postal code (ZIP+4).

B.b Inserting Mailing Notations

Mailing notations add information to a business letter. For example, the mailing notations CERTIFIED MAIL or SPECIAL DELIVERY indicate how a business letter was sent. The mailing notations CONFIDENTIAL or PERSONAL indicate how the person receiving the letter should handle the letter contents. Mailing notations should be keyed in uppercase characters at the left margin two lines below the date.[2] Figure B-3 shows a mailing notation added to a block format business letter.

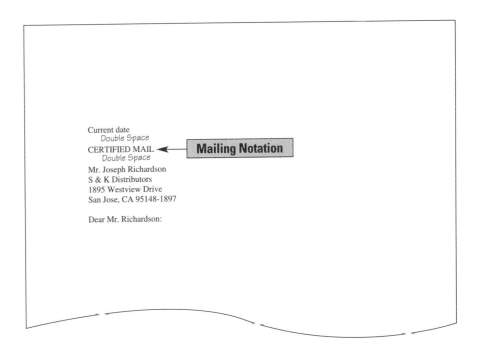

Current date
Double Space
CERTIFIED MAIL ◀──── **Mailing Notation**
Double Space
Mr. Joseph Richardson
S & K Distributors
1895 Westview Drive
San Jose, CA 95148-1897

Dear Mr. Richardson:

FIGURE B-3
Mailing Notation on Letter

B.c Formatting Envelopes

Two U.S. Postal Service publications, *The Right Way* (Publication 221), and *Postal Addressing Standards* (Publication 28) available from the U.S. Post Office, provide standards for addressing letter envelopes. The U.S. Postal Service uses optical character readers (OCRs) and barcode sorters (BCSs) to increase the speed, efficiency, and accuracy in processing mail. To get a letter delivered more quickly, envelopes should be addressed to take advantage of this automation process.

appendix
B

Table B-1 lists the minimum and maximum size for letters. The post office cannot process letters smaller than the minimum size. Letters larger than the maximum size cannot take advantage of automated processing and must be processed manually.

Dimension	Minimum	Maximum
Height	3½ inches	6⅛ inches
Length	5 inches	11½ inches
Thickness	.007 inch	¼ inch

The delivery address should be placed inside a rectangular area on the envelope that is approximately ⅝ inch from the top and bottom edge of the envelope and ½ inch from the left and right edge of the envelope. This is called the **OCR read area**. All the lines of the delivery address must fit within this area and no lines of the return address should extend into this area. To assure the delivery address is placed in the OCR read area, begin the address approximately ½ inch left of center and on approximately line 14.[3]

The lines of the delivery address should be in this order:

1. any optional nonaddress data, such as advertising or company logos, must be placed above the delivery address
2. any information or attention line
3. the name of the recipient
4. the street address
5. the city, state, and postal code (ZIP+4)

The delivery address should be complete, including apartment or suite numbers and delivery designations, such as RD (road), ST (street), or NW (northwest). Leave the area below and on both sides of the delivery address blank. Use uppercase characters and a sans serif font (such as Arial) for the delivery address. Omit all punctuation except the hyphen in the ZIP+4 code.

Figure B-4 shows a properly formatted business letter envelope.

QUICK TIP

Foreign addresses should include the country name in uppercase characters as the last line of the delivery address. The postal code, if any, should appear on the same line as the city.

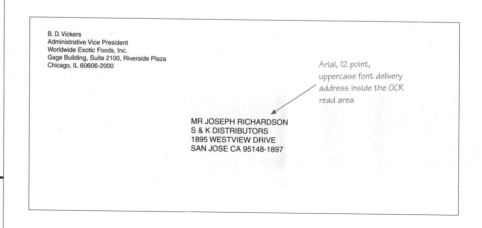

B. D. Vickers
Administrative Vice President
Worldwide Exotic Foods, Inc.
Gage Building, Suite 2100, Riverside Plaza
Chicago, IL 60606-2000

Arial, 12 point, uppercase font delivery address inside the OCR read area

MR JOSEPH RICHARDSON
S & K DISTRIBUTORS
1895 WESTVIEW DRIVE
SAN JOSE CA 95148-1897

FIGURE B-4
Business Letter Envelope

B.d Formatting Interoffice Memorandums

Business correspondence that is sent within a company is usually prepared as an **interoffice memorandum**, also called a **memo**, rather than a letter. There are many different interoffice memo styles used in offices today, and word processing applications usually provide several memo templates based on different memo styles. Also, just as with business letters that are sent outside the company, many companies set special standards for margins, typeface, and font size for their interoffice memos.

A basic interoffice memo should include lines for "TO:", "FROM:", "DATE:", and "SUBJECT:" followed by the body text. Memos can be prepared on blank paper or on paper that includes a company name and even a logo. The word MEMORANDUM is often included. Figure B-5 shows a basic interoffice memorandum.

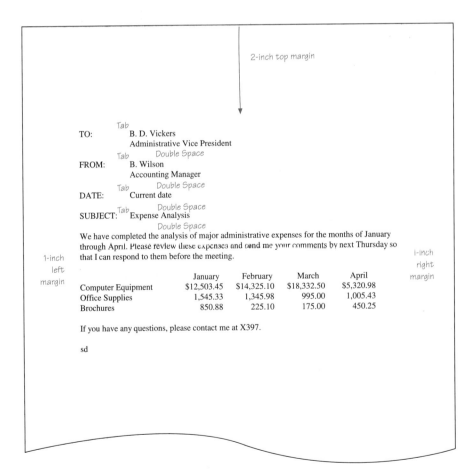

FIGURE B-5
Interoffice Memorandum

appendix
B

B.e Formatting Formal Outlines

Companies use outlines to organize data for a variety of purposes, such as reports, meeting agenda, and presentations. Word processing applications usually offer special features to help you create an outline. If you want to follow a formal outline format, you may need to add formatting to outlines created with these special features.

Margins for a short outline of two or three topics should be set at 1½ inches for the top margin and 2 inches for the left and right margins. For a longer outline, use a 2-inch top margin and 1-inch left and right margins.

The outline level-one text should be in uppercase characters. Second-level text should be treated like a title, with the first letter of the main words capitalized. Capitalize only the first letter of the first word at the third level. Double space before and after level one and single space the remaining levels.

Include at least two parts at each level. For example, you must have two level-one entries in an outline (at least I. and II.). If there is a second level following a level-one entry, it must contain at least two entries (at least A. and B.). All numbers must be aligned at the period and all subsequent levels must begin under the text of the preceding level, not under the number.[4]

Figure B-6 shows a formal outline prepared using the Word Outline Numbered list feature with additional formatting to follow a formal outline.

B.f Using Style Guides

A **style guide** provides a set of rules for punctuating and formatting text. There are a number of style guides used by writers, editors, business document proofreaders, and publishers. You can purchase style guides at a commercial bookstore, an online bookstore, or a college bookstore. Your local library likely has copies of different style guides and your instructor may have copies of several style guides for reference. Some popular style guides are *The Chicago Manual of Style* (The University of Chicago Press), *The Professional Secretary's Handbook* (Barron's), *The Holt Handbook* (Harcourt Brace College Publishers), and the *MLA Style Manual and Guide to Scholarly Publishing* (The Modern Language Association of America).

FIGURE B-6
Formal Outline

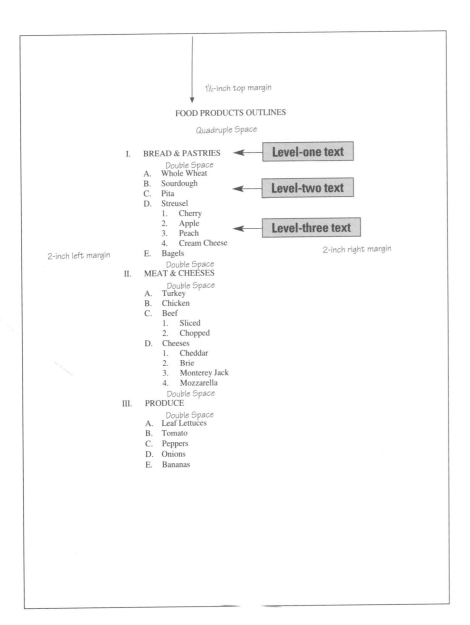

1½-inch top margin

FOOD PRODUCTS OUTLINES

Quadruple Space

I.   BREAD & PASTRIES ← **Level-one text**
       Double Space
     A.   Whole Wheat
     B.   Sourdough
     C.   Pita ← **Level-two text**
     D.   Streusel
            1.   Cherry
            2.   Apple
            3.   Peach ← **Level-three text**
            4.   Cream Cheese
     E.   Bagels
       Double Space
II. MEAT & CHEESES
       Double Space
     A.   Turkey
     B.   Chicken
     C.   Beef
            1.   Sliced
            2.   Chopped
     D.   Cheeses
            1.   Cheddar
            2.   Brie
            3.   Monterey Jack
            4.   Mozzarella
       Double Space
III. PRODUCE
       Double Space
     A.   Leaf Lettuces
     B.   Tomato
     C.   Peppers
     D.   Onions
     E.   Bananas

2-inch left margin

2-inch right margin

B.g Using Proofreader's Marks

Standard proofreader's marks enable an editor or proofreader to make corrections or change notations in a document that can be recognized by anyone familiar with the marks. The following list illustrates standard proofreader's marks.

appendix
B

Defined		Examples
Paragraph	¶	¶ Begin a new paragraph at this
Insert a character	∧	point. Ins⌃rt a letter here.
Delete	ℓ	Delete ~~these words~~ Disregard
Do not change	stet or . . .	the previous correction. To
Transpose	tr	transpose is to ⁀around⁀turn
Move to the left	[	[Move this copy to the left.
Move to the right	]	]Move this copy to the right.
No paragraph	No ¶	No ¶ Do not begin a new paragraph
Delete and close up		here. Delete the hyphen from
		pre-empt and close up the space.
Set in caps	Caps or ≡	a sentence begins with a capital
Set in lower case	lc or /	letter. This Word should not
Insert a period	⊙	be capitalized. Insert a period⊙
Quotation marks	" "	"Quotation marks and a comma
Comma	∧	should be placed here he said.
Insert space	#	Space between these#words. An
Apostrophe	'	apostrophe is what's needed here.
Hyphen	=	Add a hyphen to Kilowatt=hour. Close
Close up	‿	up the extra spa‿ce.
Use superior figure	∨	Footnote this sentence.∨ Set
Set in italic	Ital. or —	the words, _sine qua non_, in italics.
Move up		This word is too ⌐low.⌐ That word is
Move down		too ⌐high.⌐

Endnotes

[1] Jerry W. Robinson et al., *Keyboarding and Information Processing* (Cincinnati: South-Western Educational Publishing, 1997).

[2] Ibid.

[3] Ibid.

[4] Ibid.

Using Office XP Speech Recognition

Appendix Overview

You are familiar with using the keyboard and the mouse to key text and select commands. With Office XP, you also can use your voice to perform these same activities. Speech recognition enables you to use your voice to perform keyboard and mouse actions without ever lifting a hand. In this appendix, you learn how to set up Speech Recognition software and train the software to recognize your voice. You learn how to control menus, navigate dialog boxes, and open, save, and close a document. You then learn how to dictate text, including lines and punctuation, correct errors, and format text. Finally, you learn how to turn off and on Speech Recognition.

LEARNING OBJECTIVES

► Train your speech software
► Use voice commands
► Dictate, edit, and format by voice
► Turn Microsoft Speech Recognition on and off

appendix

C.a Training Your Speech Software

Speech recognition is an exciting new technology that Microsoft has integrated into its XP generation of products. Microsoft has been working on speech recognition for well over a decade. The state-of-the-art is advancing. If you haven't tried it before, this is a great time for you to experience this futuristic technology.

Voice recognition has important benefits:

- Microsoft's natural speech technologies can make your computer experience more enjoyable.
- Speech technology can increase your writing productivity.
- Voice recognition software can greatly reduce your risk for keyboard- and mouse-related injuries.

In the following activities, you learn to use your voice like a mouse and to write without the aid of the keyboard.

Connecting and Positioning Your Microphone

Start your speech recognition experience by setting up your microphone. There are several microphone styles used for speech recognition. The most common headset microphone connects to your computer's sound card, as shown in Figure C-1. Connect the microphone end to your computer's microphone audio input port. Connect the speaker end into your speech output port.

FIGURE C-1
Standard Sound Card
Headset (Courtesy
Plantronics Inc.)

USB speech microphones, such as the one shown in Figure C-2, are becoming very popular because they normally increase performance and accuracy. USB is short for Universal Serial Bus. USB microphones bypass the sound card and input speech with less distortion into your system.

USB microphones are plugged into the USB port found in the back of most computers. Windows automatically installs the necessary USB drivers after you start your computer with the USB microphone plugged into its slot.

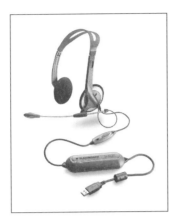

FIGURE C-2
A USB Headset (Courtesy Plantronics Inc.)

After your headset has been installed, put on your headset and position it comfortably. Remember these two important tips:

- Place the speaking side of your microphone about a thumb's width away from the side of your mouth, as shown in Figure C-3.
- Keep your microphone in the same position every time you speak. Changing your microphone's position can decrease your accuracy.

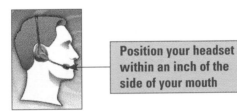

Position your headset within an inch of the side of your mouth

FIGURE C-3
Proper Headset Position

CAUTION TIP

If you see additional buttons on the Language Bar than shown in Figure C-4, click the Microphone button to hide them.

Installing Microsoft Speech Recognition

Open Microsoft Word and see if your speech software has already been installed. As Word opens, you should see either the floating Language Bar, shown in Figure C-4, or the Language Bar icon in the Windows Taskbar tray, as shown in Figure C-5.

Correction | Microphone | Tools | Write | Lined Paper | ? |

FIGURE C-4
Floating Language Bar

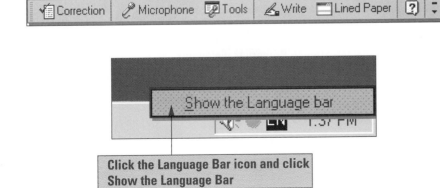

Show the Language bar

Click the Language Bar icon and click Show the Language Bar

FIGURE C-5
Language Bar Icon

appendix
C

If you can open and see the Language Bar, jump to Step-by-Step C.2. However, if this essential tool is missing, proceed with Step-by-Step C.1.

Step-by-Step C.1

| Step 1 | To install Microsoft speech recognition, open Microsoft Word by clicking **Start**, **Programs**, **Microsoft Word**. |

| Step 2 | Click **Tools**, **Speech** from the Word menu bar, as shown in Figure C-6. |

FIGURE C-6
Click Speech from the Tools menu

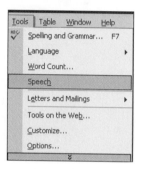

| Step 3 | You are prompted through the installation procedure. The process is a simple one. Follow the onscreen instructions. |

Training Your System

Microsoft speech recognition can accommodate many different voices on the same computer. In order to work properly, your Microsoft Office Speech Recognition software must create a user **profile** for each voice it hears—including your voice.

If you are the first user and have just installed your speech software, chances are the system is already prompting you through the training steps. Skip to Step 3 in Step-by-Step C.2 for hints and help as you continue. However, if you are the second or later user of the system, you need to create a new profile by starting with Step 1.

Step-by-Step C.2

| Step 1 | To create your own personal speech profile, click the **Tools** button on the Language Bar and click **Options**, as shown in Figure C-7. This opens the Speech Properties dialog box. |

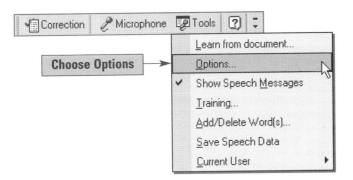

FIGURE C-7
Language Bar's
Tools Menu

Step 2   In the Speech Properties dialog box, click **New**, as indicated in Figure C-8.

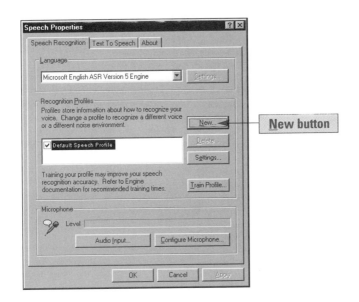

FIGURE C-8
Speech Properties
Dialog Box

Step 3   Enter your name in the Profile Wizard, as shown in Figure C-9, and click **Next>** to continue. (*Note:* If you accidently click Finish instead of Next>, you must still train your profile by clicking Train Profile in the Speech Properties dialog box.)

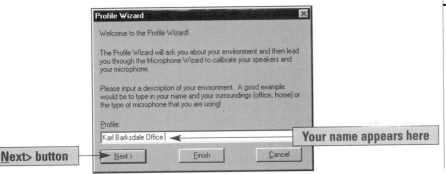

FIGURE C-9
New Profile Dialog Box

appendix
C

| Step 4 | Adjust your microphone, as explained on the Microphone Wizard Welcome dialog box, as shown in Figure C-10. Click **Next>** to begin adjusting your microphone. |

FIGURE C-10
Correctly Position Your
Microphone

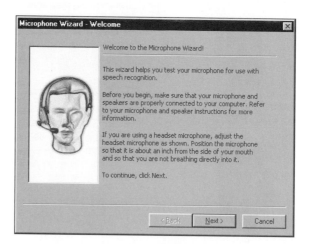

| Step 5 | Read the test sentence indicated in Figure C-11 until the volume adjustment settings appear consistently in the green portion of the volume adjustment meter. Your volume settings are adjusted automatically as you speak. Click **Next>** to continue. |

FIGURE C-11
Read Aloud to Adjust Your
Microphone Volume

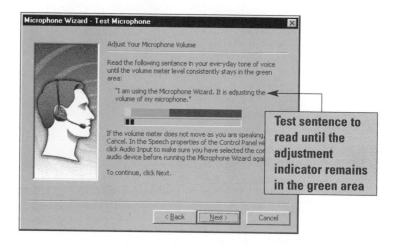

Test sentence to read until the adjustment indicator remains in the green area

QUICK TIP

Microsoft Office Speech Recognition tells you if your microphone is not adequate for good speech recognition. You may need to try a higher quality microphone, install a compatible sound card, or switch to a USB microphone. Check the Microsoft Windows Help files for assistance with microphone problems.

| Step 6 | The next audio check tests the output of your speakers. Read the test sentence indicated in Figure C-12 and then listen. If you can hear your voice, your speakers are connected properly. Click **Finish** and continue. |

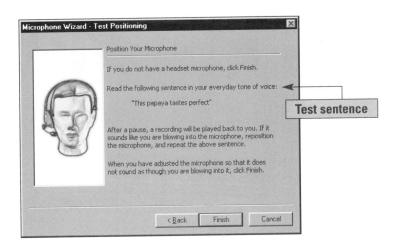

Test sentence

Read Aloud to Test Your
Sound Output

QUICK TIP

Your user file will
remember your
microphone settings
from session to
session. However, if
others use the system
before you, you may
need to readjust the
audio settings by
clicking **Tools**, **Options**,
Configure Microphone.

Training Your Software

Next, you are asked to train your software. During the training
session, you read a training script or story for about 10 to 15 minutes.
As you read, your software gathers samples of your speech. These
samples help the speech software customize your speech recognition
profile to your way of speaking. As you read, remember to:

- Read clearly.
- Use a normal, relaxed reading voice. Don't shout, but don't
  whisper softly either.
- Read at your normal reading pace. Do not read slowly and do
  not rush.

CAUTION TIP

Never touch any part
of your headset or
microphone while
speaking. Holding or
touching the microphone
creates errors.

Step-by-Step C.3

Step 1	Microsoft Office Speech Recognition prepares you to read a story or script. Read the instruction screen shown in Figure C-13 and click **Next>** to continue.

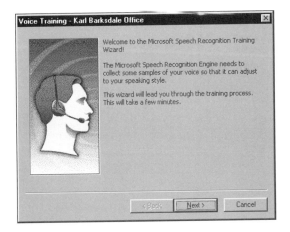

FIGURE C-13
Read the Onscreen
Instructions Carefully

Step 2	Enter your gender and age information (see Figure C-14) to help the system calibrate its settings to your voice. Click **Next>** to continue.

appendix
C

FIGURE C-14
Enter Your Gender and Age
Information

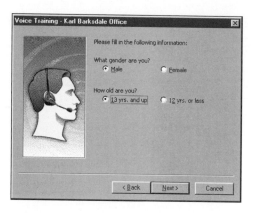

| Step 3 | Click **Sample** and listen to a short example of how to speak clearly to a computer. See Figure C-15. After the recording, click **Next>** to review the tips for the training session, and then click **Next>** to continue. |

FIGURE C-15
Listen to the Speech
Sample

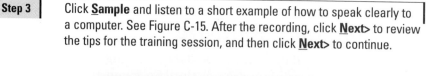

Click the Sample button and listen to learn

| Step 4 | Begin reading the training session paragraphs, as shown in Figure C-16. Text you have read is highlighted. The Training Progress bar lets you know how much reading is left. If you get stuck on a word, click **Skip Word** to move past the problem spot. |

FIGURE C-16
Software Tracks
Your Progress

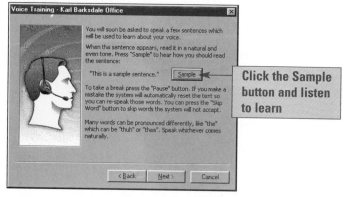

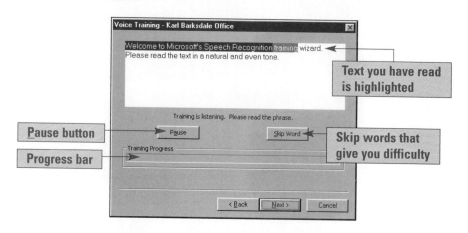

Text you have read is highlighted

Pause button

Progress bar

Skip words that give you difficulty

Step 5
The screen shown in Figure C-17 appears after you have finished reading the entire first story or training session script. You now have a couple of choices. Click **More Training**, click **Next>**, and continue reading additional scripts as explained in Step 6 (or you can click Finish and quit for the day).

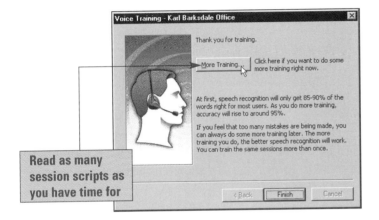

Read as many session scripts as you have time for

QUICK TIP

The more stories you read, the better. Users with thick accents, or accuracy below 90 percent, must read additional stories. You can read additional training session scripts at any time by clicking **Tools**, **Training** on the Language Bar.

FIGURE C-17
First Training Script Completed

Step 6
Choose another training session story or script from the list, as shown in Figure C-18, and then click **Next>**.

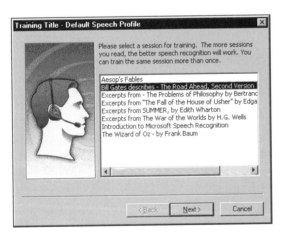

FIGURE C-18
Choose Another Story or Training Script to Read

CAUTION TIP

You must read until Microsoft Office Speech Recognition has a large enough sample of your voice to process and adjust to your unique way of speaking. Click **Pause** to take a break. However, it is best to read the entire session training script in one sitting.

Step 7
At the end of the training process, Microsoft Office Speech Recognition shows you a multimedia training tutorial (you may need to install Macromedia Flash to view the tutorial). Enjoy the tutorial before continuing.

appendix
C

C.b Using Voice Commands

Microsoft makes it easy to replace mouse clicks with voice commands. The voice commands are very intuitive. In most cases, you simply say what you see. For example, to open the File menu, you can simply say **File**.

Microsoft Office XP voice commands allow you to control dialog boxes and menu bars, and to format documents by speaking. You can give your hands a rest by speaking commands instead of clicking them. This can help reduce your risk for carpal tunnel syndrome and other serious injuries.

Before you begin using voice commands, remember that if more than one person is using speech recognition on the same computer, you must select your user profile from the Current Users list. The list is found by clicking the Language Bar Tools menu, as shown in Figure C-19.

FIGURE C-19
Current Users List

Switching Modes and Moving the Language Bar

Microsoft Office Speech Recognition works in two modes. The first is called **Dictation mode**. The second is called **Voice Command mode**. Voice Command mode allows you to control menus, give commands, and format documents.

When using Voice Command mode, simply *say what you see on the screen or in dialog boxes*. You see how this works in the next few exercises. In Step-by-Step C.4, you learn how to switch between the two modes.

Step-by-Step C.4

Step 1	Open **Microsoft Word** and the **Language Bar**, if necessary.
Step 2	The Language Bar can appear collapsed (see Figure C-20) or expanded (see Figure C-21). You can switch between the two options by clicking the **Microphone** button.

FIGURE C-20
Collapsed Language Bar

Clicking the Microphone button with your mouse turns on the microphone and expands the Language Bar.

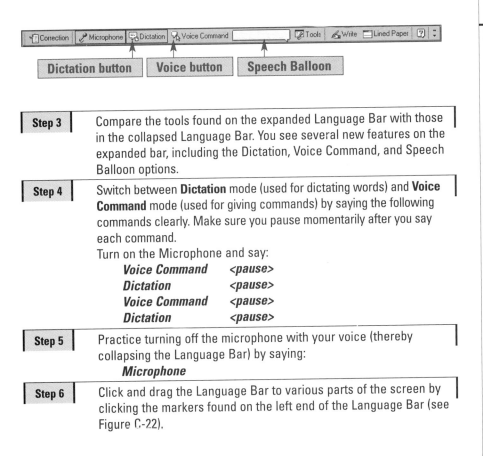

FIGURE C-21
Expanded Language Bar

Step 3	Compare the tools found on the expanded Language Bar with those in the collapsed Language Bar. You see several new features on the expanded bar, including the Dictation, Voice Command, and Speech Balloon options.
Step 4	Switch between **Dictation** mode (used for dictating words) and **Voice Command** mode (used for giving commands) by saying the following commands clearly. Make sure you pause momentarily after you say each command. Turn on the Microphone and say: *Voice Command* *<pause>* *Dictation* *<pause>* *Voice Command* *<pause>* *Dictation* *<pause>*
Step 5	Practice turning off the microphone with your voice (thereby collapsing the Language Bar) by saying: *Microphone*
Step 6	Click and drag the Language Bar to various parts of the screen by clicking the markers found on the left end of the Language Bar (see Figure C-22).

QUICK TIP

The Language Bar can float anywhere on the screen. Move the Language Bar to a spot that is convenient and out of the way. Most users position the Language Bar in the title bar or status bar when using speech with Microsoft Word.

FIGURE C-22
Move the Language Bar to a Convenient Spot

Giving Menu Commands

When you use Microsoft Office Voice Commands, your word will be obeyed. Before you begin issuing commands, take a few seconds and analyze Figure C-23. The toolbars you will be working with in the next few activities are identified in the figure.

appendix
C

FIGURE C-23
Customize Microsoft Word
with Your Voice

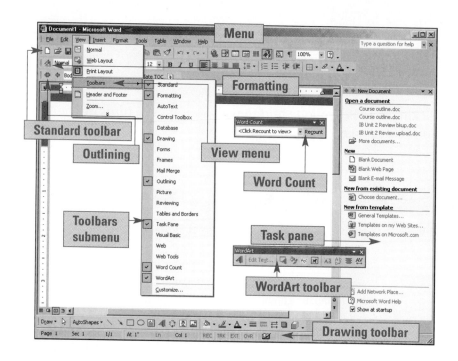

Step-by-Step C.5

Step 1	Switch on the **Microphone** from the Language Bar.
Step 2	Switch to Voice Command mode by saying: ***Voice Command***
Step 3	Open and close several menus by saying: ***File*** *(Pause briefly between commands)* ***Escape*** ***Edit*** ***Cancel*** ***View*** ***Escape***
Step 4	Close or display a few of the popular toolbars found in Microsoft Word by saying the following commands: ***View*** ***Toolbars*** ***Standard*** ***View*** ***Toolbars*** ***Formatting*** ***View*** ***Toolbars*** ***Drawing***

Step 5	Close or redisplay the toolbars by saying the following commands: *View* *Toolbars* *Drawing* *View* *Toolbars* *Formatting* *View* *Toolbars* *Standard*
Step 6	Practice giving voice commands by adding and removing the Task Pane and WordArt toolbar. Try some other options. When you are through experimenting, turn off the microphone and collapse the Language Bar by saying: *Microphone*

Navigating Dialog Boxes

Opening files is one thing you do nearly every time you use Microsoft Office. To open files, you need to manipulate the Open dialog box (Figure C-24). A dialog box allows you to make decisions and execute voice commands. For example, in the Open dialog box you can switch folders and open files by voice.

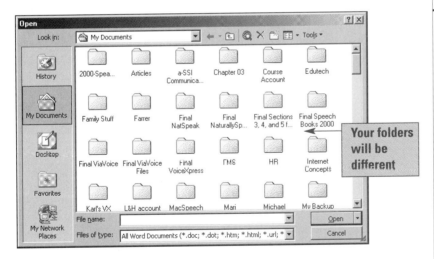

FIGURE C-24
Open Dialog Box

Step-by-Step C.6

Step 1	Turn on the **Microphone**, switch to Voice Command mode, and access the Open dialog box, as shown in Figure C-25, using the following commands: *Voice Command* *File* *Open*

appendix
C

FIGURE C-25
Say File, Open

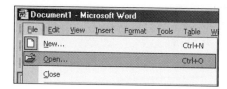

Step 2	Switch between various folder locations with your voice. In this case, you're going to switch between the Desktop, My Documents, and other folders located on the side of the Open dialog box, as shown in Figure C-26. Say the following voice commands to switch between folder locations. Pause slightly after saying each command:

Desktop
My Documents
History
Desktop
Favorites
My Documents

FIGURE C-26
Switch Between Various
Folder Locations

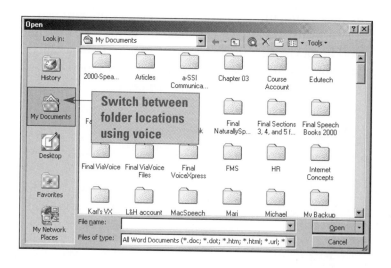

QUICK TIP

Any time a button in a dialog box appears dark around the edges, the button is active. You can access active buttons at any time by saying the name of the button or by saying **Enter**. You can also move around dialog boxes using the **Tab** or **Shift Tab** voice commands, or move between folders and files by saying **Up Arrow**, **Down Arrow**, **Left Arrow**, and **Right Arrow**. When selecting files, you'll probably find it much easier to use your mouse instead of your voice.

Step 3	You can change how your folders and files look in the Open dialog box by manipulating the Views menu, as shown in Figure C-27. Say the following voice commands to change the look of your folders and files:

Views
Small Icons
Views
List
Views
Details
Views
Thumbnails
Views
Large icons
Views
List

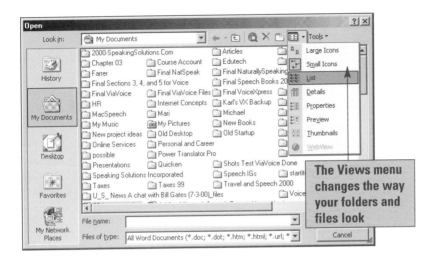

FIGURE C-27
Change the Look of Folders
with the Views Menu

| Step 4 | Close the Open dialog box by using the Cancel command. Say: *Cancel* |

Open and Count a Document

In Step-by-Step C.7, you combine your traditional mouse skills with voice skills to accomplish tasks more conveniently. Use your skills to open a file. Then, use your menu selecting technique to open the Word Count toolbar and count the number of words in a document.

Step-by-Step C.7

Step 1	Using your voice, say *File*, *Open* and select the **My Documents** folder (or the location of your Data Disk). View the folders and files in **List** view. (Review Step-by-Step C.6 if you have forgotten how to make these changes in the Open dialog box.)
Step 2	Scroll through the list of files with your mouse until you see the file called *Prevent Injury*. To open the file, select it with your mouse and say: *Open* (or you also may say *Enter*)
Step 3	As the file opens, notice that the document title is PREVENT INJURY WITH SPEECH. Speech recognition can help you avoid serious keyboarding and mouse injuries. Count the words in the article. Open the Word Count toolbar by saying the following: *View* *Toolbars* *Word Count*
Step 4	With the Word Count toolbar open, say the following command to count the words: *Recount*

QUICK TIP

To complete Step-by-Step C.7, the *Prevent Injury* document should be moved from the Data Disk to the My Documents folder on your computer.

appendix
C

Step 5	How many words are contained in the article?
Step 6	Leave the *Prevent Injury* document open for the next activity.

Save a Document and Exit Word

Saving a file will give you a chance to practice manipulating dialog boxes. Switching from the keyboard and mouse to your voice has several benefits. For example, have you heard of carpal tunnel syndrome and other computer keyboard-related injuries caused by repetitive typing and clicking? By using your speech software even part of the time, you can reduce your risk for these long-term and debilitating nerve injuries.

In Step-by-Step C.8, you change the filename *Prevent Injury* to *My prevent injury file* using the Save As dialog box.

Step-by-Step C.8

Step 1	Make sure the ***Prevent Injury*** document appears on your screen. If you closed the document, repeat Step-by-Step C.7.
Step 2	Open the **Save As** dialog box. Notice that it is a lot like the Open dialog box. Try the following commands: ***Voice Command*** *(if necessary)* ***File*** ***Save as***
Step 3	Switch to the **My Documents** folder and display the folder in **List** view as you learned to do in Step-by-Step C.7.
Step 4	Click your mouse in the **File name:** text box and type the filename or switch to Dictation mode and name the file with your voice by saying: ***Dictation*** ***My prevent injury file***
Step 5	Save your document and close the Save As the box by saying: ***Voice Command*** ***Save***
Step 6	Close the **Word Count** toolbar using the steps you learned earlier.
Step 7	Close Microsoft Word and collapse the Language Bar with the following commands: (When asked whether to save other open documents, say ***No***.) ***File*** ***Close*** ***Microphone***

C.c Dictating, Editing, and Formatting by Voice

If you have always dreamed of the day when you could sit back, relax, and write the next great American novel by speaking into a microphone, well, that day has arrived. It is possible to write that novel, a report, or even a simple e-mail message at speeds of 130–160 words per minute. However, it takes practice to achieve an acceptable level of accuracy. This section is designed to help you build accuracy.

Microsoft Office Speech Recognition is not made for complete handsfree use. You still need to use your keyboard and mouse much of the time. But, if you're willing to put in some effort, you can improve your speaking accuracy to the point that you can dramatically improve your output.

Dictating

Microsoft Speech Recognition allows you to work in **Dictation** mode when voice writing words into your documents. Switching from Voice Command mode to Dictation mode is as easy as saying ***Dictation***.

In Dictation mode, don't stop speaking in the middle of a sentence—even if your words don't appear immediately. The software needs a few seconds to process what you're saying. Microsoft Office Speech Recognition lets you know it is working by placing a highlighted bar with dots in your document, as shown in Figure C-28. A few seconds later, your words appear.

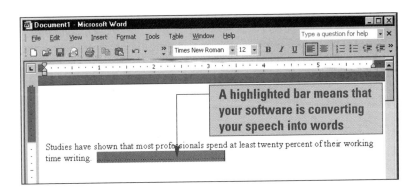

> **QUICK TIP**
>
> The best way to improve dictation accuracy is to read additional training session stories to your computer. You should read at least three to five stories. Do this by clicking **Tools**, **Current User**, and double-checking to see if your user profile name has a check mark by it. Then, click **Tools**, **Training** from the Language Bar and follow the onscreen instructions.

FIGURE C-28
Continue Talking Even If Your Words Don't Appear Instantly

appendix
C

QUICK TIP

Think about the
following as you begin
voice writing:
- Speak naturally,
  without stopping in
  the middle of your
  sentences.
- Don't speak
  abnormally fast
  or slow.
- Say each word
  clearly. Don't slur
  your words or leave
  out sounds.

During the next steps, don't be overly concerned about making mistakes. You learn some powerful ways to correct mistakes in the next few exercises. For now, experiment and see what happens.

Step-by-Step C.9

Step 1	Open **Microsoft Word** and the **Language Bar**, if necessary. Don't forget to select your user profile.
Step 2	Turn on the **Microphone**, switch to **Dictation mode**, and read this short selection into Microsoft Word. *Dictation* *Studies have shown that most professionals spend at least twenty percent of their working time writing <period> You can use speech recognition software to help you in any career you choose <period> Microsoft speech can be used in the medical <comma> legal <comma> financial <comma> and educational professions <period>* *Microphone*
Step 3	Examine your paragraph. How well did you do? Count the mistakes or word errors. How many errors did you make?
Step 4	Now delete all the text on your screen. Start by turning on the **Microphone** and then switching to **Voice Command** mode by saying (remember to pause briefly after each command): *Voice Command* *Edit* *Select All* *Backspace*
Step 5	Repeat the selection from Step 2. This time, say any word that gave you difficulty a little more clearly. See if your computer understands more of what you say this time around.
Step 6	Did you improve? Yes/No
Step 7	Delete all the text on your screen again before you continue, using the *Voice Command, Edit, Select All, Backspace* commands.

QUICK TIP

You'll need to dictate
punctuation marks. Say
the word *Period* to
create a (.), say *Comma*
to create a (,), say
Question Mark for a (?),
and *Exclamation
Mark/Point* for (!).

Using the New Line and New Paragraph Commands

In this next set of exercises, you have a chance to use the New Line and New Paragraph commands to organize text. These essential commands allow you to control the look and feel of your documents. (See Figure C-29.) It helps to pause briefly before and after you say each command.

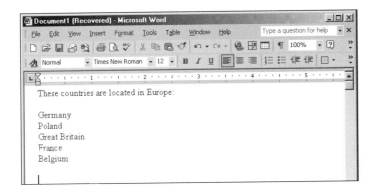

FIGURE C-29
New Line and New
Paragraph Commands
Organize Text

Step-by-Step C.10

Step 1	The New Line and New Paragraph commands help organize lists of information. Dictate the following list of European countries. Turn on the **Microphone**, if necessary, and say:

Dictation

These countries are located in Europe	***<colon> <New Paragraph>***
Germany	***<New Line>***
Poland	***<New Line>***
Great Britain	***<New Line>***
France	***<New Line>***
Belgium	***<New Paragraph>***

Step 2	Save the file in the Save As dialog box with the ***Voice Command***, ***File***, ***Save As*** commands.
Step 3	Click your mouse in the **File name:** text box and enter ***Countries of Europe*** as the filename. (*Note:* If you speak the filename, remember to switch to Dictation mode.)
Step 4	Close the Save As dialog box with the ***Voice Command***, ***Save*** commands, and then clear your screen by saying ***Edit***, ***Select All***, ***Backspace***.

Using Undo

Microsoft Office Speech Recognition offers powerful ways to make corrections and train the software to recognize difficult words, so they appear correctly when you say them again. For example, erasing mistakes is easy with the Undo command. That's the first trick you learn in this section.

The Undo command works like pressing the Undo button or clicking Edit, Undo with your mouse. You can quickly erase the problem when you misspeak. All you need to do is switch to Voice Command mode and say *Undo*.

Q U I C K   T I P

Say the word ***Colon*** to create a (:).

Q U I C K   T I P

When dictating words in a list, it helps to pause slightly before and after saying the commands, as in ***<pause> New Line <pause>*** and ***<pause> New Paragraph <pause>***.

appendix
C

CAUTION TIP

A common speech mistake occurs when speakers break words into syllables. For example, they may say **speak keen clear lee** instead of **speaking clearly.**

QUICK TIP

A key to great accuracy in speech recognition is to speak in complete phrases and sentences. Complete sentences and phrases make it easier for the software to understand what you're trying to say. The software makes adjustments based on the context of the words that commonly appear together. The more words you say as a group or phrase, the more information your software has to work with.

Step-by-Step C.11

Step 1	In this step, say the name of the academic subject, then erase it immediately with the Undo command and replace it with the next subject in the list. Erase the subject regardless of whether it is correct. Switch to Voice Command mode before saying Undo.

Dictation

Biology	*Voice Command*	*Undo*	*Dictation*
French	*Voice Command*	*Undo*	*Dictation*
American history	*Voice Command*	*Undo*	*Dictation*

Step 2	The Undo command deletes the last continuous phrase you have spoken. Say each of the following phrases, then use Undo to erase them.

To infinity and beyond	*Voice Command*	*Undo*	*Dictation*
The check is in the mail	*Voice Command*	*Undo*	*Dictation*
Money isn't everything	*Voice Command*	*Undo*	

Microphone

Correcting Errors

Correcting mistakes is obviously important. There are several ways to make corrections effectively.

Because speech recognition software recognizes phrases better than individual words, one of the best ways to correct a mistake is to use your mouse to select the phrase where the mistake occurs and then repeat the phrase. For example, in the sentence below the software has keyed the word *share* instead of the word *sure*. Select the phrase (like the boldface example) with your mouse, then say the phrase again:

What you should select: You sound **very share of yourself**.
What you would repeat: **very sure of yourself**

If you still make a mistake, select the misspoken word with your mouse and take advantage of the power of the **Correction** button on the Language Bar. Carefully read through these steps and then practice what you learned in Step 5.

Step-by-Step C.12

Step 1	If you make an error, select the mistake, as shown in Figure C-30.
Step 2	With your microphone on, say *Correction* or click the Correction button with your mouse.
Step 3	If the correct alternative appears in the correction list, click the correct alternative with your mouse.

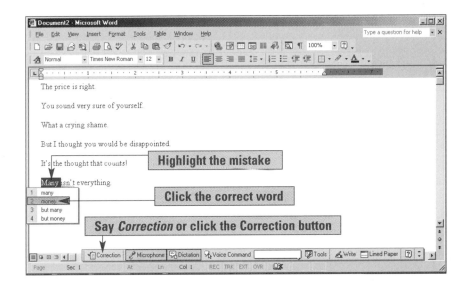

FIGURE C-30
Select the Mistake and
Say *Correction*

| **Step 4** | If the correct word does not appear, as in Figure C-31, key the correct response with your keyboard. |

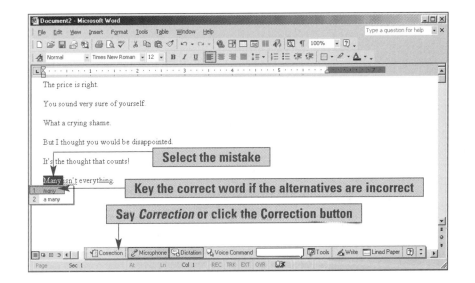

FIGURE C-31
If the Correct Word Doesn't
Appear, Key the Word

| **Step 5** | Now give it a try. Speak the following sentences. (*Hint:* Say the complete sentence before you make any corrections.) Try to correct the error first by repeating the phrase. Then, select individual word errors and use the Correction button to help you fix any remaining mistakes: |

The price is right.
You sound very sure of yourself.
What a crying shame.
But, I thought you would be disappointed.
It's the thought that counts!
Money isn't everything.

appendix
C

Formatting Sentences

After you dictate text, you can format it, copy it, paste it, and manipulate it just like you would with a mouse. In this exercise, you dictate a few sentences, and then you change the font styles and make a copy of the sentences. That is a lot to remember, so take a look at what you are about to accomplish. Review Figure C-32 to get a sneak preview of this activity.

FIGURE C-32
Dictate, Format, and Copy and Paste These Lines

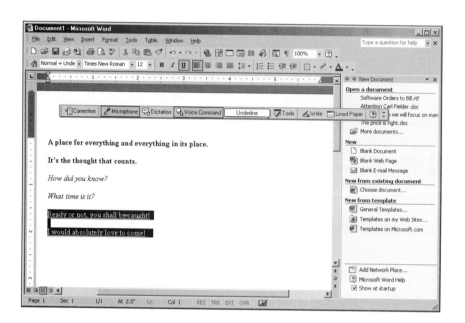

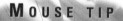

MOUSE TIP

When you correct a mistake using the Correction button, Microsoft Office Speech Recognition plays back what you said and remembers any corrections that you make. This helps to ensure that the software won't make the same mistake the next time you say the same word or phrase. Use the Correction button as often as you can. This helps to improve your speech recognition accuracy.

A few quick reminders before you begin:

- Use your mouse and voice together to bold, italicize, and underline text.
- Say the basic punctuation marks, exclamation point/mark (!), period (.), comma (,), question mark (?), semicolon (;), colon (:).
- Start a new line with the New Paragraph command.

Step-by-Step C.13

| Step 1 | Speak the following sentences, using the New Paragraph command to space between each. Do not pause in the middle of any sentence. If you make mistakes, correct them using the Correction button, as explained in Step-by-Step C.12. |

Dictation
A place for everything and everything in its place.
It's the thought that counts.
How did you know?
What time is it?
Ready or not, you shall be caught!
I would absolutely love to come!

Step 2	With your mouse, select the first two sentences and make them bold with the following commands: ***Voice Command*** ***Bold***
Step 3	Select the two questions and italicize them by saying: ***Italic***
Step 4	Select the final two exclamatory sentences and underline them by saying: ***Underline***
Step 5	Copy all the text on your screen and paste a copy at the bottom of your document by saying: ***Edit*** ***Select All*** ***Copy*** ***Down Arrow*** ***Paste***
Step 6	Print your document with the following commands: ***File*** ***Print*** ***OK***
Step 7	Close your document without saving using the ***File***, ***Close*** command and then say ***No*** when you are asked to save.
Step 8	Open a new document with your voice with the ***File***, ***New***, ***Blank Document*** commands and turn off your ***Microphone*** before you continue.

Adding and Training Names

Your speech software can remember what you teach it as long as you follow these simple steps. When you click Add/Delete Word(s) from the Tools menu, the Add/Delete Word(s) dialog box opens. This is a very powerful tool. It allows you to enter a name or any other word or phrase, click the **Record pronunciation** button, and record your pronunciation of the word or phrase.

Step-by-Step C.14

Step 1	Click **Tools**, **Add/Delete Word(s)** from the Language Bar, as shown in Figure C-33.

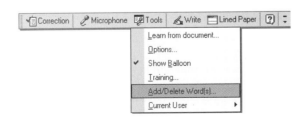

FIGURE C-33
Click the Add/Delete Word(s) Option

appendix
C

| **Step 2** | Enter your name into the **Word** text box as shown in Figure C-34. |

FIGURE C-34
Enter Your Name in the
Word Text Box

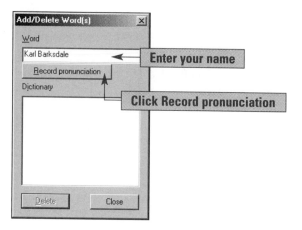

QUICK TIP

If your speech
recognition software
doesn't hear you
properly, your name
does not appear in the
Dictionary. If this
happens, try again.
When the system has
accepted your pronun-
ciation of the word, the
name appears in the
Dictionary.

| **Step 3** | Click the **Record pronunciation** button and say your name aloud. |
| **Step 4** | Your name appears in the Dictionary list. Double-click your name to hear a digitized voice repeat your name. (See Figure C-35.) |

FIGURE C-35
Add/Delete Word(s)
Dialog Box

CAUTION TIP

If your name doesn't
appear properly when
you say it, return to the
Add/Delete Word(s)
dialog box, select your
name, then click the
Record pronunciation
button and re-record the
correct pronunciation of
your name.

Step 5	Close the Add/Delete Word(s) dialog box by clicking the **Close** button.
Step 6	Return to Microsoft Word, turn on your **Microphone**, switch to **Dictation** mode. Say your name several times and see if it appears correctly.
Step 7	To improve your accuracy, it's important to add troublesome words to your dictionary. Pick five words that have given you difficulty in the past. Train the software to recognize these words as explained in Steps 1 through 6. As you add and train for the pronunciation of those words, your accuracy improves bit by bit.

C.d Turning Microsoft Speech Recognition On and Off

Microsoft Office Speech Recognition isn't for everybody—at least not in its present form. It requires a powerful CPU and a lot of RAM. It also takes a quality headset. If you don't have the necessary hardware, chances are speech recognition isn't working very well for you.

Perhaps you are simply uncomfortable using speech software. You may be an expert typist with no sign of carpal tunnel syndrome or any other repetitive stress injury. Whatever your reason for choosing not to use Microsoft speech software, it is important to know how to disable the feature.

There are two ways to turn off your speech software. You can minimize the toolbar and place it aside temporarily, or you can turn it off entirely. If you decide you want to use speech recognition at a later time, you can always turn it back on again.

Turning Off Speech Recognition

Microsoft Speech Recognition allows you to minimize the Language Bar, putting it aside temporarily. Minimizing places the Language Bar in the taskbar tray in the form of the Language Bar icon. After the Language Bar has been minimized, it is then possible to turn the system off altogether. To see how this is accomplished, follow Step-by-Step C.15.

Step-by-Step C.15

| Step 1 | Open **Microsoft Word** and the **Language Bar**, if necessary. |
| Step 2 | Click the **Minimize** button on the Language Bar, as shown in Figure C-36. |

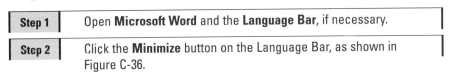

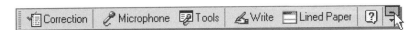

FIGURE C-36
Click the Minimize Button on the Language Bar

appendix
C

Step 3 When you minimize for the first time, a dialog box explains what is going to happen to your Language Bar, as shown in Figure C-37. Read this dialog box carefully, then click **OK**.

FIGURE C-37
Read This
Information Carefully

Step 4 Right-click the **Language Bar** icon in the taskbar. Several options appear, as shown in Figure C-38. Click **Close the Language Bar**.

FIGURE C-38
Right-Click the Language
Bar Icon

Step 5 Another dialog box opens to explain a process you can follow for restoring your speech operating system after you have turned it off. Click **OK**. The system is turned off and your language tools disappear, as shown in Figure C-39. Close Word. (*Note:* If you click **Cancel**, you return to normal and can continue using the speech recognition system by opening the Language Bar.)

FIGURE C-39
Click OK to Turn Off
Speech Recognition

Turning On Speech Recognition

There are several ways to turn your speech recognition system back on. Follow Step-by-Step C.16.

Step-by-Step C.16

| Step 1 | Open **Microsoft Word** and click **Speech** on the **Tools** menu, as shown in Figure C-40. Your speech recognition software is restored and you can begin using it again. |

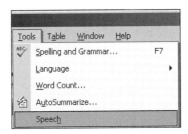

FIGURE C-40
Click Speech on the
Tools Menu

If your speech software did not restore itself after Step 1, continue with Steps 2 through 5.

| Step 2 | Click the **Start** button, **Settings**, **Control Panel**. Then double-click the **Text Services** icon to open the Text Services dialog box, as shown in Figure C-41. |

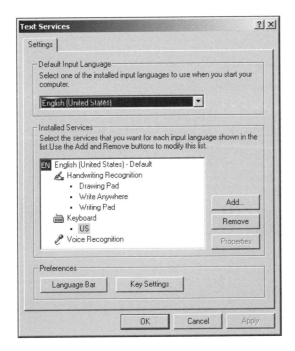

FIGURE C-41
Click Language Bar in
the Text Input Settings
Dialog Box

appendix
C

| Step 3 | Click **Language Bar** in the Text Services dialog box. |

| Step 4 | In the Language Bar Settings dialog box, click the **Show the Language bar on the desktop** check box to insert a check mark, as shown in Figure C-42. |

FIGURE C-42
Language Bar Settings
Dialog Box

| Step 5 | Click **OK**, then exit and restart your computer. The speech software should be restored and you can begin speaking again. (*Note:* If the Language Bar is still missing after you launch Word, try selecting Tools, Speech one more time.) |

Index

B

background
add image, PI 58–59
custom, PI 60
graphic, PI 59
hide, PI 58
barcode sorters (BCSs), AP 15
Basic Search, OF 28, OF 30
bitmap picture, PI 47
block format
letter, AP 13
modified, AP 14
border, PI 101, PI 111
Boolean operators, OF 43
bullets, PI 13
graphical, PI 37–38
levels, PI 27–29
demote, PI 28
first-level, PI 29
next-level, PI 28
previous-level, PI 29
promote, PI 28
second-level, PI 29
move, PI 31
rearrange in outline tab, PI 31
slide, PI 13–14, PI 31
symbols, PI 35
text, PI 27–29
button, active, AP 35

C

calendar, OF 3
category axis, PI 124, PI 134
cell, PI 101
format, PI 105–106
chart, OF 3, PI 122–149
add, PI 123–125
data label, PI 138
datasheet, PI 124
display, PI 129–130
format, PI 128–136
key data, PI 126–128
legend, PI 124, PI 129
hide, PI 138
Options dialog box, PI 135
pie, PI 136–137
placeholder, PI 123
type, PI 130–131
dialog box, PI 131
check box options, AP 8
check spelling. *See* spell check.
Chicago Manual of Style, AP 18
clicking, OF 8
clip art
add, PI 147
insert from Microsoft Clip Organizer, PI 47–50
edit, PI 51
placement, PI 51
Clip Organizer, PI 47–50
window, PI 49

indent, PI 106–108

marker, PI 106

Insert Clip Art task pane, PI 48

insert image, PI 55–56

insertion point, PI 32, PI 33

IntelliMouse, OF 4

Internet

accessing, OF 38, OF 44

connecting to, OF 38, OF 39

evaluating information from, OF 39

searching, OF 42–43, OF 44

using, OF 37–43, OF 44

Internet Explorer, OF 38–43, OF 44

Internet files, temporary, OF 41

Internet use, PI 16

Internet Service Provider (ISP), OF 38, OF 44

interoffice memos, formatting, AP 17

intranet, OF 3

ISP. *See* Internet Service Provider.

J

journal, OF 3

K

keyboard shortcuts, OF 8, OF 12, OF 21

L

landscape orientation, PI 182–183

Language Bar, AP 23, AP 24, AP 25, OF 4, OF 5, PI 5

minimizing, AP 45

moving, AP 31

switching modes on, AP 30–31

Language Bar icon, AP 23, AP 46

layout, PI 5, PI 13

change slide, PI 56

legend, PI 124, PI 129

hide, PI 138

letterhead, AP 13

letters, minimum and maximum dimensions, AP 16

line

color, PI 80–81

options, PI 83

spacing, PI 33–35

Links bar, AP 6, OF 40, OF 42

Log On to Windows dialog box, AP 2

M

Magellan Internet Guide, OF 43

mail merge, OF 7

mailing notations, AP 15

margin

set internal, PI 106–108

Maximize button, AP 4, OF 5, OF 6

memorandums, formatting, AP 17

P

page orientation, PI 182–183

paragraph spacing, PI 33

paste
object, PI 75–76

pen options, PI 153

Pentium processor, OF 4

personal information manager (PIM), OF 3

picture
format, PI 51
tab, PI 81
toolbar, PI 51

phone book, OF 3

pie chart, PI 136–137
data labels, PI 138
format, PI 137–138
plot area, PI 140–141
pull out slice, PI 140
rotate, tilt, and change height, PI 139, PI 141

placeholder, PI 5
chart, PI 123
notes, PI 9
selected text, PI 32
subtitle, PI 4
table, PI 100
text, PI 58
title, PI 4, PI 58, PI 10

pointing, OF 8

portrait orientation, PI 182

PowerPoint 2002, OF 3, OF 4, OF 6, OF 7, OF 9, OF 10, OF 11, OF 14, OF 15

preselect range, PI 126

presentation OF 3, OF 10
close, PI 10
create from
AutoContent Wizard, PI 5–6
Design template, PI 11–12
existing slides, PI 164–165
navigate through, PI 7
open, PI 27
prepare, PI 172
audience handout, PI 176–177
speaker notes, PI 173–176
preview, PI 178–182
print, PI 183
audience handout, PI 185–186
notes page, PI 185
Outline view, PI 184–185
selected slides, PI 183–184
rehearse, PI 157–161
plan, PI 157–158
practice, PI 158
prepare, PI 158
research, PI 158
save, PI 14–15, PI 16
for Internet use, PI 16
side-by-side, PI 164–165

preview
image, PI 53
presentation, PI 178
print, PI 178–182

Previous Slide button, PI 6

privacy/security issues, OF 39

S

save
  changes, PI 16
  presentation, PI 14–15, PI 16
Save command, PI 14
Save As
  command, PI 14–15
  dialog box, PI 15
Save as Web Page command, PI 16
ScreenTip, PI 4, OF 7, OF 13
scroll, OF 8
  bar, PI 6
  button, PI 6
search
  engines, OF 42
  button, PI 48, PI 49
  options, OF 28
  text, PI 48
Search button, OF 42
Search task pane, OF 27, OF 28
selecting, AP 8
sentences, formatting with speech
  recognition, AP 42
server, OF 38
shading
  styles, PI 81
shape, PI 72–73
  add text, PI 84
    AutoShapes, PI 84–86
    text box, PI 86–87
  change—of AutoShape, PI 83–84
  connect, PI 77–79
  connector line, PI 79

  draw, PI 73–74
  format, PI 80
SHIFT + F1 shortcut, OF 12, OF 13, OF 15
shortcuts
  ALT + F4 (close application), OF 14
  F1 (help), OF 12, OF 15
  Favorites, OF 40, OF 41, OF 42
  for Toolbars menu, OF 25, OF 26
  hyperlinks, OF 28
  keyboard, OF 8, OF 12, OF 21
  menu, AP 8
  menu, OF 25
  SHIFT + F1 (What's This?), OF 12, OF 13,
    OF 15
  task pane, OF 7, OF 10
  to Web page, OF 42
shortcut menu, PI 152
Show Smart Tag Actions button, OF 31
single-click environment, AP 8
Size command, OF 6
sizing handles, PI 32
slide, OF 3, OF 10
  add, PI 27, PI 28, PI 30
  background image, PI 58–59
  bullet, PI 13–14, PI 31
  change layout, PI 56
  chart, PI 123–125
  current and total number, PI 4
  Design task pane, PI 11–12
    animation scheme, PI 156–157
  edit, PI 26–45
  format, 26–45
  Layout task pane, PI 13, PI 56
  master, PI 36